Memory and Foresight in the Celtic World

Perspectives from the Late Medieval through Modern Periods

GW0049916?

Sydney Series in Celtic Studies

Dr Pamela O'Neill and Professor Jonathan Wooding, Series Editors

The Sydney Series in Celtic Studies publishes monographs and edited collections of original research in the field of Celtic Studies including archaeology, art, history, law, languages and literature. The series encompasses early and medieval subjects, as well as the modern Celtic nations with their diasporas, and encourages innovative approaches to traditional questions in its major field.

1 *Early Irish Contract Law* by N. McLeod
2 *The Celts in Europe* by A. Cremin
3 *Origins and Revivals: Proceedings of the First Australian Conference of Celtic Studies* by G. Evans, B. Martin & J. M. Wooding (eds)
4 *Literature and Politics in the Celtic World: Papers from the Third Australian Conference of Celtic Studies* by P. O'Neill & J. M. Wooding (eds)
5 *Celtic-Australian Identities: Irish- and Welsh-Australian Studies from the 'Australian Identities' Conference, University College Dublin, July 1996* by J. M. Wooding & D. Day (eds)
6 *Nation and Federation in the Celtic World: Papers from the Fourth Australian Conference of Celtic Studies* by P. O'Neill (ed.)
7 *Between Intrusions: Britain and Ireland between the Romans and the Normans* by P. O'Neill (ed.)
8 *Exile and Homecoming: Papers from the Fifth Australian Conference of Celtic Studies* by P. O'Neill (ed.)
9 *Celts in Legend and Reality: Papers from the Sixth Australian Conference of Celtic Studies* by P. O'Neill (ed.)
10 *Language and Power in the Celtic World: Papers from the Seventh Australian Conference of Celtic Studies* by A. Ahlqvist & P. O'Neill (eds)
11 *Celts and their Cultures at Home and Abroad: A Festschrift for Malcolm Broun* by A. Ahlqvist & P. O'Neill (eds)
12 *The Land beneath the Sea: Essays in Honour of Anders Ahlqvist's Contribution to Celtic Studies in Australia* P. O'Neill (ed.)
13 *Late Medieval Irish Law Manuscripts: A Reappraisal of Methodology and Content* by R. Finnane
14 *Medieval Irish Law: Text and Context* by A. Ahlqvist & P. O'Neill (eds)
15 *Grammatical Tables for Old Irish* compiled by A. Ahlqvist
16 *Germano-Celtica: A Festschrift for Brian Taylor* by A. Ahlqvist & P. O'Neill (eds)
17 *Fir Fesso: A Festschrift for Neil McLeod* by A. Ahlqvist & P. O'Neill (eds)
18 *Prophecy, Fate and Memory in the Early and Medieval Celtic World* by J. M. Wooding & L. Olson (eds)

Memory and Foresight in the Celtic World

Perspectives from the Late Medieval through Modern Periods

Edited by Lorna G. Barrow and Jonathan M. Wooding

Sydney Series in Celtic Studies 19

SYDNEY UNIVERSITY PRESS

First published by Sydney University Press
© Individual contributors 2020
© Sydney University Press 2020

Reproduction and communication for other purposes
Except as permitted under the Act, no part of this edition may be reproduced, stored in a retrieval system, or communicated in any form or by any means without prior written permission. All requests for reproduction or communication should be made to Sydney University Press at the address below:

Sydney University Press
Fisher Library F03
University of Sydney NSW 2006
Australia
sup.info@sydney.edu.au
sydneyuniversitypress.com.au

A catalogue record for this book is available from the National Library of Australia.

ISBN 9781743327159 (paperback)
ISBN 9781743327142 (epub)
ISBN 9781743327173 (mobi)
ISBN 9781743327166 (pdf)

Cover image: Celtic gravestone at Waverley Cemetery, Sydney. Photograph by Jonathan M. Wooding.
Cover design by Miguel Yamin.

Contents

Introduction: Wishful Returns and Futures Foreseen

Lorna G. Barrow and Jonathan M. Wooding

This book, together with its companion volume, *Prophecy, Fate and Memory in the Early and Medieval Celtic World* (Sydney Series in Celtic Studies 18), marks the relaunch of the venerable Sydney Series in Celtic Studies, now under the aegis of Sydney University Press, with its renewed mission to 'encourage innovative approaches to traditional questions in its major field'. The choice of themes and topics in both volumes speaks to our ambition to innovate without compromise to the scholarly values that are essential to our discipline.

It is not surprising to find a strong investment in the past in Celtic communities. And where dislocation and migration have been frequent in the recent experience of the Celtic nations, it is also not surprising that longing for a home of enduring memory is also strong—sometimes provoking what Jing Wu describes as 'a symbolic denigration of change and a wishful return to the stability of the past'.[1] Memory is one of the stronger themes in recent historiography of the Celtic nations.[2] In

---

1 Wu, Jing 2006 Nostalgia as Content Creativity: Cultural industries and Popular Sentiment, *International Journal of Cultural Studies* 9, 359–68: 360.
2 See, for example, Frawley, O. editor 2010–14 *Memory Ireland*, 4 vols, Syracuse NY: Syracuse University Press; Beiner, Guy 2018 *Forgetful Remembrance: Social Forgetting and Vernacular Historiography of a Rebellion in Ulster*, Oxford and New York: Oxford University Press.

Celtic tradition the qualities of vision and foresight have also, however, been celebrated,[3] so we have added this theme to our collection to offset any impression that Celtic nations are rooted only in tradition. In juxtaposing these themes we are not seeking either to invoke clichés of 'visionary Celts' or of cultures whose soul is sought only in remote regions.[4] Studies in the present volume find vision in urban renewal, as well as in studies of science and philosophy. Other studies here find creativity in literature, not through passive memories of Celtic languages, but active and highly nuanced ones. All the contributions evince a diverse approach to Celtic cultural and linguistic identities, which they explore through detailed case studies.

Cultural Identities and Visions

Two studies concerning Scotland, which open our collection, respectively speak strongly to our two themes. In the first, Sybil Jack's study of the Highland parish of Laggan, the letters and books of Anne MacVicar Grant (1755-1838) are used to enlighten the modern-day reader as to a world that was in many ways lost through the period of the Highland Clearances; a lost language, the break-up of family, type of work and the breakdown of Highland culture.[5] In her analysis Jack reinforces how the memory of life of long ago is passed on in 'oral story-telling traditions, fact and myth blurring within'—even tracing the way such mutable memories of Highland culture are invoked in

---

3   MacLeod, Sharon Paice 2012 *A Study of Traditional Belief with Newly Translated Prayers, Poems, Psalms and Songs,* Jefferson NC: McFarland 25–38; Henderson, Lizanne, and Cowan, Edward J. 2001 *Scottish Fairy Belief,* East Linton: Tuckwell 8–34.

4   On the 'visionary Celt': Sims-Williams, P. 1986 'The Visionary Celt', *Cambridge Medieval Celtic Studies* 11, 71–96; on remoteness, with special attention to Highland culture, see Ardener, E. 1987 Remote Areas: Some Theoretical considerations, *Anthropology at Home,* edited by A. Jackson. London: Tavistock Press, 38–54.

5   Grant, Anne MacVicar 1809 *Letters from the Mountains, Being the Real Correspondence of a Lady, Between the Years 1778–1807,* edited with notes and additions, by her son. J. P. Grant, Esq. In two volumes, London: Longman, Brown, Green and Longmans.

modern television. Jack reflects on how we remember the fact and fiction in the present day, and the difference between the respective tasks of the novelist and the historian:

> Historians, however, generally seem to pick and choose from the texts available. The strangeness of the past, that is, must be mediated by what the auditor can accept. Literary writers can be more inclusive in their presentations. While for them the past should not be comfortable, the reader must have some sympathy for or abhorrence of the subject. Hence the relationship between history and literature is strained as symbols are selected and abandoned.

In this Highland culture, around the turn of the nineteenth century, there was also a healthy respect for the capacity for supernatural foresight, as Mrs Grant notes amongst the various other superstitions she encountered in her life in the Highlands.[6] Around the same time as Mrs Grant was living in the Highlands, in the Lowlands a different type of foresight could be found. Tessa Morrison explores the vision of Robert Owen (1771–1858), a Welshman and self-made industrialist, best known for his reforms to the village of New Lanark, Southern Scotland, in 1800. Here he formed a partnership with the Chorlton Twist Company, which owned the cotton mills. Faced with housing shortages, he came up with the idea of 'Villages of Unity and Cooperation'. Morrison argues that: 'Owen's concepts of urbanisation revealed great foresight, although they have not been fully utilised yet, they remain controversial', and remain 'relevant to current proposals to improve urban housing and design'. Central to Owen's vision were his ideas on education, training and environment, which he believed formed the character of an individual. A particular contribution of Morrison's study is her reconstructions of Owen's intricate designs, from descriptions found in architectural works of

---

6   Grant, Anne MacVicar 1811 *The Superstitions of the Highlanders of Scotland: To their origins and tendency to which are added translations from the Gaelic*, 2 volumes, London: Longmans, Hurst, Rees, Orme and Brown.

the time, which give a vivid sense of how fully Owen envisaged this program of change.[7]

Cairns Craig, in a wide-ranging reflection, explores the tension between, on the one hand, reconstructions of Gaelic traditions and, on the other, approaches to the 'Celtic' that appear resistant both to the culture of modernity and 'to the actualities of past history'. He observes that the scientific side cannot be treated as a fixed benchmark, as 'the "new" sciences like anthropology—underwent radical revisions, so that what had seemed to be scientific "fact" in one decade was re-interpreted as pseudo–scientific fiction in the next'. He identifies, through the influence of David Hume's philosophy of mind, the aesthetic influence of 'associationism' on the reception of the Ossian cycle of James Macpherson (1736–96), in which

> the mind is released from its practical considerations and, in a state of 'reverie', traces a stream of associated memories whose unimpeded passage through the mind is constitutive of the experience of beauty or sublimity.

Thus, in Craig's analysis:

> The 'Celtomania' which Macpherson's Ossianic poems initiated was not the product of Macpherson's turning his back on modernity and on science: what he did was to adopt the most original modern conception of the 'science of man' ... It was precisely the modernity by which an apparently ancient past was shaped that made it so influential.

Like Jack in her study, Craig finds nuances in the distinction between literary and historical visions:

---

7   For example from: Whitwell, Stedman 1972 Description of an Architectural Model for a Community upon a Principal of United Interests as Advocated by Robert Owen, *Co-operative Communities: Plans and Descriptions*, edited by *Kenneth E. Carpenter*, New York: Arno Press.

a fiction can have as powerful effects as a supposedly empirical fact; indeed, in the human world, fictions are at least as potent as 'facts', and imagined memories as potent as fictions ... The mythic figures of Ossian and Cuchulain, as recovered by Macpherson and recreated by Yeats, become a force in the making of modern Ireland: memory recovered can thus become a future foreseen.

Will Christie explores the tension between the celebrated poet Dylan Thomas (1914–53) and his Welshness. Being raised in a culture immediate to Welsh-speaking Wales, but not himself a Welsh speaker, Thomas's affinity for rural Wales conflicts with many of the disparaging comments he made about it. Christie notes the contestable claims for Thomas's inheritance of Welsh culture from his imposing great-uncle, the bard and rural agitator Gwilym Marles (1834–79). He also documents the unshakeable desire of critics to link Thomas's prosody to its—indeed strikingly similar—counterparts in medieval Welsh bardic poetry. Christie, accordingly, finds Thomas's Welshness an elusive, but still tangible identity. One influence of which he is confident is an increasing nostalgia 'usually, but not always, self-ironic or framed as an indulgence', that was heightened by the destruction wrought on his native Swansea in WWII and which coincided with his retreat to live in the heartland of the Welsh language, during and after the war.

After these expansive studies of social life and literature, Dymphna Lonergan turns our attention to more atomised vehicles of memory in her study of the legacy of Irish words in Irish-English. In a data-rich study, she shines a strong light on the contexts in which words are transmitted into present use, including the sometimes changing forms in which they have been remembered over the modern period. She reflects on why some words initially adopted in English have been for different reasons returned to their Irish spellings, whilst others not. Of broad interest to critics of literature in English should be her close study of the use of Irish by James Joyce (1882–1941) in his novels *Ulysses* and *Finnegan's Wake*—which makes an interesting counterpoint to Will Christie's assessment of Dylan Thomas, as Joyce's interest in the Irish language was more overt than any interest Thomas had in Welsh. In a close study of Joyce's subversive uses of individual Irish words in

English phrases, as well as what appear to be deliberate misspellings, Lonergan distinguishes Joyce's literary English as his

> native language, not the English of England. Joyce's voice was an Irish one, made up of obsolete English words and anglicised Irish words but also the Dublin echoes of a Celtic language that was still in full voice elsewhere in Ireland. He feared the nets involved with the Irish language revival movement, but he could not possibly have escaped its linguistic influence, nor would he have wanted to.

Lonergan thus offers a quietly subversive approach to the question of how Anglo-Irish writing is 'Irish', in a nation where the native language is in minority—'regardless of the number of native speakers … this language duality is part of being Irish and of being an Irish writer'.

Coins are another vehicle of memory that we might describe as 'atomised'. John Kennedy considers the Celtic imagery of modern coins from a range of countries. Some of these—Ireland, the United Kingdom (Scotland, Wales, Northern Ireland and England), the Isle of Man and Continental Europe—are places with present or ancestral Celtic cultures. Coins from the Democratic Republic of the Congo and Fiji, however, offer some more abstruse causes for remembering Celtic warriors and artists. Whereas words are sometimes inconspicuous vehicles of memory, coins are a more public one, but it is poignant to observe that we live in a time in which coins themselves are very soon likely to become only historical artefacts.

Scottish Diasporas

The remaining eight chapters in this collection all concern the 'diasporas' of the Celtic nations. Most of these—consistent with the base from which this collection was assembled—focus on Australia. Those who formed the diasporas in countries such as Australia were often from the remoter parts of the Celtic home nations. Some of the more colonised of Europeans, they themselves became colonisers in new countries.

If we are inclined to associate the idea of diaspora culture in the modern era chiefly with the economic marginalisation—or just plain eviction—of rural people,[8] we should remember that before the eighteenth century, however, the more common reason for migration was either political exile or the desire for advancement through military service. Elizabeth Bonner's chapter on the fifteenth-century military diaspora of Scottish soldiers to France gives an interesting perspective on one group of the latter type, that made their lives in France in the service of Charles VII King of France (reign 1422–61). The context was the Auld Alliance, a military agreement dating from 1295 between the kingdoms of Scotland and France, and which endures today from a cultural perspective.[9] Bonner uses archival resources, along with the work of Philippe Contamine, to highlight the lives of these soldiers.[10] This chapter raises issues about how these military men are remembered from an historiographical perspective, while also proposing some interesting ideas about how primary sources housed on both sides of the English Channel can be utilised in more profitable ways to give a more complete picture of their lives, and the legacy that has endured over the centuries to the present day. Further explored are material memories of this group of Scots in particular, buildings, towns and the Scottish diaspora patchworks.

---

8   See for example, Mark-Fitzgerald, Emily 2013 *Commemorating the Irish Famine: Memory and Monument*, Liverpool: Liverpool University Press; Ó Gráda, Cormac 1999 *Black 47 and Beyond: The Great Irish Famine in History, Economy and Memory*, Princeton, NJ: Princeton University Press; Prentice, Malcolm 2008 *The Scots in Australia*, Sydney: University of NSW Press; Richards, Eric 2016 *The Highland Clearances: People, Landlords, and Rural Turmoil*, Edinburgh: Birlinn.

9   Bonner, Elizabeth 1999 Scotland's 'Auld Alliance' with France 1295–1560, *History* 84 (273) 5–30; MacDougall, N. 2001 *An Antidote to the English: The Auld Alliance, 1295–1560*, East Linton: Tuckwell.

10   Contamine, Philippe 1992 Scottish Soldiers in France in the Second Half of the Fifteenth Century: Mercenaries, Immigrants or Frenchmen in the making? *The Scottish Soldier Abroad, 1247–1967*, edited by Grant Simpson, Edinburgh: John Donald 16–30; see also Contamine, Philippe 1972 *Guerre, état et société à la fin du Moyen Age: études sur les armées des rois de France, 1337–1494*, Paris: La Haye-Mouton.

James Donaldson's contribution offers a study of life in the Scottish Highlands in the eighteenth and early nineteenth centuries and the economic challenges that led, at home and in the colonies, to the loss of the old way of life as well as the decline in the Gaelic language. In Donaldson's analysis, this was because English, especially in its written form

> as a vehicle of commerce and trade, was more universally understood. Many Gaelic speakers in Perthshire could not read their own Gaelic language nor indeed write it. Thus, on these very boundary edges of changing culture within Scotland itself, where the Gaelic language was becoming lost and the Celtic culture placed into severe decline, the place of memory and shared recollection between those Highland Celts people left behind the moving frontiers of change, must have remained in subsequent years, the sad remnants of an altered pattern of life and an almost forgotten cultural past.

In Donaldson's close analysis of life at both ends of the migration routes he draws upon close detail of the language, religion and literacy of Highland areas from the parish records in the Old and New Statistical Accounts of Scotland,[11] along with the shipping records that, *inter alia*, give detailed information related to literacy and language. Of particular interest for studies of Celtic culture is Donaldson's detail of the maintenance of Gaelic in NSW rural communities when well removed from their homelands.

Hugh Boyd Laing (1889–1974) was a Gaelic-speaking emigrant who was born in South Uist. After graduating from the University of Glasgow, he migrated to Australia in 1913, where he worked as a schoolteacher in Western Australia. He published a short volume of 'poetry, story and reminiscence' in Gaelic, *Gur Tir Mo Luaidh* ('To the

---

11 *Old Statistical Account of Scotland 1791–1799* edited by John Sinclair, 21 Vols, Edinburgh: William Creech; *New Statistical Account, by the Ministers of the Respective Parishes under the Superintendence of a Committee of the Society for the Benefit of the Sons and Daughters of Clergy*, Edinburgh: Constable 1834–45.

Land of my Praise'), in 1964. Many people in Australia remember the scandalous events whereby particular immigrants were excluded from Australia for failing a language test. This, by the *Immigration Restriction Act* of 1901, was not specified as requiring to be in English, but only a European language and in two instances (1927 and 1934) it was set in Scottish Gaelic with the deliberate intent that the examinees would fail.[12] Katherine Spadaro translates here Laing's Gaelic reminiscence of the 1927 episode, in which he participated, concerning three men who jumped ship in Bunbury from a South African vessel. Spadaro's poignant analysis of this compelling narrative highlights the ambiguities of Laing's position. He was an immigrant who was accepted within the Anglo-Australian community—unlike those being tested. But he was still not entirely of that community. He is cautious of his own memory of his native language, but surprised it was valued as a 'European' language in this context:

> I told him there was a female scholar at the High School who was very knowledgeable and fluent in German and French, and perhaps these would do the trick. He said they would not. The German language was still similar to the Dutch language which a number of the people of South Africa used, and, if we gave a dictation in German, there was a risk the Africans might not fail. As well as that, he knew that one of them had spent three years in Mauritius where French was spoken.
>
> As we were losing hope of finding a language that would be suitable, he asked if I knew another European language, and I told him I thought I could read Scottish Gaelic, although I had not spoken it for over fourteen years. He knew very little about Gaelic, and he asked where the people were who spoke it, and whether it was a kind of English, like the funny English he heard people from Glasgow speaking ...

---

12   Jupp, J. 2007 *From White Australia to Woomera: the Story of Australian Immigration*, 2nd edition Cambridge; New York: Cambridge University Press 8–18; see also The *Immigration Restriction Act* of 1901: https://www.legislation.gov.au/Details/C1901A00017

Irish-Australia

The remaining four studies in this collection explore aspects of the history of Irish-Australian life. Val Noone's contribution considers the Australian descendants of the Donegal O'Donnells and the ancestry of Dr Nicholas O'Donnell, the Melbourne-based leader of the Australian United Irish League (UIL) and a towering figure among Irish-Australian nationalists at the turn of the twentieth century. Noone's is one of a number of recent studies that have stepped beyond these topics to seek a more holistic vision of O'Donnell's life and career.[13] After an address to Adelaide members of the UIL in 1909, O'Donnell made some rather injudicious comments on contemporary O'Donnells, whom he branded 'perverts, back sliders and unionists'.[14] From this starting-point, Noone leads us into an exploration of O'Donnell's own intensive journey to authenticate his family's own claims, which he came to doubt in the course of his researches, that he was a descendant of the O'Donnells of Ulster. O'Donnell is noted as a pioneer of the Gaelic League in Australia and a scholar who corresponded with leading figures of the Celtic Studies in his era, most notably with Patrick Dinneen, the lexicographer who gave Irish its first dictionary. We gain a different vision here of those exchanges, inasmuch as they intertwined with a desire to explicate what he found to be a problem of history in his only family memories. As Noone observes, however, the mark of O'Donnell's scholarship was 'a critical handling of evidence'. His careless remarks in Adelaide soon inspired him to

> shift the public debate to encouraging his audience in the Australian Irish press to care 'not so much about tracing his descent to a great ancestor as proving by his life for Ireland and

---

13 See for example Geary, L. M. 2016 Nicholas Michael O'Donnell (1862–1920): A Melbourne Medical Life, *Australasian Journal of Irish Studies* 16, 13–29; Noone, V. editor 2017, *Nicholas O'Donnell's Autobiography*, Ballarat: Ballarat Heritage Services.

14 For the historical context: McGettigan, Darren 2005 *Red Hugh O'Donnell and the Nine Years War*, Dublin: Four Courts Press, 2005; Morgan, Hiram 1993 *Tyrone's Rebellion: The Outbreak of the Nine Year's War in Tudor Ireland*, Woodbridge: Boydell.

the race that he has endeavoured to be worthy of the patriots of the past, and to emulate their high aspirations, cheerful sacrifices, and noble deeds'.[15]

Noone's study sheds new light on the scholarly interests and political vision of a character who has often been selectively remembered mainly for his philological attainments.

Two contributions, by Richard Reid and Anne-Maree Whitaker, respectively deal with the performances and antiquarian displays of ecclesiastical and revolutionary nationalists. Reid tells the story of Cardinal Patrick Francis Moran and the 1904 St Mary's Cathedral Fair, one of many attempts that Moran made to harness public sentiment in the Irish-Australian community towards the completion of the grand, half-completed, cathedral he had inherited in Sydney. It was obvious that Moran was from the start of his career in Australia going to enforce an Irish Catholic tradition. This, he did through spectacle, while constructing an Irish Catholic past that he wanted his Australian flock to remember. Reid, quoting James Donovan, states that Moran's arrival in Sydney was heralded by quite a show of Irish symbolism, leaving no one in any doubt of his Irishness.

Reid reflects on three events where Moran was the central focus or organiser: the dedication/opening of St Patrick's cathedral on 31 October 1897; the St Patrick's Day procession in Sydney in 1901, and the central presentation at the great St. Mary's Cathedral Fair in September 1904. These events allowed for Moran, through the use of spectacle and rhetoric, to push the idea of an Irish Catholic 'Empire'. Moran was a noted scholar of Irish antiquity—one of genuinely academic attainments. The 1904 displays included replicas and facsimiles of objects that elevated the memory of the early/medieval Irish church, its centrepiece a full-scale replica of the high cross at Monasterboice in Co. Louth. These objects were there to create a link between the Australian Irish Catholics and the 'ancestors who have passed away into the night of oblivion, the simple Irish Catholics of one thousand years ago', thereby, forging a memory of a time before English occupation in Ireland.

---

15   *Southern Cross* 14 May 1909.

Anne-Maree Whitaker's chapter focuses on the commemorations in Sydney of the 1916 Rising. As she observes:

The Easter Rising not only shook the British Empire's foundations and enthused independence movements everywhere, it was also a pivotal event in the movement towards Irish Independence. As such its remembrance and commemoration over the period of a century reflect the evolving relationship between the Irish past and the present.

The 1916 Rising dramatically changed the landscape of Irish-Australian nationalism. As Noone observes, it brought O'Donnell's political career to an end, as it did that of many who had been leading figures of Irish nationalism in Australia at the turn of the century. The church had managed to claw its way into the commemorations of the centenary of 1798 and the reburial of the rebel Michael Dwyer, who is buried in the grand '98 Monument at Waverley in Sydney, but from 1929 onward the Waverley site would become the focal point of rituals led by republican veterans. Whitaker uses material that is now available as a result of the 2016 centenary to make links between the little-known families in Australia that were active participants in the 1916 rising, and who migrated to Australia as a result—with their roles only remembered in sections of the community. The documentation here of the stories of James Daly and May Gahan (later O'Carroll) and their families is an important study that notes their significant contributions to 1916, Australian politics, and the maintenance of a continuous commemoration of the rising since 1929.[16]

Performance is also at the heart of Janet Mollenhauer's study of Irish dance and immigration to Sydney, where she finds that 'Irish dancing has provided … modes of mnemonic connection to Ireland'.

The process of migration, whether by convict ship or aeroplane, is a rupture of the continuity of life: the psyche searches for the

---

16   Further on this topic also see now Reid, R., Kildea, J. and MacIntyre, P. 2020 *To Foster an Irish Spirit: The Irish National Association of Australasia 1915–2015.* Melbourne: Anchor Books.

familiar and the beloved, and finds comfort in the shared
memories of home, which are brought to life, or embodied, when
people dance. The dancing is a nexus of past and present, memory
and currency; it is a way of retaining links with the former life
while simultaneously working out a new identity in the current
circumstances of life.

An explanation of what Irish dancing is and how it is performed is
related as an 'embodiment of Ireland and Irishness' thus serving as 'a
locus for the propagation and perpetuation of memories of Ireland'.
Mollenhauer includes interviews conducted with recent immigrants
to Australia who are part of the Irish dancing scene in Sydney. Here
nostalgia allows individuals and societies to remember, either
singularly or collectively, their history. Her study, though based in her
fieldwork amongst modern dancing communities, also productively
theorises the memory dimension of dancing, using the ideas of Jens
Brockmier, Jing Wu and Svetland Boym among others.[17] This chapter
concludes by noting that memory has become globalised and that it is
'impossible to understand the trajectories of memory outside the global
frame of reference'.[18] Modern communication makes the experience of
late twentieth- and twenty-first-century migrants very different from
that of earlier times.

A particular strength of these thirteen reflections on Celtic memory
and foresight is their strong reach into a striking range of sources as
well as disciplines, including anthropology, architecture, history,
lexicography, literature, numismatics and philosophy. Together they
make a diverse, critical, approach to aspects of Celtic culture and identity.

17   Brockmeier, Jens 2002 Remembering and Forgetting: Narrative as Cultural
      Memory, *Culture and Psychology* 8 (1), 15–43; Wu 359–368; Boym, Svetlana
      2001 *The Future of Nostalgia*. New York, NY: Basic Books.
18   Assman, Aleida & Conrad, Sebastian 2010 *Memory in a Global Age:
      Discourse, Practices and Trajectories,* Basingstoke, Palgrave Macmillan 2.

1

Fable and Fiction in the Creation of Contemporary Beliefs about the Past in Scottish Life

Sybil Jack

> We, in the ages lying
> In the buried past of the earth,
> Built Nineveh with our sighing,
> And Babel itself with our mirth;
> And o'erthrew them with prophesying
> To the old of the new world's worth;
> For each age is a dream that is dying,
> Or one that is coming to birth.[1]
> (Arthur O'Shaughnessy, 1844–81)

Accounts of the more distant past have been handed down mainly in oral story-telling traditions, fact and myth blurring within. This paper looks at one remote Highland parish— Laggan—in an attempt to establish how Scots in different periods established the history that gave them identity. It examines how they incorporated the elements from the past and the gifts, like second sight, that supposedly distinguished the Scot from other races. Were these accounts of the Highlands a

---

1 O'Shaughnessy, Arthur 1874 Ode, *Music and Moonlight: Poems and Songs*, London: Chatto and Windus 2, lines 17–24.

mere historical creation?[2] It will conclude by briefly indicating how present-day fiction has reworked aspects of the spiritual world that imbued the older stories.

History is a difficult subject to pin down. Post-modern discussions sometimes doubted there could be accurate representation of the past, which implied that fiction set in the past was as valid as history. It may have obtained its justification from Erwin Schrödinger:

> Every man's world picture is and always remains a construct of his mind and cannot be proved to have any other existence, yet the conscious mind itself remains a stranger within that construct, it has no living space in it, you can spot it nowhere in space.[3]

In what sense then is history the authority for the literal representation of 'reality'?[4] The frontier between story and history is hard to pinpoint and some see fiction as a legitimate method of ascertaining the truth about human beings in society and time. Is there such a thing as recoverable historical reality from which was removed, as the Enlightenment hoped, all fable, inherited notions and invention. Or is the novel, as Brian Hamnett suggests, an intellectual and ideological response to cultural change?[5] Since history is primarily concerned with written texts, how far do or can such texts reflect 'what actually happened', especially when the object is the minutiae of the daily life of 'unimportant' groups or unrecorded people?[6] How are we to achieve what Henry Grey Graham hoped for when approaching the social life of Scotland in the eighteenth century:

---

2   Withers, Charles 1992 'The Historical Creation of The Scottish Highlands', *The Manufacture of Scottish History* edited by Ian Donnachie & Christopher Whatley, Edinburgh: Polygon 143–56.

3   Schrödinger, Erwin 2012 *What is Life? With Mind and Matter an Autobiographical Sketch,* Cambridge: Cambridge University Press 122.

4   Withers 150.

5   Hamnett, Brian 2011 *The Historical Novel in Nineteenth-Century Europe: Representations of Reality in History and Fiction,* Oxford University Press, ch. 1.

6   This approach is necessarily influenced by Hayden White for which see White, Hayden V. 1973 *Metahistory: The Historical Imagination in Nineteenth-Century Europe,* Baltimore MD: Johns Hopkins University Press.

It is in the inner life of a community that its real history is to be found—in the homes, and habits, and labours of the peasantry; in the modes, and manners, and thoughts of society; what the people believed and what they practised; how they farmed and how they traded; how the poor were relieved; how their children were taught, how their bodies were nourished, and how their souls were tended.[7]

How indeed are we to evaluate reports like those written about Scotland by appalled visiting English people about:

regions where the inhabitants spoke an uncouth dialect, were dressed in rags, lived in hovels, and fed on grain, with which he fed his horses; and when night fell, and he reached a town of dirty thatched huts, and gained refuge in a miserable abode that passed for an inn, only to get a bed he could not sleep in, and fare he could not eat.[8]

What is to be done with traditions orally passed from generation to generation, particularly in the Scottish Highlands where they were the common study of clan identity? And perhaps most crucially is memory reliable—are my memories accurate or are they invented?

Along with archaeology, history in practice requires creative and imaginative leaps of understanding in order to retrieve the past. In many cases, what we read, whether written by historians or litterateurs is as Tom Griffiths says, 'construct[ed] ... out of a lifelong dialogue between past evidence and present experience.'[9] There is constant tension with what has been called the landscape of history.[10] Historians are able to switch between time and space in a variety of ways that serve

7   Graham, Henry Grey 1899 Introduction, *Social Life of Scotland in The Eighteenth Century*, Vol. I, London: Adam And Charles Black vi.
8   Graham 2.
9   Griffiths, Tom 2016 *The Art of Time Travel: Historians and their Craft*, Carlton, Vic.: Black Inc. 10.
10 Gaddis, John Lewis 2002 *The Landscape of History: How Historians Map the Past,* Oxford: Oxford University Press, *passim*.

particular purposes but are effectively abstractions, and the historian's ability to reflect past reality is more limited than we often think.

How far should we accept a typical clan approach like that of Andrew Jervise writing about the Lindsays in 1853:

> Though traditions of the Lindsays are not so plentiful in the district as they were of old, when the hills and dales and running brooks were more or less associated with stories of their daring and valour, enough remains to show the almost unlimited sway which they maintained over the greater portion of Angus, and a large part of the Mearns. Like the doings of other families of antiquity, those of the Lindsays are mixed with the fables of an illiterate age; and, though few redeeming qualities of the race are preserved in tradition, popular story ascribes cruel and heartless actions to many of them. Still, extravagant as some of these stories are, they have not been omitted, any more than those relating to other persons and families who fall within the scope of this volume; and, where such can be refuted, either by reference to documentary or other substantial authority, the opportunity has not been lost sight of.[11]

This sort of account, inspired by aspects of Thomas Pennant's popular eighteenth-century tours, gives an idea of superstitions acceptable to the 'cultivated' people of the time.[12]

Recent history has started to distinguish between different parts of the Highlands and to suggest that they were more closely involved in the wider society of the kingdom by the sixteenth century than is usually accepted.[13] This, however, is not a new insight. There was a common view of the Highland social custom already expressed in the early sixteenth century by John Major who wrote:

---

11   Jervise, Andrew 1853 *The History and Traditions of the Land of the Lindsays in Angus and Mearns with notices of Alyth and Meigle,* Edinburgh: Sutherland and Knox vi.

12   Pennant, Thomas 1772 *A Tour in Scotland* 1769 (2nd edition), London: White.

13   Kennedy, Allan 2014 *Governing Gaeldom: The Scottish Highlands and the Restoration State, 1660–1688,* Leiden: Brill 17–30.

here is kinship of blood among these tribes; their possessions are few, but they follow one chief as leader of the whole family (*caput progenei—ceann ciimidh*) and bring with them all their friends and dependants.[14]

It was what Mrs Grant also said at the end of the eighteenth century, speaking primarily of Laggan where she was living as the wife of the local clergyman:

> You always hear Highlanders talk of countries; but did I ever tell you what our countries are? Not by any means parishes, counties or any such divisions ... but a habitable track, divided by rocks, mountains and narrow passes ... inhabited by a particular clan. These ... differ in looks, language and manners, more that you can imagine possible; nay they affect to differ; for bordering clans often live in bitter and jealous rivalship and though individuals love and sometimes marry each other, the general dislike continues ... [15]

Laggan in Badenoch was in the nineteenth century described as 'one of the most interior districts of Scotland'.[16] It was the largest of the

---

14 Major, John 1892 *A History of Greater Britain as well England as Scotland compiled from the ancient authorities by John Major by name indeed a Scot, but by profession a theologian 1521* translated from the original Latin and edited with notes by Archibald Constable, Edinburgh University Press for the Scottish History Society 334, 358–9.

15 Grant, Anne MacVicar 1809 *Letters from the Mountains, Being the Real Correspondence of a Lady, Between the Years 1778–1807*, edited with notes and additions, by her son. J. P., Esq. 2 vols, London: Longman, Brown, Green and Longmans I.250 (this is the Boston Greenough and Stebbins edition).

16 MacBain, Alexander 1922 *Place Names of the Highlands and Islands of Scotland, with Notes and Forward by W. J. Watson*, Stirling: MacKay 189: 'one of the most interior districts of Scotland; it lies on the northern watershed of the mid Grampians, and the lofty ridge of the Monadhlia range forms its northern boundary, while its western border runs along the centre of the historic Drum-Alban. Even on its eastern side the mountains seem to have threatened to run a barrier across, for Craigellachie thrusts its huge nose forward into a valley already narrowed by the massive form of the Ord Bain

Badenoch parishes and perhaps the last to be altered by 'progress' in the eighteenth century, although eighty people had been evicted from Aberarder in 1770 as a result of Ewen Macpherson's forfeiture of the estate in the 1745.

There are various reasons for choosing to focus on Laggan, perhaps the principal one being that it may be the source of much that we assume about wider Highland history. This was where James Macpherson, the 'discoverer' (or inventor) of Ossian lived and returned to end his life, so this is where one might envisage him finding his myths and poems in the Highland seats.

> Can we read beneath the surface of the text … woods stocked with wildfowl and the mountains behind them … the natural seat of the red-deer and roe … his [the clan chief] commands … partook more of the authority of a father … [17]

Here was a man who although he feared that Jacobitism was lost, produced material about a past in which the old Celtic highland spirit lived on, a Gaelic world where the old order of the warriors and heroes, the spirit, romanticism and traditions of the people, of a pre-modern life without corruption, survived.[18] Then we have Anne MacVicar, Mrs Grant, the minister's wife, whose writing on the Highlands were widely read in Britain and America around 1800.[19]

Another significant author whose impressions of the Highlands was at least partly formed in Laggan was William Forbes Skene, later

---

and the range of hills behind it. This land of mountains is intersected by the river Spey, which runs midway between the two parallel ranges of the Grampians and the Monadhlia'. There are similar accounts in the nineteenth-century statistical accounts, such as Cameron, Rev. Donald 1845 *New Statistical Account of Scotland,* Parish of Laggan XIV.417

17 *The Poems of Ossian the Son of Fingal* 1792, translated by James Macpherson, Edinburgh: J Robertson 346.

18 Gibbs, Chris 2006 The New Britons: Scottish Identity in the 18th and 19th Centuries. Napoleon Series. https://www.napoleon-series.org/research/society/c_scottishidentity.html

19 Grant, Anne MacVicar 1811 *The Superstitions of the Highlanders of Scotland: To their origins and tendency to which are added translations from the Gaelic,* 2 volumes, London: Longmans, Hurst, Rees, Orme and Brown.

Historiographer Royal for Scotland whose *Celtic Scotland* (1876–80) has been described as the most important contribution to Scottish history written during the nineteenth century.[20] He, in 1825, boarded with the minister Mackintosh Mackay, who was a Gaelic scholar and oversaw the printing of a Gaelic dictionary. And perhaps, since we are in Australia, we should note that Mackay himself—a rather neglected figure—may have brought those ideas to Australia since he emigrated in 1853 and was a key figure in the Presbyterian movement there until he left in 1861, preaching as he often did in Gaelic and eulogising the Highland character.[21]

Later accounts suggest that what became Laggan was inhabited from a very long time ago as there are 'on lofty plateaux and hill sides the marks of early cultivation, the ridges and the rigs or ftannagan.'[22] As Dun-Da-Lamh is two miles from Laggan and recent archaeology shows Iron Age—or earlier—material, we can assume constant inhabitation from distant times. But that may be all we can say. Not even a dim light can be shed on the forgotten societies that died away. As Bruce Webster says, 'lost kingdoms can rarely be reanimated, we have only a tangle of confusion and contradictory fragments.'[23]

Although MacBain and Skene squabbled over the ownership and descent of the lordship of Badenoch,[24] not much written material survives for Laggan before the later Middle Ages and then it is mostly formal grants, but stories have been handed down. Clan Chattan were believed to be the native Celtic inhabitants of the area. The now ruined St Killen's church of Logykenny or Laggan is considered to be one of the

---

20 Skene, William Forbes 1876–80 *Celtic Scotland, a History of Ancient Alban*, 3 vols. Edinburgh: Douglas.
21 *The Banner* (Melbourne) 10 January 1854.
22 MacBain, Alexander 1889–90 'Badenoch: Its History, Clans and Place Names', *Transactions of the Gaelic Society of Inverness* 16, 148–97. In Laggan the names of Macpherson family members do not start until mid-seventeenth century.
23 Webster, Bruce 1997 *Medieval Scotland: The Making of an Identity* Basingstoke: Palgrave Macmillan 29–30; See also Moffat, Alistair 2011 *The Faded Map: Lost Kingdoms of Scotland* Edinburgh: Birlinn, where he is more concerned with southern Scotland.
24 Fraser-Mackintosh, Charles 1877 The Depopulation of Aberarder in Badenoch 1770, *Celtic Magazine* 33, 418–26

21

oldest in the land. Ard Merigie, was 'the height for rearing the standard.'
Apparently, the area was held

> sacred from the most remote antiquity, and is reported by
> tradition to be the burial-place of seven Caledonian kings, who
> lived about the period when the Scots, driven northwards of the
> Tay by the Picts, held their seat of government at Dunkeld.[25]

Nearby is also Loch an Righ. The kings, it is said, and their retinue,
hunted on the banks of the lake for the greater part of almost every
summer.[26] Its original inhabitants were the MacDonalds and Kennedys
and smaller clans and families such as the MacGregors, the
Macphersons, Macintoshes, Cattanachs, Clerks and MacIntyres,[27] but
not until a list of heads of families in 1679 do we start to have
substantial documentary evidence of the inhabitants.[28]

Alan Macpherson by a careful analysis of the Register of Marriages
and Baptisms in the Parish of Laggan for the period between 1775 and

---

25 Webster, David 1819 *A Topographical Dictionary of Scotland,* Edinburgh:
    Peter Hill 3.
26 Churches of the Medieval Diocese of Moray by Cushnie enterprises:
    https://bit.ly/35IV6AR.
27 See various works by Macpherson, Alan G., especially 1967 An Old Highland
    Parish Register: Survivals of Clanship and Social Change in Laggan,
    Invernesshire, 1775–1854, *Scottish Studies* 11, 149–92. By the fifteenth century it
    was Huntly who possessed all the land in Badenoch. Its inhabitants were the clan
    Chattan amongst the 'Wild Scots' and said to be native Celts. By the late sixteenth
    century, the Macintoshes were dominant in the area and bitterly opposed to the
    Gordons. They obtained the land after Huntly was forfeit in 1572. They were
    opposed by the Macphersons who also claimed to lead clan Chattan.
28 Macpherson notes that a list of the heads of families in Laggan in 1679, may help
    genealogists and as an example lists Cluny—Duncan Macpherson of Cluny,
    James Macpherson there, William vic Iain vic Andrew there, Dougal Oig there,
    John Macgillivray there, Donald Mac Coil Oig there, John Miller there, John
    Miller his son there, Allister Macgillivray there, Kenneth Mor there, Angus Mac
    Ian Mor there, William Mac Ian vic William there, William Mac David, tailor
    there, Allister Maclennan there, Duncan Mac Coil Oig there, Donald Mac Ewen
    Dhu vic Keir there. See Fraser-Mackintosh, Charles, 1897 Antiquarian Notes,
    Historical, Genealogical and Social (Second Series) Inverness-Shire, Parish by
    Parish, https://bit.ly/2HqbOet; https://bit.ly/2HeN2hL

1854 shows what the social patterns were. His painstaking work has provided us with a solid basis for the population of the area. He has shown a high degree of endogamy within the clan before the eighteenth century. This helped maintain continuity of possession and so presumably of social practice:

> the whole social spectrum in the parish, from country lairds such as Macpherson of Cluny and Macpherson of Glentruim, through lesser tacksman families, to the host of humbler small tenants and farm servants who formed the majority in the community. Besides farmers, grieves and farm servants the economic structure of the population is found to include the parish minister, the parish schoolmaster, traditional tradesmen such as millers, blacksmiths, carpenters, tailors and shoemakers, country merchants, and after 1800—the shepherds and gamekeepers of the new economy. [29]

He rightly believed that his use of it in this manner led to a further breakthrough in understanding the traditional Highland way of life. His analysis leads him to a definition of clan life that differs from the one we see as canonical. The social structure of the Highlands was one of

> cantonal communities composed of a number of distinct clans or extended kin-groups, the dominant clan of one district usually extending in particular lineages (*sliochdan*) into adjacent districts where these then assumed the position of a dependent or minor clan (*clann*) in that community. It was this interlocking cantonal and community structure that was referred to in the disturbed years of the early eighteenth century as the 'clan system'. Its fundamental units were the local lineages associated with particular farms or groups of farms in which rights of ancient possession were acquired and asserted through conjoint tenure and the practice of runrig.[30]

---

29   Macpherson, An Old Highland Parish 120.
30   Macpherson, Alan G. 1984 The Community in Laggan: Marriage Patterns, *Journal of Historical Geography*, 10(1), 1–14.

He is also able to show from an attested document, dated 31 May 1678 how the forests and the powers of the foresters helped the heads of the local clans maintain control over the lands.

Let us turn to the descriptions that Anne MacVicar, Mrs Grant, who was for over twenty years resident in the parish as the wife of the minister, wrote in letters to her friends.[31] Literary convention required her to speak diffidently of these letters in which she had been trying to give her Lowland friends an idea of what is the core self-identity of the Highlanders:

> they are genuine but broken and interrupted sketches of a life spent in the most remote obscurity ... much is lost by the necessity of withholding those parts which contained most of narrative and anecdote.[32]

The second London edition starts 'reality was the prop on which I leant' ... and further on speaks of distinguishing 'the durable pencil of truth from the watercolours of fiction.'[33] Her letters in fact, as Graham wanted, give a pleasant account of daily life—as she perceived it—of events such as the departure of the ordinary people for the uplands in spring and their return in August.

Her works were influential on 'romantic' images of the Highlands before Walter Scott, who was a friend of hers and encouraged her to write. In her letters she describes the locals who 'so faithfully ... preserve and so accurately detail 'the tales of the times of old and the songs of the bards'[34] She was said in the early years of the nineteenth century to be 'one of the idols of literary society both in London and Edinburgh'[35] who was subsequently accused of 'having idealised the character and manners of her countrymen' and saw life through

---

31 She was no feminist—and argued forcibly against Mary Wollstonecraft's ideas in her letters.
32 Grant, *Letters* I.5
33 Grant, *Letters* I.7
34 Grant, *Letters* I.53.
35 Paston, George 1901 *Little Memoirs of the Eighteenth Century,* New York: E. P. Dutton 237ff.

rose-coloured glasses. Such were comments like this on the Highlanders—they had:

Plentiful lack of wealth and an abundant scarcity of knowledge but our common people have not often low sordid notions, cant phraseology, nor the callous hardness that marks that class of mind ...

She originally came to somewhere quite unfamiliar to her. On 14 August 1779, five years after she arrived, she acknowledged the help she had received from her mother-in-law in settling in, 'I should have been lost and bewildered on my entrance on such a new scene as the government of more than half a dozen country servants and the complicated economy of a farm ... like the neighbours.'[36] At a different time she recounts her own business.

August 27 1787. You Lowlanders have no idea of the complicated nature of Highland farming and of the odd customs which prevail here. Formerly from the wild and warlike nature of the men and their haughty indolence, they thought no rural employment compatible with their dignity unless indeed the plow. Fighting, hunting, lounging in the sun, musick and poetry were their occupations; for the latter, though you would not think it, their language is admirable This naturally extended the women's province both of labour and management. The care of the cattle was peculiarly theirs ... [problems ... when her shepherd is in one glen and her dairymaid in another with her milk-cattle.]
I shall, between fancy and memory, sketch out the diary of one July Monday. I mention Monday being the day that all dwellers in glens come down for the supplies. Item at four o'clock Donald arrives with a horse loaded with butter, cheese and milk. The former I must weigh instantly. He only asks an additional blanket for the children, a covering for himself; two milk tubs, a cog. and another spoon, because little Peter threw one of the set in the burn; two stone of meal, a quart of salt; two pounds of flax for the

---

36   Grant, *Letters* I. 218.

spinner, for the grass continues so good that they will stay a week longer. He brings the intelligence of the old sow's being the joyful mother of a dozen pigs, and requests something to feed her with. All this must be ready in an hour; before the conclusion of which comes Ronald, from the high hills, where our sheep and young horses are all summer, and only desires meal, salt, and women with shears, to clip the lambs, and tar to smear them. He informs me that the black mare has a foal, a very fine one, but she is very low and I must instantly send one to bring her to the meadows. Before he departs the tenants who do us services come; they are going to stay two days in the oakwood, cutting timber for our new byre, and must have a competent provision of bread, cheese and ale for the time they stay. [and then her work for the children and her husband urging her to go with him for a walk][37]

She always spoke well of her in-laws, writing of Castle Grant:

... the amiable propensity of this family, to cherish the inferior gentry and their humble relations who' dwelt under their shadow ... attached many of them, by the double tie of kindred and feudal subjection. ... Never surely was power so gently used of protection so gratefully acknowledged ... [it] affords one of the most pleasing views of human nature that can be met with.[38]

At other times she writes of passing events. In July 1786 she noted:

roups (sales) then are a source of great amusement here and a very expensive one to the roup-makers. At the dissolution of any family, by the death or removal of its head, it is customary here to send letters of invitation to all the connexions ... to countenance the ceremony ... an expectation, warranted by old custom, that these allies ... will purchase things rather beyond their value [39]

---

37   Grant, *Letters* I.237, 256–7.
38   Grant, *Letters* I.240.
39   Grant, *Letters* I.247–9.

The more she got to know them, the more she admired the Highlanders, pleased with unservile courtesy in the lower class 'because we don't expect it.'[40] There were oddities 'A Highlander never sits at ease at a loom; 'tis like putting a deer in the plow.'[41] What she stresses most is family commitment to one another. 'Since bad seasons and new modes of farming have impoverished the peasantry, I do not think there is a poor tenant in this parish but what is in some measure supported by his children. And there is no instance of one failing in this tender retribution.'[42] The problem with this intense commitment to family however was that it made it difficult for anyone, however benevolent, to settle amongst them. They would prefer the most insignificant of third cousins if there was a problem. The ties of blood and the duties of relationship were more important than anything. They were, she wrote, 'poor with a better grace than other people'. She was impressed that the old 'serve for song-books and circulating libraries, so faithfully do they preserve and so accurately detail the tales of the times of old and the song of the bards.' And she felt she was recording a lifestyle that was 'fast gliding into the mist of obscurity and will soon be no more than a remembered dream'.[43]

Mrs Grant was writing as the major departure of many in the clearances was beginning and change was altering appearances.[44] She speaks of 'Inverness ... from the odd looking hill of Tommin-a-heurich ... the fertile shires of Ross and Murray indulge the eye with a boundless view of gentlemen's seats, seated generally under the shelter of eminences and surrounded with wood plantations (for the gentry here are great improvers ...'[45]

---

40   Grant, *Letters* I.26.
41   Grant, *Letters* I.241.
42   Grant, *Letters* II.89.
43   Grant, *The Superstitions* I.5.
44   Fraser-Macintosh, The Depopulation of Aberarder 418–26; Ramsey, William J. 2002–4 Construction, Contention and Clearance—Life in 18th century Badenoch, *Transactions of the Gaelic Society of Inverness* 63, 337–57.
45   Grant, *Letters* I.169.

How accurate is she?[46] Clearly her presentation is affected by her philosophical ideas but it seems a fair reflection when one looks at the other records.[47]

Another thing too we get in such literary accounts—images of how the forests round about were managed.[48] Elizabeth Grant in her autobiography provides a lively account of the process—the numbers involved, the way the logs were prepared, and the water managed:

> The number of people employed in the forest was great. At this winter season little could be done beyond felling the tree, lopping the branches, barking the log, while the weather remained open … The logs prepared by the lopper had to be drawn by horses to the nearest running water and there left in large quantities till the proper time for sending them down the streams. It was a busy scene all through the forest … this driving lasted till sufficient timber was collected to render the opening of the sluices profitable. Formerly small saw-mills had been erected wherever there was sufficient water-power, near the part of the forest where the felling was going on, and the deals when cut were carted down to the Spey … It was picturesque to come suddenly out of the gloom of the pine-trees, on to a little patch of cultivation near a stream with a cottage or two and a saw-mill at work, itself an object of interest in a rude landscape … In order to have a run of water at command, the sources of the little rivers were managed artificially [49]

---

46 She writes of Knoydart [it]is the asylum of the catholicks; all who live in the country are of that profession, and, wonderful to tell, a gentleman of family, great learning, genteel manners. And most spotless life, a bishop of their communion spends his life in this truly savage abode; he has no other motive but the desire of doing good to those who can make him no adequate recompense. There too in the most secluded recess of these wilds, in a corner so obscure that the sun can scarce shine on it, is a seminary, where boys are educated for the priesthood (that is prepared for foreign seminaries) through very great poverty and hardship. *Letters* I.95

47 See Jack, Sybil 2007 Keeping the Faith: the Catholic Mission in the Highlands 1560–1800, *Journal of the Sydney Society for Scottish History* 11, 40–64.

48 Fowler, John 2002 Introduction, *Landscapes and Lives: The Scottish Forest Through the Ages* Edinburgh: Canongate.

She goes on to describe at length the way the timber was carried into the water and how rafts were made at the Spey by the Ballindalloch men to carry the floats further.[50]

Surprisingly, we get relatively little about the superstitions in Anne MacVicar's letters—although she wrote that she had 'learned to listen to stories of apparitions and predictions with as much indulgence though with less credulity than N. B. Halhed.'[51] She refers to the *Bean Nighe*, for instance, the washer woman at the ford created when a woman died in childbirth; they became this sort of fairy ghost and remained in such a state until the day they normally would have died.[52] Or, in passing, speaks of

> like our witches, who, when in pursuit of a devoted object of vengeance, dare not cross a running water, that being a boundary by the laws of "magick irremediable"; a very comfortable regulation this for good nautical Christians.[53]

She was in fact remarkably tolerant of what she noted, writing of the store of ghost and visions, whom they kept like Teraphim [these were the biblical idols in the Old Testament evidently used for divination] in their secret chambers and were afraid to acknowledge yet unwilling to resign.[54] From her knowledge, she alleged that

> on all occasions where I have had this kind of second-hand acquaintance with them, are in a high degree moral, rational, and prudent and give the best advice imaginable [55]

---

49 Grant, Elizabeth (of Rothiemurchus) 1911 *Memoirs of a Highland Lady,* edited by Lady Strachey, London: John Murray 218–29.
50 Grant of Rothiemurchus 235.
51 Nathaniel Brassey Halhed was an orientalist and linguist who worked in Bengal.
52 Grant, *Letters* II.9.
53 Grant, *Letters* II.121.
54 Grant, *The Superstitions* I.16.
55 Grant, *The Superstitions* I.225.

Spirits were never seen by more than one person at a time and permitted to do so for sin committed by the visitant.[56]

In her essay on Highland superstitions she puts the beliefs into categories. The first danger to be guarded against, then, was the power of fairies in taking away the infant, or its mother; the locals saw the need for baptism and other rites to protect it[57] and the folly of boasting of the health or beauty of the child.

Then there was the danger of its being carried off in sleep—the attendant took a bible and went thrice round it, waving all the time the open leaves and adjuring all the enemies of mankind, by the power and virtue contained in that book, to 'fly instantly to the Red Sea &c.'.[58] Dreams of the dead occurred if grief is too great, and the appearance of dead children to smooth the bed of their parents, she sees as understandable—and perhaps, something she experienced herself or was expected to.[59]

Most interesting perhaps is the account of the local Laggan spirit who was put to rest by her husband preaching on the spot where she normally appeared. This was the meagre and haggard woman, known as the Caillich Rua. Grant tells us the story. She had a lover whom her brother in consequence of some feud attacked and killed. She buried him in one of those fairy hillocks in some spot which neither friend nor enemy could discover. She never spoke afterwards, nor could be prevailed on to re-enter the dwelling of her father. When she died or whether she died at all was never ascertained. Still the shade wandered in mournful silence and still appeared to all in the tribe, to which she herself belonged, as she seemed to retain some resentment towards them although she never annoyed anyone. Finally, Mrs Grant's husband, the minister, carried out a service in the presence of all local dwellers and she was evidently put to rest and the minister was very angry at the suggestion that he had banished her.[60]

---

56 Grant, *The Superstitions* I.214.
57 Grant, *The Superstitions* I.164
58 Grant, *The Superstitions* I.166. See also 165, 167 (the evil eye), 169 ('God save the bairn or the beast'), 225 ('mountain ghostes').
59 Grant, *The Superstitions* I.181-2.

Can such accounts, in fact, enable historians to present impartial reconstructions of events, in accordance with what is known of the mental and emotional climate of the place and period? Ann MacVicar writes as a conservative Presbyterian woman and her letters may help the historian penetrate thought processes that differ from the present. Her approach is governed by the public discourse of the time in which she wrote and simultaneously helps form cultural memory and transform images of the past. She is visibly influenced by her perception of her audience.

Historians, however, generally seem to pick and choose from the texts available. The strangeness of the past, that is, must be mediated by what the auditor can accept. Literary writers can be more inclusive in their presentations. While for them the past should not be comfortable, the reader must have some sympathy for or abhorrence of the subject.[61] Hence the relationship between history and literature is strained as symbols are selected and abandoned.

What, therefore, is the function of a novel in relation to history—is it re-imagining what history cannot or strengthening the myths of the past?[62] How do ways of looking at the past get created? Does the storyteller retrieve the past or does she recreate it? Are we concerned with fictitious history rather than historical fiction and what role does imaginative writing play in recreating our experience of the past?[63] This does not have a single simple answer.

Historical novelists, just like historians, approach their subject in different ways. Are we to see Scotland's history as falsified by Walter Scott,[64] or laud Scott as the stimulator of necessary human imagination?[65] Or treat his work as an aspect of legal consolidation

---

60 Grant, *The Superstitions* I.269–70. For the appearance of less well-meaning ghosts—vigils and appearances 228–30; 284 those who smelled the smell of cooking or heard the sound of pipes ... from the fairy hills.
61 Griffiths 14, quoting the American historian Richard White.
62 Craig, Cairns 1999 *The Modern Scottish Novel: Narrative and the National Imagination*, Edinburgh University Press 157.
63 Lascelles, Mary 1980 *The Story-Teller Retrieves the Past Historical Fiction and Fictitious History* Oxford: Clarendon Press 112–3.
64 Craig 117.
65 Lascelles, *passim*.

that paradoxically resulted in a belief in what was seen, however improbable.[66]

Some like Allan Massie avoided the problem of 'reality' by writing as a past storyteller himself—telling the story of Augustus as an account given by the man himself to his heirs, and the story of Arthur in similar ways, presenting the myths as a part of a separate narrative.[67] Neil Gunn adopts an alternative approach putting the images of the past into the mind of the present-day archaeologist in *The Silver Bough*. It seemed to him 'that Mrs Mackenzie and Mrs Cameron carried on a way of life that was the essence of the traditional inheritance of long periods of human living'.[68] Then there are those who like Diana Gabaldon in her *Outlander* series effectively adopt and adapt the beliefs about fairyland transport between one place or time and another. The idea of a portal to another dimension—outlandish and otherlandish where 'the stones' are the passage—is a popular present-day fantasy.

The way choice of subjects in historical fiction shifts suggests that the readers' interests play a part—and so does the medium. What is clear is the extent to which their images stay in our minds. Laggan, however, has shaped our image of the Highlands in a much more forceful way than I have here described—it is Glenbogle in 'The Monarch of the Glen' TV series.

---

66 Wickman, Matthew 2013 *The Ruins of Experience: Scotland's "Romantick" Highlands and the Birth of the Modern World*, Philadelphia PA: University of Pennsylvania Press.
67 Massie, Allan 1986 *Augustus*, London: Bodley Head; in the preface to his volume on Arthur, Massie says that it 'purports to be a translation of a narrative written by the medieval scholar and astrologer Michael Scott: Massie, Allan 2003 *Arthur the King*, New York: Carol and Graf.
68 Gunn, Neil 2003 [1948] *The Silver Bough*, Dunbeath: Whittles Publishing, Chapter 12.

2

Robert Owen and Villages of Unity and Cooperation: a New Concept of Urbanism

Tessa Morrison

By the beginning of the eighteenth century the Industrial Revolution had begun to scar the British landscape with polluting factories. This destruction of the environment is epitomised by William Blake's poem in *Milton* when he looked for Jerusalem among those 'dark Satanic mills'. The Industrial Revolution had caused endemic social problems and a national housing crisis. In 1800, self-made Welsh industrialist Robert Owen formed a partnership with the Chorlton Twist Company to purchase the cotton mills at the village of New Lanark, in southern Scotland. Although Owen was a junior partner he was also the manager and could implement many reforms in the village and its society. Although he attempted to achieve a political solution for factory reform and conditions his concerted efforts failed to make any real changes to the conditions of industrial workers and their families. In 1817 Owen was asked by the 'Committee of the Association for the Relief of the Manufacturing and Labouring Poor' to give his views of the causes of the national distress. From this point, Owen turned his energies away from factory reform, where he had had very little success, into what he perceived to be a practical solution to the crisis—Villages of Unity and Cooperation. This paper considers how Owen's concept of the Villages of Unity and Cooperation was a new concept in self-contained urbanism, which appears to be radical in its approach. Although no Village of Unity and Cooperation was built in the manner that he had conceived, his new urbanism concept was highly influential throughout the nineteenth century and into the twentieth and twenty-first centuries. Owen's concepts of urbanism revealed great foresight, although they have not been fully utilised, yet they remain controversial. In 2015 the Scottish Government Reporter dismissed an appeal lodged against the refusal of planning permission for a £500 million development of a town, Owenstown, in southern Scotland, designed to Owen's principles. Although his concepts are 200 years old, they remain relevant to current proposals to improve urban housing and design.

Although the Industrial Revolution made the most dramatic and rapid changes to the environment, the change in the pattern of village life in the countryside began much earlier. In the discussion between Thomas More; Peter Gilles, the town clerk of Antwerp; Cardinal Morton; and philosopher and traveller Hythlodaeus in Book One of *Utopia* (1516), Hythlodaeus stated:

> Your sheep which are ordinarily so meek and require so little to maintain them, now they begin (so they say) to be so voracious and fierce that they devour even the people themselves: they destroy and despoil field, houses, towns.[1]

Hythlodaeus referred to the growing need for fine wool for the production of expensive clothes for the gentry and clergyman. The estate owners 'enclose everything as pasture, they destroy homes, level towns, leaving only the church as a stable for the sheep'.[2] In the early sixteenth century farmers were thrown out of smallholdings; men, women, orphans, widows and small children became homeless to produce wool.

By the seventeenth century the process of land reform through 'enclosure' had become widespread. This process saw the estate owners enclose the common land that was used as common grazing land by the villagers, which had a devastating effect on villagers since they

---

1   Miller, Clarence H. 2001 translator, *Thomas More: Utopia*, New Haven CT: Yale University Press 22.

2   *Thomas More: Utopia* 22.

depended upon these common lands to sustain their livestock. Most of the villagers worked as labourers on neighbouring farms. However, this employment was inconsistent throughout the year. They supplemented their meagre wages through other means, such as small-scale farming. They generally lived on small plots from one to four acres with certain pastoral rights to the common land.[3] Through the loss of their pastoral rights to the common ground they could no longer sustain their own framing practices and had to increasingly rely on their employment as labourers to sustain their living. In turn, they had to relinquish grazing stock as a result of the enclosures and this in turn led to a reduction in their future income.[4]

By 1710, 47 per cent of the commons in Britain had been enclosed.[5] These enclosures had been accomplished with the help of Acts of Parliament. With an increasing population in Britain there was a need to produce food and the enclosures intensified to accommodate demand. The development of agricultural mechanisation and industrialisation increased the need for more land under agriculture. Eventually the controversy that surrounded enclosures led to the Enclosure Consolidation Act of 1801 (sometimes referred to as General Enclosure Act), which recognised the accelerated pace of the enclosures over the previous century. This Act entitled villagers to compensation for the loss of the commons but generally it supplied less arable and smaller plots of land as compensation and villagers were obliged to provide expensive fencing for their allotments. It was a case of very little and far too late, and was considered a 'dismal half measure',[6] since by 1801 there were few commons left. Although the enclosures had been denounced by the Church there was no political will to oppose them.

With the new efficiencies in farming, such as new fertilisers, crop rotation, irrigation systems and mechanisation, a significant proportion of the rural population was displaced and there was a systematic

---

3   Moffit, Louis 2013 *England on the Eve of Industrial Revolution*, London: Taylor and Francis 106.
4   Chambers, J. D. and G. E. Mingay 1966 *The Agricultural Revolution 1750–1888*, London: B. T. Bradford 19.
5   Overton, Mark 1996 *Agricultural Revolution in England: The Transformation of the Agrarian Economy 1500–1850*, Cambridge University Press 148.
6   Chambers and Mingay 121.

reduction in the number of rural villages through depopulation and demolition. The consequence of enclosure was a depopulation of the countryside and an increase in the urban population. However, enclosure was not the only reason for depopulating of the countryside. The Agricultural Revolution made possible the Industrial Revolution which further displaced many of the villagers. The enclosures forced the villagers into towns, increasing the urban population. However, as urban dwellers they fuelled more demand for food and commodities. The need for more commodities in turn fuelled the need for technological change to support increasing and more efficient production.

Spinning wool, cotton or flax was a stable industry in many cottage homes and was a major occupation of many women in both weaving and spinning districts in the first half of the eighteenth century.[7] These cottage proto-industries occurred in the countryside among the villagers and subsidised their meagre incomes from their small farms. The goods produced in cottage industries were mainly textiles with mass-marketing potential but also included other products such as gloving, straw plaiting, glass, leather and metalwork.[8] Proto-industrialisation represented a clear distinction between town and country. The manufacturing was executed in the country while the towns were centres of trade and commerce. In some regions, the demand of the market outstripped the available labour source, thus introducing changes in industrial organisation and techniques to meet the demand with less labour. This accommodation to meet demand led to the factory-based process of mass production.[9] The proto-industries were distributed throughout the countryside in mills that were highly mechanised and employed hundreds, and in some establishments, thousands, of weavers, who worked long hours under poor conditions but were able to generate cheaper products than the cottage industries.

---

7   Moffit 179.
8   Houston, Rab and Snell, K. D. M. 1984 Proto-Industrialization? Cottage Industry, Social Change, and Industrial Revolution, *The Historical Journal* 27, 473–92: 473.
9   Clarkson, L. A. 1985 *Proto-industrialisation: The First Phase of Industrialisation,* London: Macmillan 27.

The development of these weaving and spinning technologies from the 1730s increased production through mechanisation. By the mid-eighteenth century, the first water-powered mills were being used. These mills could produce as much as one hundred horsepower and they continued to be used well into the nineteenth century.[10] However, with each development in technology different social problems emerged. Because the water-powered mills required a significant volume of water, the mills were typically situated in the countryside beside rivers or creeks and as a result they were located on sites where there was no significant town and sometimes no town at all. Often the accommodation was no more than a dormitory-style building which would hold up to 500 people. With the development of steam engines, factories became more efficient and began to be developed in cities. For cities like Manchester, growth in the Industrial Revolution was exponential, with the population in 1773 of only 22,481 reaching 142,026 by 1831.[11] Scotland was slower to utilise the new technologies of the Industrial Revolution and it is commonly agreed that the Scottish Industrial Revolution began with the appearance of Scottish mills at Penicuik in Midlothian and at Rothesay, Bute, in the 1770s.[12] The industrial town of Glasgow had a population of 23,500 in 1755; by 1801 this had increased to 83,000 and thirty years later it was 202,000. Glasgow overtook Edinburgh to become the largest city in Scotland.[13]

The map of urban distribution in Britain radically changed in the late eighteenth century. Cities became larger and sprawling, towns were created where no town existed before and village life was rapidly being eroded, and in many areas villages disappeared. The patterns of employment changed from agriculturally based to industrial based. The displaced villagers moved to new industrial villages or to the slums in

---

10   Lindsay, Jean 1960 An Early Industrial Community: The Evans' Cotton Mill at Darley Abbey Derbyshire, 1783–1810, *The Business History Review* 34 (3), 277–301.

11   Lloyd-Jones, Roger and Lewis, Merv 1998 *British Industrial Capitalism Since The Industrial Revolution*, London: University College London Press 25.

12   Whatley, Christopher A. 1997 *The Industrial Revolution in Scotland*, Cambridge: Cambridge University Press 33.

13   Newman, Gerald and Brown, Lesley Ellen 1997 *Britain in the Hanoverian Age, 1714–1837: An Encyclopedia*, New York: Garland Press 291.

the city to become factory workers as they no longer could sustain their living in the country. The return of thousands of demobbed soldiers from the French Wars searching for employment and, after the collapse of the Irish economy in 1815, waves of Irish workers also seeking employment, further added to increased urbanisation and urban poverty.[14]

A consequence of this was that architectural pattern books began to be produced in an attempt to improve living conditions through mass and inexpensive housing. Architects such as John Wood the Younger of Bath and London architect Joseph Gandy produced some of the earliest architectural pattern books to resolve the housing crisis.[15] However, most of these designs were individual cottages and the few villages they designed were impractical for an industrial model. Many attempts were made to abate the social evils, and health and housing problems of the Industrial Revolution.

In 1784, New Lanark Mills was established by David Dale, in South Lanarkshire Valley, southern Scotland. It was located close to the Falls of Clyde, a well-known tourist attraction among the late eighteenth-century romantics that supplied a suitable power source for the cotton mills.[16] In this isolated location acquiring labour was an extremely difficult process and in the 1780s labourers were accessed who found difficulty getting employment elsewhere. To make up the scarcity of labourers, Dale applied to the superintendents of the parish poor in the most populous towns such as Glasgow to send him children, but at a very early age. Around one-third of Dale's workforce were pauper apprentices. The New Lanark Mills soon became the largest of their kind in Scotland. Dale was known as a man of eminent philanthropy, and it is claimed that he had the happiness of these children much at heart.[17] He also employed

14   Lloyd-Jones and Lewis 22.
15   Gandy, Joseph Michael 1805 *The Rural Architect,* London: John Harding; Gandy, Joseph Michael 1805 *Designs for Cottages, Cottage Farms and Other Rural Buildings,* London: John Harding; Wood, John [of Bath, the Younger] 1806 *A Series of Plans for Cottages or Habitations of the Labourer Either in Husbandry, or the Mechanic Arts,* London: J. Taylor.
16   Donnachie, Ian and Hewitt, George 1993 *Historic New Lanark: The Dale and Owen Industrial Community since 1785,* Edinburgh University Press.
17   [Anon.] 1813 Important Reformation Effected in the Moral Habits of the Workmen at the Lanark Mills, *Belfast Monthly Magazine* 10 (58), 364; Owen,

Highlanders who had been victims of the land clearances and enclosures. When one of the mills burnt down in 1788,[18] he continued to pay the wages of the labourers while the mill was being rebuilt. Dale also established schools for the children at his own expense and was considered to be an enlightened and benevolent employer.[19]

In 1800, Robert Owen became a junior partner with Chorlton Twist Company, and instigated the purchase of New Lanark Mills from the elderly David Dale. Owen had a one-ninth interest in the partnership. The Company proceeded to purchase New Lanark in South Lanarkshire Valley, southern Scotland, close to the Falls of Clyde that supplied the power for the mills. Although he was a minor partner, after a few months Owen became the sole manager of New Lanark with a stipend of £1000 per annum.

When he became manager of the mill the total population of the village of New Lanark was 1519, and 1334 of these villagers worked in the mills.[20] There were 500 parish children that lived and worked at the mill, aged from five to ten.[21] They worked thirteen hours a day with only one and a quarter hours allowed for meals. At 7:30 to 9:00 pm, the end of a long working day, they received an extremely rudimentary education, which included religion, reading and some writing. For children who were too young to work, under five years old, there were two days of schooling per week. The 500 children lived in one house and three children to a bed. Although conditions appear to have been harsh Dale had laid out a plan that preserved the health, well-being and morals of the children who had no parents and very few opportunities. According to Owen the children were well provided for and they had spacious, clean, and well-ventilated accommodation, and their food was ample and

Robert 1991 (1813–16), A New View of Society, *Robert Owen, A New View of Society and Other Writings*, edited by Gregory Claeys, London: Penguin 1–91: 31.

18   Donnachie and Hewitt.
19   Robinson, A. J. 1971 Robert Owen, Cotton Spinner, New Lanark, 1800–1825, *Robert Owen: Prophet of Poor*, edited by Sidney Pollard and John Salt, London: Macmillan 151.
20   Donnachie and Hewitt 25.
21   Owen, Robert 1857 *The Life of Robert Owen: Written by Himself*, London: Effingham Wilson 60.

of the best quality.[22] However, Owen came to the conclusion that no amount of good accommodation, kindness, food or elementary education could make up for the long hours and in some cases physical disabilities that the work inflicted upon these children.[23] He therefore decided to engage no more paupers as apprentices and to dispense with the existing indentures as they ran out.[24]

David Dale had been very popular in New Lanark and in the beginning, Owen as a 'foreigner' from Wales working for an English company, was mistrusted. Owen planned fundamental changes to the village in the work practices and in the education of the children and workers. The keystone to his philosophy was his education system. The principle behind Owen's education system was that education was a means to the formation of character and the possession of happiness. Character can be given not just to the individual but to any community. He claimed that children 'may be formed collectively into any human character.'[25] Owen strongly believed that the character of man was made for him by education, training and environment. His mantra was 'that human character is formed *for*, and not *by*, the individual.'[26] This mantra was central to Owen's ' science of surrounding' as well as his socialism. He believed that moral responsibility, free will and the myth of equal opportunities were based on the false concept of human nature and ignored its social conditions. In short, social conditions were a greater part of forming the human character than the individual's human nature.

As manager of New Lanark, Owen set out to reform not only the factory conditions but also the housing and community conditions. He created sports facilities, provided pensions, sick pay and accident relief.[27]

---

22 Owen, A New View of Society 31.
23 Owen, Robert 1949 On the Employment of Children in Manufactures, in *A New View of Society and Other Writings*, edited by G. D. H. Cole, London: J. M. Dent and Sons.
24 Owen, *The Life of Robert Owen* 61.
25 Owen, A New View of Society, 12.
26 Owen 1991 (1817) A Further Development of the Plan for the Relief of Manufacturing and Labouring Poor, *A New View of Society and Other Writings*, 136–58: 140.
27 Berend, Tibor Iván 2013 *An Economic History of Nineteenth-Century Europe: Diversity and Industrialisation*, Cambridge University Press 169.

He improved the housing of the village where most families lived in one-room apartments and these were replaced by two-room apartments. Prior to Owen becoming manager the village shops had a monopoly and charged high prices for poor-quality food. These were replaced by community stores that sold high-quality food at inexpensive prices. The centrepiece of his improvements was the school or as he called it an 'Institute for the Formation of Character'. The community was slow to trust him but as the improvements to the village of New Lanark became visible and their houses became more comfortable their prejudices against this 'foreigner' began to soften. When the American embargo against Britain and France was in force in 1806, which was imposed in response to violations of American neutrality, New Lanark Mills closed for four months. Instead of laying off the workforce Owen continued to pay his workforce for the full duration of the closure and this cost the company £7000 for the time of unemployment.[28] New Lanark became a model industrial village that attracted thousands of visitors every year to see Owen's successful enterprise. These visitors included the Grand Duke Nicholas, who later became the Czar of Russia, and he was reported to be so impressed with what he saw at New Lanark he attempted to induce Owen to follow him to Russia.[29]

Owen set out his ideas in A New View of Society, which began in 1813. It was a series of essays that outlined his views on education and the general character of any given community. It set out principles for reform that were directed to the entrepreneur, manufacturers and government. The final essay was dedicated to His Royal Highness the Prince Regent and it considered how the current levels of abject poverty, disease and misery disadvantaged the nation as well as the individual.[30] Although he attempted to ameliorate a political solution for factory reform and conditions, he promulgated that the minimum age of children working in a factory was to be ten years old and that those aged under ten were not to be employed. Additionally, he promoted the concept that those over ten years old would have their

---

28   Owen, *The Life of Robert Owen* 64.
29   Sargant, William Lucas 1860 *Robert Owen and His Social Philosophy*, London: Smith, Elder and Co. 83.
30   Owen, *A New View of Society* 62–92.

hours reduced to ten and three-quarters hours per day. Unfortunately, his efforts failed to make any real changes. However, in 1817 Owen, as a successful manager of a model industrial village of a commercial enterprise with a strong educational curriculum for the villagers, was asked by the 'Committee of the Association for the *Relief of the Manufacturing and Labouring Poor*' to give his views of the causes of the distress.

In 1817, he published a *Report to the Committee of the Association for the Relief of the Manufacturing and Labouring Poor.* The report considered not just the causes of the distress, but presented what Owen perceived to be a practical solution that would relieve the national distress. He first conceded that there were three main solutions to the current crisis, each taking different directions. They were

> 1st, The use of mechanism must be greatly diminished; or,
> 2nd, Millions of human beings must be starved, to permit its existence to the present extent; or,
> 3rd, Advantageous occupations must be found for the poor and unemployed working classes: to whose labour mechanism must be rendered subservient, instead of being applied, as at present, to supersede it.[31]

Owen believed that the nation and individuals had benefited greatly under existing commercial systems with the use of mechanical power and diminishing its use would be detrimental to the nation's economy and individual wealth, thus the first option was not viable. The second option was equally detrimental as it would be 'an act of gross tyranny were any government to permit mechanical power to starve millions of human beings'.[32] Therefore, the only option that he felt should be considered was the third. He proceeded to describe a way that the poor and working classes could be advantageously employed, which supported mechanical improvements, and conditions which would

---

31 Owen, Robert 1817 *Report to the Committee of the Association for the Relief of the Manufacturing and Labouring Poor,* London [no publisher named] 6–7.
32 Owen, *Report to the Committee* 7.

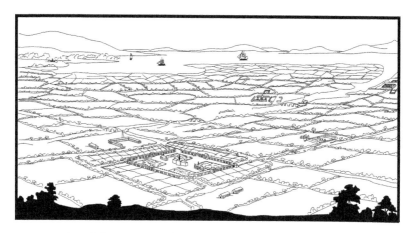

Figure 2.1 Owen's frontispiece with the first depiction of the Villages of
Cooperation and Unity

have enhanced the employment and living standards of the poor and
working classes.

*Report to the Committee of the Association for the Relief of the
Manufacturing and Labouring Poor* was the first of many writings on
what he called Villages of Unity and Cooperation. It incorporated his
ideas that were mapped out in The New View of Society and he also
produced an economic plan for a society, a description of an ideal
community and the design for a village that would enhance the
standard of life for the inhabitants. The plan would be conducive for
education, health and the production of agricultural and
manufacturing goods. These villages would be mainly agricultural, with
some industrial production. They would initially be set up from
philanthropic donations, but eventually the village would be
self-sufficient and any excess in their agricultural or industry
production would be sold to pay for the running costs of the
community.

The frontispiece of *Report to the Committee of the Association for
the Relief of the Manufacturing and Labouring Poor* was an image of
Villages of Unity and Cooperation (see Figure 2.1). The village was
square and was able to accommodate 1200 inhabitants. The buildings

43

that created the outer square were the accommodation wings. Within the square were public buildings, which divide into two parallelograms. The centre building contained the public kitchen, mess rooms, and everything concerned with the economical preparation of food and comfortable eating. The other central buildings consisted of schools, other lecture rooms and a place of worship. The four accommodation wings were separated into rooms for the married, which consisted of four rooms in each; each flat sufficiently large to accommodate a man, his wife, and two children below three years of age. The fourth side was designed for dormitories for all the children exceeding two in a family, or above three years of age. In the centre of this side of the square were apartments for those who would superintend the dormitories: at one extremity was the infirmary; and at the other a building for the accommodation of strangers who may come from a distance to see their friends and relatives. In the centre of two sides of the square were apartments for general superintendents, a clergyman, schoolmasters, surgeon, and the third wing was required for the use of the establishment and the running of the village. On the outside, and at the back of the houses around the squares were gardens; bounded by roads immediately beyond these, on one side, were buildingw for mechanical and manufacturing purposes. The slaughterhouse and stables were separated from the establishment by plantations. There were 1000 to 1500 acres of agricultural land surrounding the village.

The image is crudely drawn and is not attributed to an architect. It is possible Owen drew it himself. In the background of the village are two other villages towards the right-hand side of the image. From this image, it is clear that he perceived this style of village spreading throughout the countryside, although he did not state this view until 1832 when he was asked what he would do if he were Prime Minister of England.[33] *The Times* published a short article with a ground plan in 1817 (see Figure 2.2) which clarified his design.[34] He perceived that this form of village and production would become widespread throughout Britain, thus resolving the national housing crisis.

---

33   Owen, Robert 1832 Robert Owen's Reply to the Question 'What Would You Do, If You Were Prime Minister of England?', *Cowen Tracts* 6.
34   Owen, *Report to the Committee.*

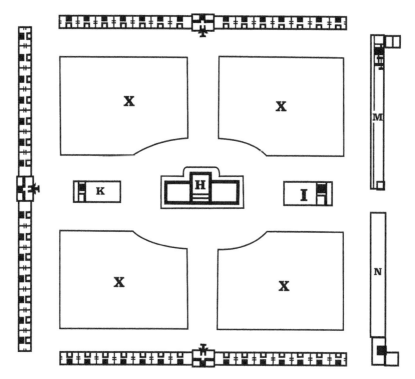

Figure 2.2 Ground plan of Owen's Village of Cooperation and Unity: H – public kitchens, I – schoolroom, lecture rooms and chapel, K – public were for adults, library, committee room et cetera, M – dormitory for boys, N – dormitory girls, T – dwellings of families, X – gardens.

Owen attempted to capture public interest in his vision with the report and *The Times* article. Every day that his concept was mentioned in the newspaper he would purchase 30,000 copies and send them to every parliamentarian from both Houses as well as to parish ministers, magistrates, bankers, and to anyone he thought would be able to support his scheme.[35] Although it did attract some interest it also

---

35   Cole, G. D. H. 1965 *The Life of Robert Owen,* London: Frank Cass & Co. 188.

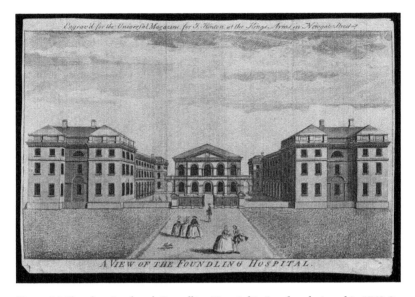

Figure 2.3 Theodore Jacobsen's Foundling Hospital in London designed in 1742 ©
Victoria and Albert Museum, London

attracted a great deal of criticism and the Village of Unity and
Cooperation became known as 'the parallelogram of paupers'.[36] The
idea of segregation and the enclosed buildings within a square was
associated with prisons and workhouses. An example of a workhouse
designed by an architect was Theodore Jacobsen's Foundling Hospital
in London designed in 1742 (see Figure 2.3), which Owen would have
been familiar with. However, there were many workhouses that were
not designed but were buildings with a wall constructed around them.[37]

Owen believed that the existing arrangements in society meant
that the principles of Christianity could never be bought into action
since the social environment was an impediment. Owen stated that in

36   Harrison, John F. C. 2009 *Robert Owen and the Owenites in Britain and
     America: The Quest for the New Moral World* London: Routledge 183.
37   Morrison, Kathryn 1999 *The Workhouse: A Study of Poor-Law Buildings in
     England*, London: English Heritage.

attempting to unite the key principles of Christianity and society: 'you may as well attempt to unite oil and water; individualised man, and all that is truly valuable in Christianity are so separate as to be utterly incapable of using throughout all eternity.'[38] It was only by creating the 'correct' social conditions and environment that human nature could be formed to accommodate these key principles.

In *A New View on Society* Owen urged that only the government could accept responsibility for providing the structure of national education that covered all classes and all stations of a child's education. Owen chastised educational reformers such as Andrew Bell and Samuel Whitbread for the obviously Christian rationales of their initiatives in popular education. This revealed that Owen's views were far from those of Orthodox Christians and that he believed that Christianity was fundamentally incompatible with the empirical truth of character forming and environmental determinism of his education reforms.[39] Key to his reforms was Owen's belief that all religions had been founded on the ignorance of mankind and served to the detriment of society and that the correct form of education could negate these detrimental effects. In 1829, he stated his long-held view that all religions

> are directly opposed to the never-changing laws of our nature; that they have been, and are, the real source of vice, disunion, and misery of every description; that they are now the only real bar to the formation of a society of virtue, of intelligence, of charity in its most extended sense, and of sincerity and kindness among the whole human family; and that they [religions] can been no longer maintained except through the ignorance of the mass of the people and the tyranny of the few over that mass.[40]

---

38 Owen, *The Life of Robert Owen* 112.
39 Thompson, Noel and Williams, Chris 2011 *Robert Owen and his Legacy*, Cardiff: University of Wales Press 97.
40 Owen, Robert and Campbell, Alexander 1852 *The Evidences of Christianity: A Debate Between Robert Owen, of New Lanark and Alexander Campbell, Containing an Examination of the 'Social System,' and all the Systems of Skepticism of Ancient and Modern Times*, Cincinnati: E. Morgan & Co. 31.

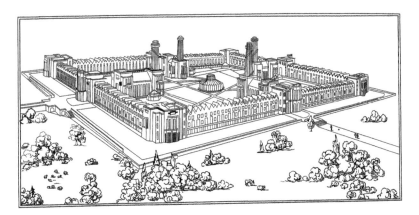

Figure 2.4 Stedman Whitwell's design for Owen's Villages of Unity and Cooperation

The resolution to a better society was to turn around that society and form the character of the next generation of children. This required the separation of those children from their families at a very early age, so they were not corrupted by this 'vice, disunity and misery of every description'.

Owen's report to the Committee of the Association for the Relief of the Manufacturing and Labouring Poor changed radically the society of the working poor and shocked many people. New Lanark was always seen as controversial because of Owen's educational agenda, but it was still seen as an ideal industrial and commercial community. The Villages of Unity and Cooperation Plan was something distinctly radical and what he was proposing was neither industrial nor commercial. Owen became known as a 'visionary' in a derogatory sense and he was unable to effectively promote his plan to the government. In 1820, Owen decided to support the venture himself with the assistance of other philanthropists. He submitted a prospectus for a Village of Unity and Cooperation to be established in the Middle Ward of the County of Lanark, which was outlined in *A Report to the County of Lanark of a Plan Relieving Public Distress, and Removing Discontent*.[41] However, the plan was rejected in June 1821. Disillusioned, Owen turned to America in 1824 and he took with him his architect, Stedman Whitwell, and a six-foot model of

Figure 2.5 Reconstruction by author of the centre of Whitwell's design

the Village of Unity and Cooperation.[42] Owen embarked on a lecture tour and he gained permission from President John Quincy Adams to display the model for six weeks in an ante-room at the White House,[43] although by then the architectural design by Whitwell had undergone significant changes (Figure 2.4).

In the 1817 model the kitchen and eating areas were in the middle of the ground plan with two buildings on either side that catered for

---

41   Owen, Robert 1821 *A Report to the County of Lanark of a Plan Relieving Public Distress, and Removing Discontent,* Glasgow: Wardlaw and Cunningham.
42   Armytage, W. H. G. 1971 Owen and America, *Robert Owen, Prophet of the Poor: Essays in Honour of the Two Hundredth Anniversary of His Birth,* edited by S. Pollard and J. Salt, London: Macmillan 214–38: 218.
43   Oved, Iaacov 1993 *Two Hundred Years of American Communes,* Piscataway NJ: Transaction Publishers 113.

the education of the children and the adults. In Whitwell's design the centre was now a conservatory (see Figure 2.5) and four buildings surrounded each side of it. These were for the kitchens and eating areas, and educational buildings. In addition, buildings for gymnasiums and baths had been added near to each of these buildings. Placing the garden in the centre of the complex, which does parallel Thomas More's utopian cities with their centralised garden, strengthens Owen's concept of the utopian village. However, it is impossible to know whether it was Owen or Whitwell's idea to change the ground plan. Nevertheless, Owen approved of the plan and promoted it through his lecture tours in America. The four large internal buildings each had a massive tower that had multi-purposes. They were intended to form astronomical observatories and for this purpose they had an external spiral staircase. Halfway up the tower were clocks that were illuminated by gaslight at night. There were also powerful reflectors powered by gas that radiated light downwards and illuminated the internal courtyard at night. There were also chimneys for the kitchens and for the underground transport system. The square was on an elevated platform and underneath the square was a subway that led to the storerooms and to the rail system. The rail system formed a complete circuit of the establishment and had four central stopping points, each under the main public buildings. This rail system also connected the village with other villages and towns. Whitwell's plan integrated the most modern features into the Villages of Unity and Cooperation.

Owen continued to promote his ideas in America. He purchased a pre-existing community from the Rappites in Indiana called Harmony. George Rapp was a German ecclesiastical Lutheran who had come to America in 1805 to escape religious persecution in Germany for his unique brand of Pietism. The community in Indiana was their second community and was established in 1814; however, the weather conditions of Harmony did not suit their agricultural requirements. By 1825, when Owen purchased Harmony, the town consisted of 150 log cabins, community stores, a tavern and the town was surrounded by cleared land for farming. The new community became known as New Harmony. The pre-existing buildings remained, and Owen's son William oversaw the initial developments in New Harmony. However, there were problems in securing building materials for further development.[44]

However, the architectural problems of New Harmony were insignificant compared to the political ones. New Harmony soon became a centre of education for children but the concept of separating children from their parents at three years of age was unpopular. It also caused divisions within the community. By 1828 various factions developed in the community that differed on key issues such as education, religion, and common property. The community soon began to fail. Whitwell's plan was never built; however in 1830, Whitwell published his plan in *Description of an Architectural Model*. Although Owen continued to promote these villages they were never realised. Nevertheless, they were highly influential.

The Owenite movement began to build a strong following among the working classes. They used Mechanics Institutes, which had been established to provide adult education on technical subjects for working men, as venues for lectures to promote the concept of Villages of Unity and Cooperation. In 1826, author, and for a short time radical parliamentarian of Sheffield, James Silk Buckingham, and philanthropist and author John Minter Morgan, both ardent Christians, met with Owen to discuss the Villages of Unity and Cooperation[45] as they wished to adapt Owen's plan but to integrate Christian principles into their plans. In *The Christian Commonwealth* published in 1849 Morgan promoted a self-supporting village that would be established on not less than 1000 acres, and 300 families would support themselves and defray the expenses of the establishment.[46] The design of the village was based on Owen's original plan. Although Owen actively campaigned for donations to establish the villages, he failed to secure enough funding.[47]

---

44 William Owen, quoted in Armytage 218.
45 Batchelor, Peter 1968 The Origin of the Garden City Concept of Urban Form, *Journal of the Society of Architectural Historians* 28, 184–200: 191.
46 Morgan, John Minter 1849 *The Christian Commonwealth*, London: Phoenix Library.
47 Armytage, W. H. G 1958 John Minter Morgan's Schemes, 1841–1855 *International Review of Social History* 3, 26–42.

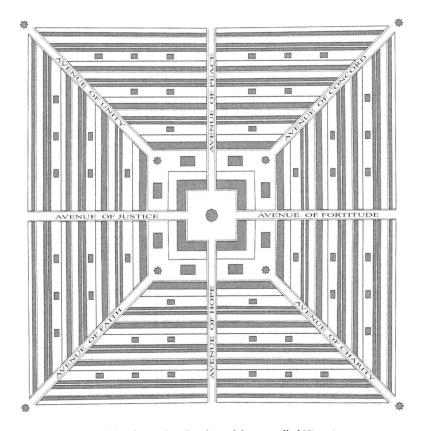

Figure 2.6 Ground plan for Buckingham's model town called Victoria

Buckingham moved away from philanthropy and attempted to corporatise these villages through a share system, and only shareholders could live in the town with a minimum shareholding of £20 which could be paid off over time. He would form a new association that would be incorporated by an Act of Parliament. The town and its surrounding agricultural land would be 10,000 acres and it would accommodate 10,000 inhabitants. It was an extremely hierarchical plan with the working classes on the outside circuit of housing in densely packed housing and wealthy merchants in the centre circuit in large, luxurious terraces. It was highly symmetrical and incorporated many of Owen's Village of Unity and Cooperation features (see Figure 2.6). Like Owen he perceived that these villages would spread throughout the countryside, radically changing the living and work practices of the country.

The plans of Morgan, Buckingham and later ones by Robert Pemberton[48] were all heavily influenced by Owen and all became branded as 'utopian' in an extremely derogative sense. Pemberton promoted a similar education system to Owen, although Pemberton took the concept of separating the community and creating a better environment even further. He removed the entire community away from what he called the 'Kingdom of Mammon'. His community would be isolated and located in New Zealand, a country he had never been to.

In his eighties Owen had converted to Spiritualism which appeared to contradict his lifelong insistence on logic and rational thought. However, his concept of education and his mantra 'that human character is formed for, and not by, the individual' remained as strong as it had been in the early days of New Lanark. His social environmentalism, the forming of a society and community through the education and development of human character, was a central key to his urban concepts. On his 84th birthday in 1855 he gave a speech on the importance of education, reintegrating what he had said many years before. In response to this speech Pemberton published *An Address to the Bishops and Clergy* in 1855, which strongly linked himself with Owen and his brand of social environmentalism. Owen claimed, 'I find Mr Pemberton more advanced in knowledge of these all-important subjects than any one now living.'[49] Throughout Owen's life his views on the forming of the ideal community of unity and cooperation through urban planning and education never wavered.

The utopian label that had been attached to Owen, Morgan, Buckingham and Pemberton was strengthened with the publication of Frederick Engels's *Socialism: Utopian and Scientific* in 1880.[50] However,

---

48 Pemberton, Robert 1985 *The Happy Colony*, New York: Garland.
49 Owen, Robert 2005 (1855) Letter to Prince Albert Dated 10 October 1855, *Owenite Socialism: Correspondence II: 1839–1858*, edited by Gregory Claeys, Abingdon: Routledge 366.
50 Frederick Engels 2006 *Socialism: Utopian and Scientific*, New York: Mondial.

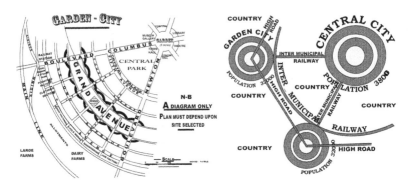

Figure 2.7 Ebenezer Howard's diagrams of the garden city and satellite cities

in 1899 Ebenezer Howard published *Tomorrow: A Peaceful Path to Real Reform,* reissued in 1902 under the title of *Garden Cities of Tomorrow.*[51] Howard presented Owen's concepts as a new third alternative to the lifestyles presented in the town or country; he considered a town–country option that had originally been established by Owen. Howard was careful to avoid the 'utopian' label. In his books that outlined his concepts of the garden city he did not produce specific plans, only conceptual schematics.

In his diagrams, he clearly specified that these drawings were 'a diagram only – plans must depend upon site' (Figure 2.7). There was not a specified layout of the town. Howard formed the Garden City Association in 1899, which led to the Garden City Movement. The first garden city was constructed in England at Letchworth in 1903. It was to be built to the concepts outlined in *Garden Cities of Tomorrow.* In 1919 the second garden city was built in Britain at Welwyn, Hertfordshire. However, the concept spread and was reproduced in America,[52]and Australia.[53] Although they were originally influenced by Owenite

51   Howard, Ebenezer 1965 *Garden Cities of Tomorrow,* London: Faber & Faber.
52   Schaffer, Daniel 1981 Garden Cities for America: The Radburn Experiment, PhD. thesis, State University of New Jersey.
53   Fletcher, Meredith 2002 *Digging People up for Coal,* Melbourne University Press.

concepts of social housing, by the twentieth and twenty-first centuries these towns had moved away from Owen's community concept and become sought-after properties and prime real estate within commuting distance of large cities. Although cooperative housing has become a movement throughout the world and its influence is rooted in the nineteenth century with Owen's work, it remains small scale and relatively unknown. However, there has recently been increased interest in revitalising Owen's original ideas on urbanism.

In the last decade, there has been a program to revise Owen's true legacy with plans for an Owenite town for South Lanarkshire. The plan consists of 3200 affordable houses and the community would be enlightened by Owen's Village of Unity and Cooperation. It is planned that the housing will be prefabricated to reduce costs, which will assist in the affordability for young families. The site selected is 2000 acres and the town itself will cover 400 acres, leaving a significant green belt. Owenstown aims to be carbon neutral and to provide energy for heating and power through renewable means. It would include offices and commercial spaces, restaurants, shops, land and buildings for industry, as well as two new primary schools and one secondary school. The aim is to create 5000 new jobs, 3000 permanent jobs, in a deprived area, by promoting an enterprise culture engendered by a board of the cooperative. The town would be owned and managed on a cooperative basis by its residents and all surplus funds generated would be reinvested in the community instead of being taken out by property developers or landowners. Owenstown guiding principles would engender a community that would encourage the cooperative spirit in a healthy, sustainable and low-carbon environment that would promote community involvement and ownership and encourage economic development and job creation. Although the principles of Owenstown are based on early nineteenth-century philosophies of cooperation it is concerned with twenty-first-century ideals and needs that concern the community, families and the environment.[54]

---

54 Owenstown Cooperative, Owenstown, South Lanarkshire
     http://owenstown.org/.

Figure 2.8 Owenstown Cooperative, Owenstown, South Lanarkshire

However, like Owen's proposal in *A Report to the County of Lanark of a Plan Relieving Public Distress, and Removing Discontent* in 1820, which was rejected in 1821, the Owenstown proposal was rejected in April 2014. Despite there being 1500 applications prior to lodging the application with the Council, Michael McGlynn of the South Lanarkshire Council claimed that 'The applicants had failed to show that there is demand for the form and scale of development proposed at this location.'[55] The Owenstown organisation was left with the choice of lodging an appeal or moving the proposal away from Scotland. In March 2015, the Scottish Government Reporter dismissed the appeal lodged by the Owenstown organisation against the refusal of planning permission in principle for the £500 million development of Owenstown. Solicitor

---

55 Michael McGlynn quoted in 2014 by BBC News, South Lanarkshire Owenstown New Town Plan Rejected by Councillors, https://www.bbc.com/news/uk-scotland-glasgow-west-2682163.

for the appeal before the Scottish Government Reporter Colin Innes stated: 'The planning system and the existing Development Plan is not able to handle the unique nature of Owenstown,'[56] a unique character, which stems from 1817. It appears there exists the same bureaucratic problems and lack of vision that existed 200 years ago. Although the cooperative-housing movement has moved forward, it is small and tends to be very small holdings rather than villages. Owenstown was an attempt to revitalise a truly unique urban concept established by Owen that although influential, its significance and influence has not truly been utilised. Since the rejection of the plan there has been discussion about moving the project away from Scotland, but it remains to be seen what the next step will be. However, Owen's foresight in his new concept of urbanism remains controversial, and it appears that the planning authorities are unable to comprehend the full extent of this foresight, even after 200 years.

---

56   Owenstown Cooperative, Owenstown Plans Rejected, https://bit.ly/2Rt27xA.

3
Celticism, Science and the Mnemonic Universe

Cairns Craig

In her study of *Primitivism, Science, and the Irish Revival*, Sinéad Garrigan Mattar distinguishes between 'Celticism' and what she calls 'Celtology':[1] the latter is the 'scientific' study of things Celtic, whether through philology or archaeology or anthropology, whereas 'Celticism' refers to the use—or, more often, the *abuse*—of a past assumed to be 'Celtic' but with little or nothing to do with any real past civilisation—or, indeed, with any of the actual texts which might offer us a record of those civilisations. Celticisms involve the construction of largely fictional worlds that stand in opposition to the 'facts' sought by Celtologists, and however charming the creations of the Celticists they will always attract from Celtologists accusations of fraud and falsification, or of peddling sentimental escape routes from an unpalatable present. The greater their impact, as in the case of the works that James Macpherson in the 1760s attributed to a third-century Gaelic bard, the greater the scrutiny of their claims to 'authenticity', which, if not upheld, rapidly undermine their standing in the literary canon. Thus David Hume, although originally convinced by the arguments in favour of the authenticity of the Ossianic poems,[2] wrote

---

1   Mattar, Sinéad Garrigan 2004 *Primitivism, Science, and the Irish Revival*, Oxford: Clarendon Press 21ff.

2   See Hume's letter of August 16, 1760 to Sir David Dalrymple of Newhailes, in which he cites Adam Smith as confirming that 'the piper of the Argyleshire

in 1763 to Hugh Blair, Macpherson's chief defender, urging him to gather, from ministers in the Highlands, evidence of the existence of the Gaelic originals, because

> I often hear them totally rejected with disdain and indignation, as a palpable and most impudent forgery. This opinion has indeed become very prevalent among the men of letters in London, and I can foresee, that in a few years the poems, if they continue to stand on their present footing, will be thrown aside, and will fall into final oblivion ... It is in vain to say, that their beauty will support them, independent of their authenticity: NO; that beauty is not so much to the general taste as to ensure you of this event; and if people be once disgusted with the idea of forgery, they are thence apt to entertain a more disadvantageous notion of the excellency of the production itself.[3]

Hume's scepticism has been echoed regularly by critics of Celticism. Indeed, Terence Brown's edited collection on *Celticism* (1996) is more marked by its contributors' resistance to the term than their acceptance of its relevance; as George Watson comments, the 'key to the intellectual history of Celticism is the annulment, elision or denial of history',[4] with the consequence that '"the Celtic" and "change" are seen as antithetical categories'[5] and that 'Celticisms' are therefore necessarily resistant to 'aspects of modernity such as science, technology and administration'.[6] They are equally resistant to the actualities of past history so that Brendan Ó Buachalla finds that the 'renderings of early Irish sagas' by Sir Samuel Ferguson, identified by W.B. Yeats as 'the greatest poet Ireland has produced because the most central and most Celtic',[7] 'bear no resemblance in content, tone or treatment to the original texts; he

---

Militia repeated to him all those poems which Mr Macpherson has translated, and many more of equal beauty.' Greig, J. Y. T editor 1932 *The Letters of David Hume*, Oxford University Press I.1727–1765, 329.

3 Greig, *The Letters of David Hume* 399.
4 Watson, George 1996 Celticism and the Annulment of History, *Celticism*, edited by Terence Brown, Atlanta GA: Rodopi 208.
5 Watson 210.
6 Watson 220.

uses them as mere pegs on which to hang his moralising on Victorian man.[8] As the sciences that Carrigan Mattar groups under the heading of 'Celtology' progressed during the nineteenth century, conflict between science and Celticism became inevitable, with the result that the two 'co-exist in an unhappy disequilibrium':

> The scientists fought stolidly against the threat of Celtomania which *littérateurs* insistently raised, whilst the writers themselves continually protested their scientism, even as they reaffirmed the basic tenets of romantic Celticism.[9]

Mattar herself sees the tension between Celticism and Celtology as driving the artistic development of the Irish Revival, forcing its major writers into redefinitions that displace 'romantic primitivism' for a literary modernism in which the primitive is savage rather than noble. Suggestive though this argument is, it works by maintaining a fundamental opposition between scientific 'fact' and the products of the literary 'imagination', and by assuming that this opposition can only be tested at the level of the truth or falsity of the 'content' of the literary work. Literary works are, in effect, to be judged by how far they accord with the facts as uncovered by Celtologists. In the period of literary 'Celtomania', however, the truth claims of science itself—both the established sciences like 'natural philosophy' and the 'new' sciences like anthropology—underwent radical revisions, so that what had seemed to be scientific 'fact' in one decade was re-interpreted as pseudo-scientific fiction in the next. The most famous victim of these changes was 'aether': as James Clerk Maxwell noted in his contribution to the ninth edition of the *Encyclopaedia Britannica*,

7   Frayne, John P. editor 1970 *The Uncollected Prose by W. B. Yeats, Vol. 1, The Poetry of Sir Samuel Ferguson—II*, London: Macmillan 103.
8   Ó Buachalla, Brendán 1987 The Gaelic Background, *Samuel Ferguson: A Centenary Tribute*, edited by Terence Brown and Barbara Hayley, Dublin: Royal Irish Academy 35.
9   Mattar 23–4.

Aethers were invented for the planets to swim in, to constitute electric atmospheres and magnetic effluvia, to convey sensations from one part of our bodies to another, and so on, until all space had been filled three or four times over with aethers ... The only aether which has survived is that which was invented by Huygens to explain the propagation of light. [10]

That final 'aether' was, of course, itself to become redundant with Einstein's publications of 1905. Something which had been a stable part of the physical world as understood by natural philosophy since before Newton had, quite literally, disappeared out of existence: the very objects of science, and the objectivity they implied, had changed; they had crossed the boundary between fact and fiction. The opposition between 'Celticism' and 'Celtology' on which Mattar's argument is based is not between the fictional and the factual, but between differing accounts of authority and authenticity, of presumed causes and their effects. A fiction upon which people act—'did that play of mine send out/Certain men the English shot?'[11]—becomes a purported 'fact' of history, a potential cause *in* history, as stubborn as any '-ological' truth.

II

When David Hume published the first volume of his *Treatise of Human Nature* in 1739, it was subtitled as 'an attempt to introduce the experimental method of reasoning into moral subjects', and thus claimed to be the foundation of 'the science of Man'.[12] Ironically, of course, it set in doubt the most fundamental category of the 'experimental Method', the category of 'cause', which was turned from

---

10   Maxwell, James Clerk 1878 Ether, in *Encyclopædia Britannica Ninth Edition* 8.568–72.
11   Yeats, W. B. 1950 The Man and the Echo, *Collected Poems*, London: Macmillan 393.
12   Hume, David 1888 *A Treatise of Human Nature*, edited by L. A. Selby-Bigge, Oxford: Clarendon Press xix.

an explanatory force assumed to be operative in the world into a regular conjunction in the human psyche:

> The efficacy or energy of causes is neither plac'd in the causes themselves, nor in the deity, nor in the concurrence of these two principles; but belongs entirely to the soul, which considers the union of two or more objects in all past instances. 'Tis here that the real power of causes is plac'd … [13]

And what governs the 'soul' in its identification of 'cause' is the 'association of ideas'—'a kind of ATTRACTION, which in the mental world will be found to have as extraordinary effects as in the natural'.[14] The 'association of ideas' is thus established as having a comparable role in 'the mental world' that gravity has in the Newtonian account of the physical world: association is the fundamental principle by which the phenomena of consciousness are organised. This would have surprised John Locke, who had introduced the notion of the 'association of ideas' into British philosophy in order to explain why men, whom he considered to be rational creatures, could nonetheless disagree about what ought to be evident truths:

> Some of our ideas have a natural correspondence and connexion one with another: it is the office and excellency of our reason to trace these, and hold them together in that union and correspondence which is founded in their peculiar beings. Besides this, there is another connexion of ideas wholly owing to chance or custom: ideas, that in themselves are not all of kin, come to be so united in some men's minds, that it is very hard to separate them; they always keep in company, and the one no sooner at any time comes into the understanding, but its associate appears with it; and if they are more than two, which are thus united, the whole gang, always inseparable, show themselves together.[15]

---

13   Hume, *Treatise* 166.
14   Hume, *Treatise* 12–13.
15   Locke, John 1824 *An Essay Concerning Human Understanding, The Works of John Locke in Nine Volumes,* London 12th edition, part 1, ch. xxxiii 5, 419.

For Locke, association is the accidental uniting of ideas in the mind as a result of custom or education, producing disruptive 'gangs' which cannot be policed by reason; for Hume, on the other hand, 'reason is, and ought only to be the slave of the passions',[16] and the passions are themselves shaped and intensified by the process of association, since 'two different associations, of impressions and ideas, by uniting their forces, may assist each other's operation'.[17]

The 'association of ideas' was to become, in the nineteenth century, in the works of James Mill, Herbert Spencer and Alexander Bain,[18] the foundation of the new science of empirical psychology, but in the eighteenth century it was to have its most immediate impact on theories of 'taste' and, in particular, on the understanding of what happens in the mind when it judges something as being 'beautiful' or 'sublime'. By the time of Archibald Alison's *Essays on the Nature and Principles of Taste* in 1793, association had become the encompassing explanation for all aesthetic[19] experience:

When any object, either of sublimity of beauty, is presented to the mind, I believe every man is conscious of a train of thought being immediately awakened in his imagination, analogous to the character or expression of the original object. The simple perception of the object, we frequently find, is insufficient to excite these emotions, unless, according to common expression, our imagination is seized, and our fancy busied in the pursuit of all those trains of thought, which are allied to this character or expression.[20]

---

16   Hume, *Treatise* 415.
17   Hume, *Treatise* 306.
18   Mill, James 1829 *Analysis of the Phenomena of the Human Mind*, was revised and reissued by John Stuart Mill, with the help of Alexander Bain in 1869; Spencer, Herbert 1856 *Principles of Psychology* was several times revised before 1890; Bain, Alexander 1855 *The Senses and the Intellect* and 1859 *The Emotions and the Will* went through several revised editions before Bain's death in 1903.
19   'Aesthetic', of course, was a word which only came into use in the nineteenth century, but I will use it hereafter to designate what, in the eighteenth century, would have been referred to as 'taste'.
20   Alison, Archibald 1811 *Essays on the Nature and Principles of Taste*, 2nd edition, Edinburgh: Bell & Bradfute. Essay 1, 4–5.

Even among those who did not accept the sceptical implications of Hume's metaphysics, his associationist account of the mind helped explain how a response of 'taste' is different from any other kind of experience: in aesthetic experience the mind is released from its practical considerations and, in a state of 'reverie', traces a stream of associated memories whose unimpeded passage through the mind is constitutive of the experience of beauty or sublimity. Each successful work of art will inspire a train of associations unique to a particular individual, and the intensity of the experience will depend on the memory resources that can be released and sustained in a connected chain, which is why those with the richest memories—often, therefore, the most educated—will have the most powerful aesthetic experiences; the work of art so experienced will itself then become an addition to the memory resources on which an individual can call, thus further enriching any future aesthetic experience. Association not only explains how, to one observer, a landscape is simply a place of utility for grazing animals or for growing crops, while to another it is a scene of beauty, it also accounts for how two observers may both attribute 'beauty' to the same object and yet have very different individual experiences of it, and make very different judgments as to *how* beautiful it is. Alison's theory is often treated as though it were an endpoint which would be made redundant by Romantic notions of the 'creative imagination', but in fact associationist accounts dominated much nineteenth-century thinking about art and continued to shape what artists and writers hoped to achieve by their works until well into the twentieth century.[21]

One of the earliest applications of associationist principles to a work of literature is to be found in Hugh Blair's *Critical Dissertation on the Poems of Ossian*, first published in 1763. Blair argued that Ossian's [or Macpherson's] poetic method was fundamentally associationist:

Very often two objects are brought together in a simile, though they resemble one another, strictly speaking, in nothing, only

---

21   See Craig, Cairns 2007 *Associationism and the Literary Imagination: From the Phantasmal Chaos,* Edinburgh University Press, especially ch. 1, 'Kant has not Answered Hume'.

because they raise in the mind a train of similar, and what may be called, concordant ideas; so that the remembrance of the one, when recalled, serves to quicken and heighten the impression made by the other.[22]

And Blair points out something in the Ossianic poems that would become the foundation of theories such as Alison's:

Such analogies and associations of ideas as these, are highly pleasing to the fancy. They give the opportunity for introducing many a fine poetical picture. They diversify the scene: they aggrandize the subject; they keep the imagination awake and sprightly. For as the judgment is principally exercised in distinguishing objects, and remarking the differences among those which seem like; so the highest amusement of the imagination is to trace likeness and agreements among those which seem different.[23]

Blair here deploys two of the most important consequences of associationist aesthetics: first, the aesthetic experience depends on the *activity* of the perceiving mind as it generates new trains of association on the basis of identifying likenesses in the poet's imagery; second, the resource required for this activity is a well-stocked *memory*, since the more memories that are aroused the greater the mental *activity* and therefore the more intense the aesthetic experience.

These associationist principles were, of course, assumed to be universally true of the art of all times, but once they were identified they began to influence the ways in which art was structured, foregrounding those effects which offered the largest stimulus to memory. Macpherson's *Fragments of Ancient Poetry* offered its readers characters and scenes that had, unlike classical literature, no pre-existing associations: readers' minds had to be, in Alison's words, 'busied in the pursuit of all those trains of thought, which are allied to this character

---

22   Gaskill, Howard (editor) 1996 *The Poems of Ossian and Related Works*, Edinburgh University Press 382.
23   Gaskill, *Poems of Ossian* 383.

or expression'; the very limitedness of what a 'fragment' offered provided the focal point for the generation of unanticipated associations which could, in turn, spring further unexpected associations into life:

> The manner of composition bears all the marks of the greatest antiquity. No artful transitions, nor full and extended connection of parts; such as we find among the poets of later times, when order and regularity of composition were more studied and known; but a style always rapid and vehement, in narration concise even to abruptness, and leaving several circumstances to be supplied by the reader's imagination.[24]

Even when Macpherson published the more connected narrative of *Fingal*, the style displayed the same rapid, vehement abruptness, the same sudden digressions—as, for instance, in Book VI, when the action suddenly switches to the story of Trenmor, 'great grandfather to Fingal'.[25] Was this style in the nature of primitive poetry, as Blair suggests, or was it, rather, the product of Macpherson's time at the University of Aberdeen, where one of his teachers was Alexander Gerard, the first Scottish thinker to apply Hume's conception of the mind to the operations of 'taste'. In *An Essay on Taste*, published in 1759, Gerard quotes Hume's *Treatise* as part of his discussion of the sublime and concludes that,

> The sentiments of taste depend very much on *association*. So far as they proceed from this, *custom* must augment them, as custom, by adding a new principle of union, renders the connection more intimate, and introduces the related ideas more quickly and forcibly. Custom likewise begets new associations, and enables works of taste to suggest ideas which were not *originally* connected with them: and what a surprizing intenseness, the association of ideas, originally foreign, bestows on our

---

24 Gaskill, *Poems of Ossian* 354.
25 Gaskill, *Poems of Ossian* 98.

perceptions, both pleasurable and painful, is obvious in too many instances to require being enlarged on.[26]

Macpherson's style may not be a rendering of his understanding of how ancient Gaelic poetry is structured but his deliberate exploitation of the very techniques by which Gerard and Blair understood poetry to work. In other words, Macpherson had created works—as his detractors implied, without grasping the reasons for it—which would operate within the terms of a new eighteenth-century conception of the nature and workings of 'taste', one in which, as Gerard puts it,

> Sublimity of style arises, not so much from the sound of the words, though that doubtless may have some influence, as from the nature of the ideas, which we are accustomed to annex to them, and the character of the persons, among whom they are in most common use. This too is the origin of the grandeur we ascribe to objects high and elevated in place; of the veneration, with which we regard things in any direction distant; and of the superior admiration excited by things remote in time; especially in antiquity or past duration.[27]

To seal the latter point Gerard again invokes Hume, and Hume's analysis of our notions of the 'elevated', whether in nature or in society, as running in parallel with our experience of gravity:

> we feel a difficulty in mounting, and pass not without a kind of reluctance from the inferior to that which is situated above it; as if our ideas acquired a kind of gravity from their objects.[28]

---

26 Gerard, Alexander 1759 *An Essay on Taste: London, printed for A. Millar in the Strand, A. Kincaid and J. Bell in Edinburgh, with Three Dissertations on same subject by Mr. De Voltaire, Mr. D'Alembert, Mr. De Montesquieu*, Scolar Press reprint 1971, part 2, section iv, 'Of the Sensibility of Taste', 112.
27 Gerard 21.
28 Hume, *Treatise of Human Nature*, Book II, part 3, section viii 435.

The 'sense of difficulty' is even greater in relation to time and 'a considerable distance in time produces a greater veneration for the distant objects than a like removal in space', because,

> The imagination moves with more difficulty in passing from one portion of time to another, than is the transition thro' the parts of space; and that because space or extension appears united to our senses, while time or succession is always broken or divided ... The mind, elevated by the vastness of its object, is still further elevated by the difficulty of the conception; and being oblig'd every moment to renew its efforts in the transition from one part of time to another, feels a more vigorous and sublime disposition, than in a transition thro' the parts of space, where the ideas flow along with easiness and facility.[29]

Distance in time fractures the ease with which events can be associated with one another, but by doing so forces the mind into greater efforts to establish those associations which, in turn, increases the intensity of aesthetic experience.[30] Macpherson's insistence on the ancientness of the poems of Ossian underlines how well they correspond with Gerard's new poetics of sublimity, a poetics which also requires that the responsive reader must have

> such a *sensibility of heart*, as fits a man for being easily moved, and for readily catching, as by infection, any passion, that a work is fitted to excite. The souls of men are far from being alike susceptible of impressions of this kind. A hard hearted man can be a spectator of very great distress, without feeling any emotion: A man of cruel temper has a malignant joy in producing misery. On the other hand, many are composed of

---

29 Hume, *Treatise of Human Nature,* Book II, part 3, section viii 436.
30 See Gaskill, Howard 1996 Herder, Ossian and the Celtic, *Celticism,* edited by Terence Brown 257–72, for the responses in France and Germany to the 'asyndetic abruptness of folk-poetry' and the new appreciation of the 'loose and broken manner' of ancient Greek poetry, especially Pindar (261).

so delicate materials, that the smallest uneasiness of their fellow creatures excites their pity.[31]

As Blair notes, Macpherson's Ossian,

> appears to have been endowed by nature with an exquisite sensibility of heart; prone to that tender melancholy which is so often attendant on great genius; and susceptible equally of strong and soft emotions.[32]

Ossian, both warrior and bard, is by his 'exquisite sensibility of heart' endowed with all the qualities required by the new aesthetics; he is, pre-eminently, the poet both of the heart and of memory, calling up previous bards to recall, through their songs, long-dead heroes:

> Still on the darkening Lena arose in my ears the tuneful voice of Carril. He sung of the companions of our youth, and days of former years; when we met on the banks of Lego, and sent round the joy of the shell. Cromla, with its cloudy steeps, answered to his voice. The ghosts of those he sung came in their rustling blasts. They were seen to bend with joy towards the sound of their praise.[33]

The bard recalls into the present the memory of the dead, and just as the process of association recalls the past and reinvigorates it as a part of the present, so the dead acquire new life by the new associates to whom they are introduced around the bardic performance and the new associative contexts with which they can then be connected. The ghosts who flit in and out of the poem are nothing less than manifestations of the associative mind: they are called up when Ossian's mind finds something to link them with, leading the narrative into digressions that push even further back the memories which the poem can recall:

---

31 Gerard 86.
32 Gaskill, *Poems of Ossian* 352.
33 Gaskill, *Poems of Ossian* 99 (*Fingal,* Book 6).

> Mournful is thy tale, son of the car, said Carril of other times. It sends my soul back to the ages of old, and to the days of other years—Often have I heard of Comal who slew the friend he loved;[34]

In Ossianic poetry memory invokes further memories in a structure where the living and the ghostly dead seem equally real, because all of them exist only in the recollections of Ossian himself, the poet as the memorialist of his people. His is the art of memory in a double sense—as a supposedly historical character he brings back and gives voice to a past which only he can remember, but in doing so Macpherson makes him the medium by which an eighteenth-century audience can *acquire* the 'memory' of a past of which it had no previous knowledge.

Since 'beauty' however, is not inherent in any object but in the workings of the associating mind, all associationist accounts of art are threatened by the failure of memory: if an audience has no appropriate memories to connect with a particular work of art, that work will become a meaningless blank. It is this threat that Francis Jeffrey pointed to in his account of Alison's theories in the *Edinburgh Review* of 1811, when he noted of Scott's description of Loch Katrine that

> the particular train of images, by the help of which [our] general impressions may be moulded into distinct objects of emotion, is evidently altogether loose and undetermined, and must depend on the taste, dispositions and information of every different beholder.[35]

Ossian, the 'last of his race', cut off from community and communication because he has no surviving children to whom he can transmit his memories, is symbolic of that threat:

> No more shalt thou rise, O my son, to partake of the feast of Cromla. Soon will thy tomb be hid, and the grass grow rank on thy grave. The sons of the feeble shall pass over it, and shall not know that the mighty lie there.[36]

---

34 Gaskill, *Poems of Ossian* 70.
35 Jeffrey, Francis 1811 (May) *Edinburgh Review* 18 (35), 1–45: 23.
36 Gaskill, *Poems of Ossian*, 'Fingal' 103.

But as the supposedly third-century Ossian announces the coming of an obliterating amnesia, the eighteenth-century James Macpherson reverses the process and makes the forgotten memorable again.

Fiona Stafford, in her book *The Last of the Race*, takes Macpherson's Ossianic poems as a classic instance of the drama of being the *last*, a drama in which 'the death of the last bard has a finality which is hard to reject':[37]

> In the literature of the last bard, there is no real attempt to cross the boundary between the primitive and the civilized, and the bard must remain with his race, preserved at an earlier stage of society. The poetry is in part a fictitious memorial to the lost race, protecting the last man in an ideal world which could never be destroyed since it had already vanished.[38]

The point of Macpherson's poetry, however, is that the last bard has not vanished: he has returned. When the Welsh family on their tour of the new United Kingdom in Tobias Smollett's *Humphrey Clinker* (1771) reach the Highlands, the landscape, once empty of memories, becomes full of them:

> We have had princely sport in hunting the stag on these mountains—These are the lonely hills of Morven, where Fingal and his heroes enjoyed the same pastime; I feel an enthusiastic pleasure when I survey the brown heath that Ossian wont to tread; and hear the wind whistle through the bending grass—When I enter our landlord's hall, I look for the suspended harp of that divine bard, and listen in hopes of hearing the aerial sound of his respected spirit—The poems of Ossian are in every mouth.[39]

This is not a 'real' memory, of course, since it is derived from literature, but then neither were Ossian's, since many of them were derived from

---

37   Stafford, Fiona 1994 *The Last of The Race: The Growth of a Myth from Milton to Darwin*, Oxford: Clarendon Press 94.
38   Stafford 93.
39   Smollett, Tobias 1985 *The Expedition of Humphry Clinker*, edited by Angus Ross, Harmondsworth: Penguin 277.

the tales of the bards who preceded him. Once reactivated, a 'recovered memory' acts in exactly the same way as a real memory: it populates the landscape and makes it aesthetically pleasing, and it has the benefit of being a shared rather than a private memory—it is 'in every mouth'. The dying and expiring memories of Ossian, the character in Macpherson's poem, become the real and living memories of eighteenth-century aesthetic experience: the dramatic structure of the poem as a narrative of decline and death is negated by its form, which is of resurrection and revival, a resurrection and revival that replicates the structure of the associationist aesthetic.

The 'Celtomania' which Macpherson's Ossianic poems initiated was not the product of Macpherson's turning his back on modernity and on science: what he did was to adopt the most original modern conception of the 'science of man', with its stadial conception of historical progress and its implications of the differences between the mentalities of the primitive and the modern, and used the new psychology that underpinned Hume's analysis of the mind to intensify an aesthetics of memory. It was precisely the modernity by which an apparently ancient past was shaped that made it so influential. Even if his claims for the authenticity of the original poems were untrue, the form in which they were cast was designed to achieve the sublimity that the mind experiences in overcoming the strangeness and the lack of easy progression that Hume describes as characteristic of our sense of the past. In form, the poem itself is like the ghosts it records—the continual recall and re-embodiment of that which has, apparently and finally, passed away. Stafford's account of the 'last bard' is, in other words, only half true, for the last man is not the end of the story as long as the story can be recovered and restated, creating a new and living memory in an entirely different world. As long as the poetry can generate new associations, the last bard will survive in the memories of eighteenth-century readers, and the writings they then produce, haunted by Ossianic characters, will continue to populate the memories of the living with the ideas and emotions of the past. Macpherson's Ossianic poetry is the first of many associationist works that both dramatise and defy the threat of oblivion, melancholically grieving over a past that has been forgotten but in so doing finding routes to raise those lost memories to new and vigorous life.

III

Associationist accounts of the mind are pervasive in late-nineteenth-century anthropology, and nowhere more so than in that most influential Scottish contribution J. G. Frazer's *The Golden Bough*. Frazer's grand division of primitive magic into the Homoeopathic—based on perceived similarities between things in the world—and the Contagious—resulting from direct human contact with those things—is, at base, a practical implementation of the association of ideas:

> If my analysis of the magician's logic is correct, its two great principles turn out to be merely two different misapplications of the association of ideas. Homoeopathic magic is founded on the association of ideas by similarity: contagious magic is founded on the association of ideas by contiguity.[40]

Frazer's 'scientific' analysis of the primitive is founded on principles that would have been recognisable to Macpherson; when the young W. B. Yeats adopts the same terminology to explain his Celticism and his occultism, he is not using an out-of-date set of ideas but those which inform the 'ologies' of his scientific contemporaries. For Yeats, the peasantry of Ireland were not only the people who had maintained, in whatever fragmentary form, the memory of the Ossianic heroes, but were the upholders of a conception of the world which gave credence to fairies, apparitions and the power of magic: 'I believe,' he declared in an essay of 1901, 'in the practice and philosophy of what we have agreed to call magic, in what I must call the evocation of spirits.'[41] That belief was underpinned, he argued, by three doctrines:

> (1) That the borders of our mind are ever shifting, and that many minds can flow into one another, as it were, and create or reveal a single mind, a single energy

---

40   Frazer, J. G. 1922 *The Golden Bough* London: Macmillan (one volume edition) 12.
41   Yeats, W. B. 1961 *Essays and Introductions,* London: Macmillan 28.

(2) That the borders of our memory are as shifting, and that our memories are a part of one great memory, the memory of Nature herself

(3) That this great mind and great memory can be evoked by symbols.[42]

That 'great mind and great memory' are underpinned by the same principles of association which guide our little memories, and which attach symbolic significance to certain clusters of past experiences:

> they act, as I believe, because the great memory associates them with certain events and moods and persons. Whatever the passions of man have gathered about, becomes a symbol in the great memory, and in the hands of him who has the secret, it is a worker of wonders, a caller-up of angels or of devils. The symbols are of all kinds, for everything in heaven or earth has its association, momentous or trivial, in the great memory, and one never knows what forgotten events may have plunged it, like the toadstool and the ragweed, into the great passions.[43]

Just as, for Macpherson, the 'ghosts' by whom Ossian is surrounded are the manifestations, or the externalisations, of his memories as they associate present and past events, so 'magic', for Yeats, harnesses the power of association, whether wilfully sought, as by the magus, or involuntarily revealed, as in dream or revelation. Yeats's magic, like Macpherson's ghosts, corresponds with the 'scientific' account of the mind as an associating mechanism and association as the 'medium' by which memories return to give meaning to present experiences. Every symbol is a complex interweaving of associations both personal and 'extra-personal', as a result of the fact that each individual has, at some time or another, access to memories stored in the 'Great Memory' which have never been personal experiences but are nonetheless experienced personally when they are encountered. They may be what came to be known as 'engrams', memories acquired by genetic

---

42   Yeats, *Essays and Introductions* 28.
43   Yeats, *Essays and Introductions* 49–50.

inheritance from our most distant ancestry,[44] or they may be the kinds of memories that we acquire at second hand through literature, the kind of 'memories' of ancient Celtic heroes that eighteenth-century readers acquired from Macpherson's Ossianic poems.

Despite his use of the modern 'scientific' terminology of association and the suggestions of a supra-personal memory in the work of empirical psychologists, Yeats presents himself as assertively anti-scientific, because he understands by 'science' something that denies his belief in the supernatural. Thus he tells us in his autobiography that his Celticism and occultism were a response to the materialist account of the universe given by post-Darwinian scientists such as John Tyndall, whose 'Belfast Address' to the British Association for the Advancement of Science in 1874 seemed to declare that science led necessarily to a philosophical materialism: modern physics, Tyndall asserted, upheld the view of Democritus in ancient Greece that,

> The only existing things are the atoms and empty space; all else is mere opinion ... The atoms are infinite in number and infinitely various in form; they strike together, and the lateral motions and whirlings which thus arise are the beginnings of worlds.

This, says Tyndall, is 'a fair general statement of the atomic philosophy as now held'.[45] 'I have been put into a rage by the followers of Huxley, Tyndall,' Yeats noted in 'The Trembling of the Veil',[46] and he traced to that rage his own belief system, with its Celticist foundations:

> I was unlike others of my generation in one thing only. I am very religious, and deprived by Huxley and Tyndall, whom I detested, of the simple-minded religion of my childhood, I made a new religion, almost an infallible church out of poetic tradition: a

---

44 See Ward, James 1913 *Heredity and Memory*, Cambridge University Press 27ff.; this was a sustained development of an argument first touched on in his article on 'Psychology' for the ninth edition of the *Encyclopaedia Britannica* (1886).

45 Tyndall, John 1874 *Address Delivered Before the British Association Assembled at Belfast, with Additions,* London: Longmans, Green 4.

46 Yeats, W. B. 1955 *Autobiographies,* London: Macmillan 190.

fardel of stories, and of personages, and of emotions, inseparable from their first expression, passed on from generation to generation by poets and painters with some help from philosophers and theologians. I wished for a world where I could discover this tradition perpetually.[47]

Tyndall had set out to enrage the religious by his materialist view of the universe, but in fact he enraged many in the scientific community as well. Present at the Belfast address was a young man by the name of William Robertson Smith, a promising physicist who would later become a leading theologian, but would be forced from his professorship in the Free Church College in Aberdeen for his insistence on the historical nature of the Biblical text. Subsequently, he became the editor of the ground-breaking Ninth Edition of the *Encyclopaedia Britannica* to which J. G. Frazer would be a contributor. Robertson Smith was in Belfast to take notes for a group of Scottish physicists—William Thomson, later Lord Kelvin; Peter Guthrie Tait, Kelvin's co-author of the *Treatise on Natural Philosophy* (1867), which sought to replace Newton's *Principia* with a new science of energy; and James Clerk Maxwell, whose *Treatise on Electricity and Magnetism* (1873) was actually to take its place alongside Newton's *Principia* in terms of influence on subsequent science. What Robertson Smith noted was how out of date Tyndall's views were in the context of the advances in physics made by Scottish natural philosophers in the previous thirty years, advances which insisted that the universe did not consist of atoms governed by *force* but consisted instead of *energy*, an energy which was defined by its capacity for transformation: as one of Kelvin's associates, W. Macquorn Rankine, had put it in a paper delivered twenty years earlier at the 1852 meeting of the British Association for the Advancement of Science, thermodynamic[48] experiments confirmed

that all the different kinds of physical energy in the physical universe are mutually convertible; that the total amount of

---

47 Yeats, *Autobiographies* 115–16.
48 It was Rankine who had first introduced the term 'thermodynamic' into the scientific lexicon.

physical energy, whether in the form of visible motion and mechanical power, or of heat, light, magnetism, electricity, or chemical energy or in other forms not yet understood, is unchangeable; the transformations of its different portions from one of those forms of power into another, constituting the phenomena which are the objects of experimental physics.[49]

Tyndall's materialism was still part of the physics of force—atoms 'strike together, and the lateral motions and whirlings which thus arise are the beginnings of worlds'—that Thomson and Tait believed they had overthrown in their *Treatise* in the previous decade; energy physics implied that Tyndall's confidence in philosophical materialism was misplaced, for the universe was a place of unexpected transformations rather than calculable forces.

Thomson and Tait's alternative conception of the nature of the universe opens the possibility that Yeats's rejection of Tyndall was not a rejection of science but a prescient foresight of how science itself was reshaping our understanding of the workings of the universe. I say 'prescient' but it may well be that Yeats had encountered Peter Guthrie Tait's speculative riposte to Tyndall in a book of 1875 entitled *The Unseen Universe, or Physical Speculations on a Future State*, co-written with another Scottish physicist, Balfour Stewart, who became the second President of the Society for Psychical Research, an organisation whose aim was to subject claims of paranormal or supernatural experiences to empirical investigation and with which Yeats had many dealings. *The Unseen Universe* was published by Yeats's own publishers, Macmillan, who also published Frazer's *The Golden Bough*, and it is significant that *The Unseen Universe* begins not with energy physics but with an anthropological exposition of how human beings from the ancient Egyptians to the early Christians had all believed that the world was divided into 'seen' and 'unseen' dimensions. This section had been researched by Robertson Smith, who went on to be one of the most influential analysts of primitive religion and who not only

---

49   Rankine, W. J. Macquorn 1881 On the Reconcentration of the Mechanical Energy of the Universe, *Miscellaneous Scientific Papers*, edited by W. J. Millar, London: Charles Griffin 200.

co-opted Frazer to write on 'Totem' and 'Taboo' in the ninth edition of the *Britannica* but invited Clerk Maxwell, rather than Tyndall, to write the entry on 'atom'. Tait and Stewart—and, implicitly, Robertson Smith—argued that these ancient beliefs, including Christian belief and, presumably, Yeats's belief in the supernatural, could be accommodated within the new physics, despite the fact that the public perception of energy physics in the period seemed to offer only a very pessimistic outcome for the evolution of the universe. Kelvin and Tait's account of energy physics implied the universe's ultimate decline into 'heat death', when, as a result of the dissipation of energy, a uniform environment was created in which there was not enough differential to initiate action or change. As David Masson described it in his *Recent British Thought* (1865):

> By a process which has been named the Equilibration of Forces, and which is slowly going on, it seems to be foreseen that a period will come when all the energy locked up in the solar system, and sustaining whatever of motion or life there is in it, will be exhausted ... and all its parts through all their present variousness will be stiffened or resolved, as regards each other, in a defunct and featureless community of rest and death ... [Farther, Science] yet sees no other end but that all the immeasurable entanglement of all the starry systems shall also run itself together at last in an indistinguishable equilibrium of ruin.[50]

This had been a more terrifying prospect for many Victorians than the implications of Darwinian evolution—it provided, for instance, the pessimistic vision of a dying universe in H. G. Wells's *The Time Machine* (1895)—though it had not bothered Lord Kelvin since it was, in his view, entirely compatible with his Calvinist reading of the Bible. It led, however, to one of the most famous thought experiments in modern science, one which, thanks to Kelvin, came to be known as 'Maxwell's Demon', since its implications utterly disrupted the orderliness of Kelvin's conception of the workings of energy.

---

50 Masson, David 1867 *Recent British Philosophy*, 2nd edition, London: Macmillan 151–2.

Maxwell's 'demon' is an atomic-sized creature who sits by a little sliding door between two vats of gas. The vats ought to cool at the same rate as the atoms of their gases reduce in speed, but the demon watches for the moment when a hotter atom in the first chamber approaches the door and opens it so that heat is added to the second chamber; equally, when a cooler atom in the second chamber approaches the gate, the demon opens it to allow that cooler atom to enter the first chamber. The effect is that the second chamber gets warmer and the first chamber gets colder, defying the orderly cooling that ought to be brought about by the dissipation of energy predicted by the laws of thermodynamics. What Maxwell's demon reveals is that the dissipation of energy is a statistical likelihood rather than an immutable law, thus opening up the possibility that the heat death of the universe may never actually occur because of randomly chaotic reversals of energy flows.

Tait and Stewart used the implications of this extended conception of energy physics to argue both for the possible truth of belief systems based on an 'unseen universe' and for the role of energy in what I call a mnemonic universe:

> the law of gravitation assures us that any displacement which takes place in the very heart of the earth will be felt throughout the universe, and we may even imagine that the same thing will hold true of those molecular motions ... which accompany thought. For every thought that we think is accompanied by a displacement and motion of the particles of the brain, and ... we may imagine that these motions are propagated through the universe.[51]

The process by which experience is *inscribed* in the brain is one which, at the same time, *inscribes* it in the fabric of the universe: the energy that turns into memory both goes inward into the brain and outward across space. They then use Maxwell's thought experiment to suggest that the outward-flowing energy is not simply dissipated into space but, like the atoms in the two vats over which the demon presides, it is

---

51 Stewart, Balfour and Tait, Peter Guthrie 1875 *The Unseen Universe: or Physical Speculations on a Future State,* London: Macmillan 156.

transferred from one environment—the seen universe—into another, an unseen universe:

> [Each] thought that we think, is accompanied by certain molecular motions and displacements in the brain, and part of these, let us allow, are in some way stored up in that organ, so as to produce what may be termed our material or physical memory. Other parts of these motions are, however, communicated to the spiritual or invisible body, and are there stored up, forming a memory which may be made use of when that body is free to exercise its functions.[52]

Our individual memories and the energies of our thoughts are being harnessed into the greater memory of the unseen universe—one which could allow our individual identities to survive the 'energy failure' that is death.

The speculative work of two of the foremost scientists of the mid-nineteenth century run parallel with Yeats's occult Celticism. Was the 'great memory' that Yeats thought he had encountered among the peasants of Ireland but a local version of a universal scheme that allowed the 'seen' and the 'unseen' to interact with one another, as though there was a gate controlled by a demon who could allow particles of memory to transfer from one to the other? If so, then the ghosts of Macpherson's Ossianic poems who respond to their recollection in the song of the bard—'The ghosts of those he sung came in their rustling blasts. They were seen to bend with joy towards the sound of their praise'—could be memory traces inscribed in the unseen universe which are occasionally called down to interact again with the living world. Thus the worldviews underpinning eighteenth- and nineteenth-century Celticisms can be read as reflections of, rather than rejections of, the science of their times. Science, indeed, might prove to be the means of confirming Celticist imaginings, as Yeats hoped when, in 1915, he encountered 'a machine which received and amplified voices from the spirit world',[53] invented

---

52 Stewart and Tait 159.
53 Foster, R. F. 2003 *W. B. Yeats: A Life: Volume II The Arch Poet 1915–1939*, Oxford University Press 80.

by David Wilson, producing voices which, to Yeats's delight, 'all seemed anxious for us to know that there was a universal mind and that if we spoke to them, it was as but links in this mind'.[54] Had not Wilson been lost to the war, science and Celticism might have been proved to be different routes by which to investigate the same phenomena Yeats remained hopeful of such a reconciliation.

IV

The antithesis between Celticism and science as defined by Mattar is based, in part, on a misunderstanding of the processes of science, which is assumed somehow to have evacuated all elements of subjectivity in order to produce a truly 'objective' account of reality. It is also based on a misconception of the relationship between the remembered, the imagined and the real, in which it is assumed that an imagined memory is, by virtue of being doubly removed from reality, less capable of impacting on it. But a fiction can have as powerful effects as a supposedly empirical fact; indeed, in the human world, fictions are at least as potent as 'facts', and imagined memories as potent as fictions, a 'fact' that Yeats celebrated in his poem 'The Statues':

> When Pearse summoned Cuchulain to his side,
> What stalked through the Post Office? What intellect,
> What calculation, number, measurement, replied?
> We Irish, born into that ancient sect
> But thrown upon this filthy modern tide
> And by its formless spawning fury wrecked,
> Climb to our proper dark, that we may trace
> The lineaments of a plummet-measured face.

The mythic figures of Ossian and Cuchulain, as recovered by Macpherson and recreated by Yeats, become a force in the making of modern Ireland: memory recovered can thus become a future foreseen,

---

54   Foster 81.

and though social scientists and theorists of the nation may deplore the 'false' memories with which the modern world is infused,[55] the associative links forged in the past return as causes which help shape the future, forming links in a chain that imbue some memories with the apparent power of foresight.

---

55   This has become increasingly central to debates about the nature and value of the nation and of 'nationalism', from Benedict Anderson 1983 *Imagined Communities*, London: Verso, through Anthony Smith 1999 *Myths and Memories of the Nation*, Oxford University Press, to recent debates about the rise of right-wing nationalist movements in Europe.

4

'One foot in Wales and my vowels in England': the Welshness of Dylan Thomas

Will Christie

Had the ardent nationalist and co-founder of Plaid Cymru, Saunders Lewis, had his way, there would have been no place at a Celtic Studies conference for Dylan Thomas, now far and away Wales's best-known writer. Born 27 October 1914 and reared in the Anglicised suburb of Uplands in Anglicised Swansea and educated in the entirely English curriculum of the Anglicised Swansea Grammar School where the only subject he took any interest in whatsoever was—wait for it—*English*, Thomas spoke and wrote only in the English language and remained a determined monoglot throughout his short life, attempting no other language, least of all Welsh. An 'inauthentic, un-Welsh product of English linguistic colonisation', declared Lewis in a famous address to the Cardiff Branch of the Guild of Graduates at the University of Wales [Urdd Graddedigion Prifysgol Cymru Cangen Caerdydd] in 1938 entitled 'Is there an Anglo-Welsh Literature?': 'There is nothing hyphenated about him. He belongs to the English.'[1]

Lewis, a lecturer at the University College in Swansea and linguistic essentialist who advocated an organic, Welsh-speaking society, was discussing the first issue of Keidrych Rhys's ground-breaking Anglo-Welsh literary journal, *Wales*, which in the summer of 1937 had

---

1   Lewis, Saunders 1939 *Is There an Anglo-Welsh Literature?* Caerdydd: Guild of Graduates of the University of Wales 5.

opened with an experimental short story by Thomas entitled 'Prologue to an Adventure', with the first, long sentence of Thomas's story beginning on the front cover. Though Thomas himself was sceptical about the idea of an Anglo-Welsh literature, which struck him as at best irrelevant and at worst apologetic—or 'hyphenated', to use Saunders Lewis's word—nevertheless he was friends with Keidrych Rhys (Thomas would be best man at Rhys's wedding) and actively supportive of the enterprise.

Rhys's choice of Thomas as an opening flourish for a journal that would circulate and celebrate English-language writing by Welsh authors can be understood as recognition of the centrality of Thomas to this newly self-conscious cluster of talented young writers. At the same time, it can also be understood as a shrewd marketing strategy. Though only twenty-two, Dylan Thomas was already a name amongst the poetry writers and readers of both Wales and England and could number among his friends and supporters in the English literary establishment Edith Sitwell, Cyril Connolly, William Empson, Geoffrey Grigson, Stephen Spender, and T. S. Eliot. It had been this way since the publication on 18 December 1934, not long after his twentieth birthday, of an astonishingly original first volume, *18 Poems*.

In *18 Poems*, Thomas had offered the reading public a selection of the strikingly idiosyncratic poems he had been cultivating—'fluently and furiously', to quote James A. Davies[2]—in school exercise books since the age of fifteen.[3] Though he would eventually sell the notebooks in 1941, effectively renouncing them as a resource for future publications, poems drafted or written during this brief, intense period of writing would comprise the bulk of the *Collected Poems* that Thomas brought out in 1952, the year before he died in New York at the age of thirty-nine.

From the beginning of Thomas's fourth notebook of August 1933, his poems had taken on the gnomic tone, dense anatomical imagery

2   Davies, James A. 1998 *A Reference Companion to Dylan Thomas*, Westport CT: Greenwood Press 25.
3   Four of these 'notebooks' are still extant (there is a gap between July 1932 and January 1933). Held in the Poetry Library of the State University of New York, Buffalo, they were first made available to the public in an edition by Ralph Maud in 1968: *Poet in the Making: The Notebooks of Dylan Thomas*, London: J. M. Dent & Sons.

and cannibalised Christian mythology, the thrusting rhythm, obsessively regulated metrical and stanzaic forms, and the complicated half-rhyme and assonantal patterning that would become Thomas's trademark. At the same time, the notebook betrays the characteristic obsessions of the so-called 'process' poems: exploring the implication of the human body and its parts in the universal cycle of life and death and in the impersonal processes, weathers, heavens, tides, and times of an indifferent natural and industrial world. The best known and most anthologised of the process poems is 'The force that through the green fuse drives the flower', copied out or composed on 12 October 1933:

> The force that through the green fuse drives the flower
> Drives my green age; that blasts the roots of trees
> Is my destroyer.
> And I am dumb to tell the crooked rose
> My youth is bent by the same wintry fever.
> The force that drives the water through the rocks
> Drives my red blood; that dries the mouthing streams
> Turns mine to wax.
> And I am dumb to mouth unto my veins
> How at the mountain spring the same mouth sucks.

Amid the social and political turmoil of the 1930s, poems like 'The force that through the green fuse drives the flower' offered the poetry-reading public the excitement of novelty and originality, even, ironically, something like hope. For all the images of decay and death in the process poems, that is, there was an unmistakable vitality marking their strong rhythms, sonorous music, and elemental landscapes and mindscapes, their compounds and coinages. Even those who found the poems baffling—and this would become a critical issue with the publication of Thomas's next two volumes—were willing to credit him with the creation of a new and exciting language.

Compellingly, Thomas's first lines shock and disorient: 'I see the boys of summer in their ruin', 'Where once the twilight locks no longer', 'A process in the weather of the heart', 'Before I knocked and flesh let enter', 'The force that through the green fuse drives the flower', 'My hero bares his nerve along my wrist', 'From love's first fever to her plague',

'Light breaks where no sun shines', 'If I were tickled by the rub of love', 'When, like a running grave, time tracks you down', and so on. The diction is familiar enough, and so, too, is the grammar and the syntax (though this is not always the case), but we have to strain to make sense of it, to allow familiar structures to accommodate the unfamiliar, grammatically and conceptually:

> A process in the weather of the heart
> Turns damp to dry; the golden shot
> Storms in the freezing grave.
> A weather in the quarter of the veins
> Turns night to day; blood in their suns
> Lights up the living worm.
> A process in the eye forewarns
> The bones of blindness; and the womb
> Drives in a death as life leaks out.[4]

It is the same with Thomas's characteristic inversion of clichés and stock phrases: 'once below a time', 'fall awake', 'a grief ago', 'dressed to die', 'as happy as the grass was green'. The impulse to rattle or rearrange the verbal props upon which we rely in order to force language and locution on our consciousness and to compel us to rethink the world through these contortions was a reflex reaction with Thomas: he does it in his poems and letters, he does it later in his radio features and in his famous play for voices, *Under Milk Wood*.

No less characteristic was Thomas's attention to the sound that words made. The sound of a word, independent of its semantic associations, had its own sensual pleasure and affective resonance:

> The greatest single word I know is 'drome' which, for some reason, nearly opens the doors of heaven for me. Say it yourself, out aloud, and see if you hear the golden gates swing backward as the last, long sound of the 'm' fades away.

---

4   *Poet in the Making* 262.

'Drome', 'bone', 'doom', province', 'dwell', 'prove', 'dolomite'—these are only a few of my favourite words, which are insufferably beautiful to me. The first four words are visionary; God moves in a long 'o'.[5]

Again and again, Thomas attributed his urge to write to a love of the sound of words. 'What the words stood for, symbolised, or meant, was of secondary importance; what mattered was the *sound* of them', Thomas remembered of his childhood:

> And these words were, to me, as the notes of bells, the sounds of musical instruments, the noises of wind, sea, and rain, the rattle of milk-carts, the clopping of hooves on cobbles, the fingering of branches on a window pane, might be to someone, deaf from birth, who has miraculously found his hearing. I did not care what the words said, overmuch, nor what happened to Jack & Jill & Mother Goose and the rest of them; I cared for the shapes of sound that their names, and the words describing their actions, made in my ears; I cared for the colours the words cast on my eyes.[6]

Poems make sense in complex ways that exploit the ambiguity of the word 'sense' itself: they make sense out of using and changing conventional meanings, they make sense out of images that evoke ideas and feelings, and they make sense out of sounds and their complex orchestration. 'I think that one of the magical things about his reading,' said Aneirin Talfan Davies, one of Thomas's producers when the poet worked as a writer and broadcaster for the BBC, 'is that he has made people believe that they understand his poetry. He has insinuated the meaning into the reading.'[7] Whether magic or sleight of hand, what it sounded like made sense.

---

5 Thomas, Dylan 2000 *The Collected Letters*, second edition, edited by Paul Ferris, London: J. M. Dent 90.
6 From the interview with Thomas in 1951 known as 'Poetic Manifesto', as reprinted in Thomas, Dylan 1971 *Early Prose Writings*, edited by Walford Davies, London: J. M. Dent & Sons 154.
7 Thomas, David N. editor 2004 *Dylan Remembered: Interviews with Colin Edwards, Volume Two 1935–1953*, Brigend: Seren/Poetry of Wales Press 2, 148.

Light breaks where no sun shines;
Where no sea runs, the waters of the heart
Push in their tides;
And, broken ghosts with glow-worms in their heads,
The things of light
File through the flesh where no flesh decks the bones.

What Thomas was *not* doing in his poetry, moreover, only reinforced his attraction for his early readers. Boldly symbolic, he was *not* subtly expository; visionary, it seemed, not worldly; and he was sensual instead of being intellectual. If the poems were often dense and obscure, they were not erudite, hieratic, cultured, allusive—having none of the cultured élitism of Modernists like Eliot and Pound, in other words, or of the Oxford Marxists. 'The Audenesque convention is early ended,' declared Desmond Hawkins, reviewing *18 Poems* on 9 February 1935, 'and I credit Dylan Thomas with being the first considerable poet to break through fashionable limitation and speak an unborrowed language.'[8]

An 'unborrowed', 'original', 'idiosyncratic' language; a language that aspired to the condition of music: but was it Anglo-Welsh or Welsh writing in English? Saunders Lewis, as we saw, thought not. Even Keidrych Rhys had his doubts: 'Dylan's only affinity with the Gogynfeirdd [or Medieval court poets] is his vanity and use of I—I, Dylan, the poet and fucker,' he wrote to his friend Glyn Jones in a fit of pique: 'He could never become a truly representative Welsh poet. Can a poetic person with his sensitiveness ignore the industrial mess where he lives? Or am I being unduly cynical and catty?'[9]

---

8   Hawkins, Desmond 1935 Review of *18 Poems, Time and Tide*, 16:6, 206.
9   Keidrych Rhys to Glyn Jones, 14 March 1937, as quoted in Lycett, Andrew 2003 *Dylan Thomas: A New Life*, Woodstock and New York: The Overlook Press 151.

Thomas on Wales

If Rhys was being catty he was neither the first nor the only one. As Harri Garrod Roberts observes,

> From Saunders Lewis's outright rejection of Thomas's claims to Welsh nationality ... to [Katie] Gramich's reservations about Thomas's apparent collusion with English stereotyping, attempts to assess Thomas's contribution to a distinctively Welsh literature in English almost invariably feel obliged to engage with an identity politics in which the fundamental question of poetic ability cannot be easily disentangled from issues of national identity.[10]

Part of the protracted argument over the Welshness, or not, of Dylan Thomas and his writing—an argument 'framed by the contested status of Wales in relation to post-colonialism', as Nadine Holdsworth observes—is provoked by the poet's own declared indifference to—and at times, apparently, deep loathing of—the Welsh nation in which he was raised. 'Land of my Fathers! As far as I'm concerned, my fathers can keep it', Thomas is often quoted as having said.[11] He didn't, as it happens. It is a line from his script for a film entitled *The Three Weird Sisters*, and is said by the villainous Owen Morgan-Vaughan.[12] But Thomas might have said it, and indeed can be found to have said far worse: 'this arsehole of the universe, this hymnal blob, the pretty sick, fond, sad Wales,' he erupted, in a bilious parody of John of Gaunt's speech from Shakespeare's *Richard II*.[13] More publicly, in a series of dark, melodramatic fables, Thomas would create a nightmare version of rural West Wales in a fictional place he called Jarvis Valley that was unflattering to his Welsh compatriots, a grotesque, adolescent version

---

10   Roberts, Harri Garrod 2009 *Embodying Identity: Representations of the Body in Welsh Literature*, Cardiff: University of Wales Press, chapter 6.

11   See, for example, Smith, David 1988 Writing Wales, *Wales Between the Wars*, edited by Trevor Herbert and Gareth Elwyn Jones, Cardiff: University of Wales Press 186.

12   Thomas, Dylan 1995 *The Complete Screenplays*, edited by John Ackerman, New York: Applause 299.

13   In a letter to John and Bonnie Nims, 17 July 1950, *Collected Letters* 854.

of William Faulkner's Yoknapatawpha and the Welsh anti-pastoral of
Caradoc Evans.

But loathing betrays a good deal more intimacy and emotional
investment than indifference and only begs the question of Thomas's
Welshness. 'That Welsh-speaking life so consciously denied the poet at
source,' asks Walford Davies, 'could it still have exerted an influence
even on the wider reaches of his poetry?'[14]

Gwilym Marles

There was one prominent figure in the Thomas family mythology
whose memory the poet's father, D. J. Thomas, was careful to preserve,
and that was Dylan's great-uncle, the bard and radical Unitarian convert
and preacher William Thomas (b. 1834), self-named Gwilym Marles
after the Marles or Marlais, a local stream.[15] After attending the
Presbyterian College in Carmarthen, where his Unitarianism, drinking,
and theatrical habits drew the family's disapproval, Gwilym Marles won
a scholarship to Glasgow University where he established a reputation
as a poet, novelist, and pamphleteer in the Welsh language, before
returning to three Unitarian livings in Cardiganshire, where he became
more, rather than less, radical, representing the rights of local
smallholders and itinerant labourers when a conservative reaction led
to serial evictions.[16]

Gwilym Marles for many 'has been the assured, tangible link
between Dylan Thomas and Welsh poetry', to quote Tudur Hallam.[17]
But that Thomas shared his father's interest in his great-uncle is
unlikely—there is no record of his ever making the effort to read his
great-uncle's writings—nor should we exaggerate the family

---

14 Davies, Walford 1990 *Dylan Thomas*, Writers of Wales, Cardiff: University of
    Wales Press 10.
15 See Ferris, Paul 1999 *Dylan Thomas: The Biography*, second edition, J. M.
    Dent & Sons 8.
16 Lycett 9–10.
17 Hallam, Tudur 2015 'Curse, bless, me now': Dylan Thomas and Saunders
    Lewis (Chatterton Lecture on Poetry read 24 October 2014), *Journal of the
    British Academy* 3, 211–53: 244.

resemblances suggested by the bardic pose, some early hard living, and
an early death (Gwilym Marles died at forty-five). Gwilym Marles was
a self-conscious bard in the Welsh tradition, where the role carried
with it social responsibilities analogous to those he bore as a dissenting
preacher. He was driven—and broken—by politico-pastoral activities
that have no equivalent in Thomas's life. There can be no doubt that
the impulse to preach was strong in Dylan Thomas, who deployed the
language of the pulpit with oratorical ease, but rarely if ever without
a vestigial irony and reflex self-mockery. Thomas had the rhetorical
power without the social and spiritual conviction.

Certainly this is the drift of Glyn Jones's meditation on Thomas's
Welshness in his landmark text *The Dragon Has Two Tongues: Essays on
Anglo-Welsh Writers and Writing*, which came out in 1968, fifteen years
after Thomas's death:

> the idea of the wild and petted man apart seemed to remain with
> him for a long time, perhaps until his death, the man from whom
> ordinary responsibility and participation ... cannot be expected,
> who possesses nothing, no religion, no politics, no community, no
> thought, nothing, only that one gift that marks him off from his
> fellow men. I think it is difficult for a Welsh-language poet to see
> himself in this way, as a man cut off, because poetry is much more
> a part of everyday life in Welsh Wales than it is in England—and
> it was to England, or rather London, that Dylan always looked.[18]

The choice, as Jones sees it, is between a commitment to 'the everyday
life of Welsh Wales' and a Romantic isolation.

Thomas chose both—though whether that makes him a
hyphenated Anglo-Welsh or simply an artist is a moot point. From
the years 1938 and 1939 emerged a set of ten stories that were very
different in form and atmosphere from the crepuscular extravaganza
of the dark fables with which he had been testing the tolerance of the
reading public. In 'A Visit to Grandpa's', the eccentricity and fantasy
and insanity familiar from Thomas's Jarvis Valley stories become the

---

18   Jones, Glyn 1968 *The Dragon Has Two Tongues: Essays on Anglo-Welsh
     Writers and Writing*, London: Dent 186.

endearing symptoms of an estranging dementia, as a child learns to deal with the revisionary delusions of his grandfather's senile imagination. It would become one of the most successful in a future volume entitled *A Portrait of the Artist as a Young Dog* and published in April 1940, to which Thomas soon added 'One Warm Saturday' and 'The Peaches'. This last was his second literary use of his Aunt Annie and Uncle Jim Jones's farm, Fernhill, a moving story of a paid holiday on a struggling farm in West Wales taken by a city boy from a wealthy family.

The child who tells the story, however, is not the wealthy visitor and is carefully déclassé. An urban visitor to his impoverished aunt and uncle's world of rural subsistence, he is both part of, and not part of, the family of his poor relations, for whom a tin of peaches represents the height of refinement. A friend of the young boy who is the paying visitor, the narrator unwittingly gets caught up in a fight for survival and dignity in the face of the iniquities of history, society, and human weakness. In a closely observed, class-calibrated fable, Thomas is able to satirise the folly of a Nonconformist enthusiasm in the narrator's cousin, Gwilym, while at the same time understanding and figuring it as part of a socially conditioned sensibility, and as one of many distorted voices in the awkward conversation between different historical sensibilities and social classes going on in his own family, and his own Welsh society.

Thomas has gone back past an adolescent self-obsession to a vision of the artist as an almost cruelly observant, privileged child and youth—privileged by his class and privileged by his youth—around whom an interpretable world of characters and events unfolds. This visionary and revisionary transaction between the child's consciousness and an exciting and perplexing world would be one that Thomas would use again and again during and after the war in the different media in which he worked. It also, I would suggest, quite precisely positions Thomas as both part of and not part of Wales, as artistry supervenes on nationality.

The reorientation towards Wales and the past that is already well underway in the stories for *A Portrait of an Artist as a Young Dog* was only accelerated by the devastating air raids in and around Swansea early in 1941. What we get after 1941 is nostalgia—usually, but not always, self-ironic or framed as an indulgence—a nostalgia that will soon become a characteristic part of Thomas's engagement with the new and larger public represented by the audience of the BBC where his writing and recording commitments were increasing every year.

Nostalgia will also become part of a revised poetic. The poetry that was once so vigorous had started to become overwrought and dense to the point of paralysis: 'a mad-doctor's bag', he called it, stuffed to repletion with the idiosyncratic and often impenetrable symbols of his trade.[19] Readers of Thomas's next and fourth volume of verse, *Deaths and Entrances*, a product of the poet's second and final period of sustained creative activity at New Quay in 1944–45, were greeted by more accessible imagery and heard a very different music. It was as if a light had broken on the landscape of his memory and his imagination had been invaded by a wider, more inclusive pathos.

Intricately patterned by its sounds, the famous 'Poem in October' has an almost flawless syllabic count of 9, 12, 9, 3, 5, 12, 12, 5, 3, 9 in the respective lines of each stanza. Thomas's craftsmanship, careful to the point of obsessiveness, is characteristic of all his work, early *and* late. For all its apparent spontaneity, for example, an early poem like 'If I were tickled by the rub of love' has a syllabic patterning (10, 10, 10, 10, 10, 10, 6) that is as flawlessly consistent as that of 'Poem in October', ordered down to the last syllable of the last line-end word. 'I am a painstaking, conscientious, involved and devious craftsman in words,' wrote Thomas in the document which has become known as his 'Poetic Manifesto'.[20]

And it was true. Thomas, to quote Chris Baldick, was 'the most dedicated practitioner both of half-rhyme and of pararhyme' (vowel variation within repeated consonants)—both, interestingly, characteristic of Old Welsh poetry.[21] Whether discussing the discipline itself, the act of craftsmanship—in Welsh, *Cerdd dafod*, or tongue craft—or analysing specific prosodic effects, Thomas's reclamation as a Welsh poet writing in English has invariably focused on his obsessive practice. 'I'm not influenced by Welsh bardic poetry,' Thomas wrote to Stephen Spender, 'I can't read Welsh.'[22] This much we know to be true,

---

19 Thomas, *Collected Letters* 249.
20 Thomas, *Early Prose Writings* 158.
21 Baldick, Chris 2004 *The Modern Movement*, The Oxford History of English Literature, Volume 10, 1910–1940, Oxford University Press 79.
22 Thomas, *Collected Letters* 953.

but if he hoped that would be an end to it he would be as disappointed with the critical nationalists as he was with the cultural nationalists.

In other words, Thomas's ignorance of Welsh has not stopped critics writing, often persuasively, of characteristically Welsh rhythms and verse forms in his work. 'Dylan Thomas knew a great deal about *cynghanedd* and Welsh metres,' insists the twentieth-century Welsh-language poet Alan Llwyd.[23] So for T. James Jones and Mererid Hopwood—indeed, to quote Tudur Hallam,

> the similarities between Thomas's modernist poetry—his attitude towards words in particular—and the poetics of Welsh literary tradition are clearly apparent to a number of his readers familiar with *Cerd Dafod* and *cynghanedd*, i.e., the Welsh bardic tradition.

Striking similarities have been found with the fourteenth-century poet Daffydd ap Gwilym, and F. W. Bateson has compared him with the twelfth-century Cynddelw Brydydd Mawr.

On one (admittedly unique) occasion, Thomas himself warned a would-be editor of alien conventions: "'I dreamed my genesis" is more or less based on Welsh rhythms, & may seem, rhythmically, a bit strange at first.'[24] Thomas's obsessive devotion to the metrical and prosodic craft of poetry was as legendary as his drinking. As Glyn Jones points out, Thomas always 'felt the need for some sort of discipline to his verse.'[25] Like a Welsh classical poet—or like the sea in 'Fern Hill'—Thomas could only sing in chains, which were largely self-imposed. Only rarely did he flirt with traditional verse forms, but he wrote no poem without imposing often punitive technical limits on himself.

Does this make Thomas a Welsh poet? Aneirin Talfan Davies certainly thought so:

> Dylan's whole attitude is that of the Medieval bards. They gave themselves tasks. He said he knew nothing about Welsh bardic

---

23 Llwyd, Alan 1978 (Summer) Cynghanned and English Poetry, *Poetry Wales* 14, 23–58: 54.

24 Thomas, *Collected Letters* 161–2.

25 *Dylan Remembered* 2, 48.

poetry, but I often talked to him about it. You have to be wary of
Dylan—he was always laying false trails.[26]

Similarly for John Ackerman, in both Thomas and traditional Welsh
literature, 'the exuberance of the bardic personality, the liking for
ceremony and elaborate ritual, co-exist with a most craftsmanlike
devotion to composition'.[27] Thomas habitually denied the influence of
classical Welsh poetry but he shared the technical skill and verbal
gymnastics mandated by its tradition and, as Walford Davies observes,
'unvoiced national instincts (social, cultural, literary, religious) are there
in his welcoming of strictness of form'. Davies also identifies 'the Welsh
heft in Dylan's high definition inventiveness in all things verbal'.[28]

And there are other kinds of Welshness and other ways of
approaching these Welsh affinities. 'How much of Dylan
Thomas's "violent rhetoric"', for example, was 'afforced by generations
of chapel hell-fire in their Welsh blood?' asks Valentine Cunningham.[29]
Roland Mathias certainly thought so when he drew attention to the
various ways in which the tone, rhythm, and idiom of Thomas's poetry
could be seen to derive from the Welsh-speaking chapel culture of
south-west Wales.[30]

Under Milk Wood

And Under Milk Wood? Whether embraced as quintessentially Welsh or
rejected as a stereotypical Wales manufactured for an English audience,
Under Milk Wood seems to focus the contentious question of Thomas's
own Welshness. 'Within Welsh culture,' writes Nadine Holdsworth,
'Thomas and Under Milk Wood occupy an uneasy place, by turns

26 As quoted in Ferris, Dylan Thomas 104–5n.
27 Ackerman, John 1966 The Welsh Background, in Dylan Thomas: A Collection
    of Critical Essays, edited by C. B. Cox, Englewood Cliffs NJ: Prentice Hall 29.
28 Davies, Walford, Dylan Thomas 17, 25.
29 Cunningham, Valentine 1988 British Writers of the Thirties, Oxford University
    Press 67.
30 Mathias, Roland 1985 A Ride through the Wood: Essays on Anglo-Welsh
    Literature, Bridgend: Poetry Wales Press 72.

celebrated as cultural icons that have become an intrinsic part of the national imagining, but equally pilloried for offering a damaged, reductive and folksy image of Wales and the Welsh.'[31] In spite of the industry that has grown up around spotting the originals of Llareggub and its many characters, it remains a fictional place, and not just in the sense of a legal disclaimer: 'The story, all names, characters, and incidents portrayed in this production are fictitious. No identification with actual persons, places, buildings, and products is intended or should be inferred.' Thomas's characterisations are informed as much by literature as they are by his own experience, and any adequate genealogy of *Under Milk Wood* would have to include, along with Shakespeare and Dickens and James Joyce—'Joyce is there in the characters,' writes Barbara Hardy, 'he's there in the time scheme, he's there in the dream fantasy, he's there in the narrative monologues, he's there in the fun and flow'[32]—writers such as Caradoc Evans, Stella Gibbons, and Edgar Lee Masters's *Spoon River Anthology* (1915), a favourite of Thomas's in which the dead speak from a small-town graveyard.

With a cast of over seventy characters, many of them with a Dickensian distinctiveness and memorability, *Under Milk Wood* is busy with idiosyncratic life—a busyness and vitality symbolised and generated by Thomas's restlessly inventive orchestration and imagery. 'Love the words' was the one piece of directorial advice he had to offer the cast at the first full performance of *Under Milk Wood* in New York in May 1953.[33] It is this, before anything else, that establishes a continuity between Thomas's late, more popular work and the strikingly idiosyncratic forms he had entered into his notebooks in the early 1930s.

As the sheer number of characters suggests, the audience is not treated to complex characterisation, rather to effective caricature (especially effective on air and in the theatre): 'eccentrics whose

---

31 Holdsworth, Nadine 2014 Over and Beyond *Under Milk Wood*: Dylan Thomas, National Icons and Reimagining the Cultural Landscape of Wales, in her edition of *Theatre and National Identity: Re-Imagining Concepts of Nation*, London: Routledge 43.

32 Hardy, Barbara 2000 *Dylan Thomas: An Original Language*, Athens GA and London: University of Georgia Press 57.

33 See Colin Edwards's interview with Sada Thompson and Nancy Wickwire, *Dylan Remembered* 2, 226.

eccentricities, in Thomas's own words, 'are but briefly & impressionistically noted.'[34] In the end, the significance of character lies not in the parts, but in the patterns of the play, as Thomas works his contrasts and variations on the theme of human singularity and relationship. In the elaboration and contrast of the many and various characters, we are reminded once again that Thomas was a poet and, like his self-mocking persona, the Rev Eli Jenkins, 'intricately' rhyming (15), creating what John Goodby has called 'an almost mathematical web of relationships and fixed natures.'[35] But the form in the end is not mathematical, it is musical: the patterned repetitions of lyric poetry, recognising that the shape of our lives is not logical, but symphonic—or, as Raymond Williams has remarked of *Under Milk Wood*, 'polyphonic.'[36] Music, Thomas well knew, is central to poetic, indeed to all language, and *Under Milk Wood* should be thought of as divided not into acts but into movements.

Robert Pocock recalled having 'only once heard Dylan express an opinion of Welsh nationalism. He used three words. Two of them were Welsh Nationalism.'[37] Addressing the Scottish PEN in September 1948 and aware of the swell of feeling in his audience for an independent Scottish culture, Thomas was characteristically evasive, at the same time expressing what I take to be a genuine ideal of transnationality, one that avoided the reductive stereotypes of nationalist thinking: 'Regarded in England as a Welshman (and a waterer of England's milk), and in Wales as an Englishman, I am too unnational to be here at all,' he said. 'I should be living in a small private leper house in Hereford or Shropshire, one foot in Wales and my vowels in England.'[38]

For many Welsh artists and intellectuals, especially those writing in English, Saunders Lewis's sacrifice of English-language writers to an

---

34 Thomas, *Collected Letters* 906.
35 Goodby, John 2001 'Very profound and very box-office': The Later Poems and *Under Milk Wood*, *Dylan Thomas: New Casebooks*, edited by John Goodby and Chris Wigginton, Basingstoke: Palgrave Macmillan 192–220: 210.
36 Goodby 213.
37 As quoted in Fitzgibbon, Constantine 1965 *The Life of Dylan Thomas*, London: J. M. Dent & Sons 10.
38 As quoted in Tedlock, E. W. editor 1960 *Dylan Thomas: The Legend and the Poet*, London: Heinemann 8.

ideal of racial purity slid dangerously close to the more sinister versions of national socialism being cultivated on the Continent. It is too easy to forget what the word 'nationalism' conjured during the 1930s. In one of Thomas's short stories, 'Where the Tawe Flows', the 'cheerful, disreputable' Mr Roberts invokes his ideological leader: 'Heil, Saunders Lewis!' When Thomas rages against 'this arsehole of the universe, this hymnal blob, the pretty sick, fond, sad Wales', invoking Shakespeare's 'This England' speech, he is mocking that 'last refuge of a scoundrel' (Dr Johnson): patriotism. Recalling Thomas's visit to Prague in 1949 in an interview with Colin Edwards, Zdenêk Urbánek argued that Thomas 'was much more liked than other poets who were singing about the glories of their nations. We had enough of it from the Germans.'[39]

Thomas became evasive or recalcitrant when his writing was subject to any kind of labelling, whether it was artistic, cultural, or national. On the issue of his own Welshness or the Welsh affinities of his poetry, he countered Lewis's exclusive linguistic purism with a vocational purism of his own, in which the poet moved to protect his art against the contamination of an ephemeral geopolitics. His obligation, at least as Thomas saw it, was to himself and to his art. He was the observer—or, better still (because that has a quasi-scientific, analytical ring), the casual looker-on—of the period's historical and material culture. He was not its policeman or policy maker. 'To his credit,' writes Walford Davies, 'he held that the first test of a poem is its prosodic accomplishment, not its conscience.'[40]

This was and is unlikely to satisfy the nationalists, or indeed the critics who want to know about Thomas's attitude to Wales or about the Welsh roots of Thomas's literary expression and practices, the critics for whom the Welshness (or not) of his poetry turns into questions of interpretation and value. Yet for every brutal renunciation of Wales in Thomas's writing and every equivocation can be found a statement of more or less ironic recognition, not to say celebration, of his native country, though more frequently towards the end of his life. And the fact remains that most of his best poetry was written in Wales, and all his best stories and radio features were set in Wales. His 'links

---

39 *Dylan Remembered* 2, 164.
40 Davies, Walford, *Dylan Thomas* 39.

with Welsh writers', moreover, 'despite Thomas's own reservations about many of them and a general indifference to the idea of 'Anglo-Welsh' writing, became a significant element in his literary career', as James Davies points out.[41]

Insofar as the language of any poet will be found, like his or her DNA, to carry traces of an incomprehensibly complex inheritance, the interpretation of Thomas's Welsh affinities requires tact and circumspection. 'He would call himself a Welsh poet writing English poetry, because Welsh was in his blood'—so said Vernon Watkins, who, like Thomas, did not approve of the term 'Anglo-Welsh' that was becoming fashionable during his time. 'You can be wholly Welsh, and write only English poetry. And that's what Dylan did.'[42] This seems to me unexceptionable—though, because we all have to be allowed to change our mind, I am going to give the last word to Saunders Lewis, who on hearing of the news of Thomas's death in November 1953 wrote, in Welsh, that Thomas 'is the greatest Welsh poet writing in English in our time' and 'the most splendid English-speaking child Wales has produced in centuries'.[43]

---

41 Davies, Paul, *A Reference Companion* 36.
42 *Dylan Remembered* 2, 62.
43 Lewis, Saunders 1953 Dylan Thomas, *Dock Leaves* (Spring) 8–9.

5
Ireland's Lexical Memory: Irish Words in English-Language Texts, 1800–2016

Dymphna Lonergan

'Con, … I have no speech now'. When the boy asked 'what else have you got?' the girl said 'English'. When the boy asserted that surely English was speech she replied: 'If it was, surely people would understand it?'[1]

This reference to language transfer by a local girl to a servant boy on Canon Peter O'Leary's farm in nineteenth-century Ireland shows how this transfer was a lived experience for many Irish people in the eighteenth and nineteenth centuries. The new language, English, was not yet everyday speech and in many cases was not learned in a formal way. So sudden was the language transfer that the Irish still carried around in their heads Irish syntax and vocabulary that influenced the new language. For example, the word 'youse' was most likely coined as a response to many dialects of English no longer having a plural form of the second-person pronoun as Irish does (Ir. *tú* 'you', *sibh* 'you' pl.). Another feature of Irish English is how the absence of a perfect or pluperfect tense in the Irish language was managed in English. In Irish, these tenses could be made by using the words *tar éis* 'after' plus the gerund. This construct can still be heard in Ireland today even

---

1   O'Leary, Peter 1915 *Mó Sceil Fein*; English version 1970 *My Own Story*, Cork: The Mercier Press 48.

among the most educated speakers: *I'm after finishing my dinner* for 'I have just finished my dinner' or *I was just after coming home* for 'I had just come home'. As well as syntax and certain grammatical features individual Irish words were also carried into the new language either for convenience or because there was no equivalent English word. The appearance and use of these Irish words in an English-language text is the subject of this essay. They represent an aspect of language memory at play and a dual approach to language by the Irish writer. By the 'Irish writer' I mean a writer who was born and schooled in Ireland and who writes mainly in English. The importance of the Irish language is all around the Irish writer, starting with its recognition in the Constitution whose Article 8 claims:

1. The Irish language as the national language is the first official language
2. The English language is recognised as a second official language[2]

Here, in claiming Irish as the first official language of the country, English is recognised as *a*, not *the*, second official language. Ireland has been largely English speaking for hundreds of years now, but not only is its primary language still remembered, its importance continues to be reinforced. This includes the importance of the appearance of the language in print. *A Study of the Irish Text of the Constitution* in 1999 reiterated that when the Constitution is formally amended, the enrolled amendment to the Supreme Court is formatted in the Gaelic script because 'The first Irish text was enrolled in the Gaelic script and the practice has been maintained ever since'.[3] The Foreword also explains that where there is a dispute, the Irish language version will take precedent. Along with these historical and practical matters of format and dispute resolution, the Foreword to the Study includes the following:

---

2   Constitution of Ireland. Available online at https://bit.ly/2RwiCbY.
3   *Bunreacht na hÉireann A Study of The Irish Text of the Constitution*, 1999 Dublin: The Stationery Office.

The present Irish text of the Constitution illustrates the richness and antiquity of the language. Some of the terms employed in the Constitution have a lineage that can be traced back to the eighth century. Other expressions used in the Constitution relate to the modern development and adaptation of the language since the foundation of the State. The study discloses the wealth of written sources in the Irish language available to us today. The study illustrates the continuous literary tradition embodied in the modern language. On the eve of a new millennium we see that the Irish language spoken today did not begin with the revival movement initiated in 1893. The language spoken in the Gaeltacht in particular and taught in schools is the proud inheritance of a spoken tradition which has evolved over more than two millennia.

This pride in the language is not new. It has been part of centuries-old discussions on the importance and role of Irish in Ireland. One element that seems to have been present in the Irish language from early times is its unifying effect.[4] An early compilation of Ireland's history, *Lebor Gabála Érenn* ('Book of the Takings of Ireland'), claimed in the eleventh century that the Irish people were descended from a single set of ancestors and that the language itself 'is constructed from the best elements of language available at the Tower of Babel' and that the language was said to be 'the speech which is melodious and sweet in the mouth'.[5] Even as late as the beginning of the eighteenth century, the Irish language was used as a constant reminder that the dispossessed Irish people were 'descendants of glorious ancestors'.[6] In the twentieth century, the language was seen to be 'an organic connection' with the past that nourishes the 'growing plant of the future'.[7] Michael Collins, one of the foremost figures in the Irish fight for independence,

---

4   Ó Corráin, Donnchadh 1989 Prehistoric and Early Christian Ireland, *The Oxford Illustrated History of Ireland*, edited by R. F. Foster, Oxford University Press 1–52: 27.
5   Ó Corráin 27.
6   Canny, Nicholas 1989 Early Modern Ireland, *The Oxford Illustrated History of Ireland*, edited by R. F. Foster 161–212: 159
7   Brennan, Martin SJ 1969 Language, Personality and the Nation, *A View of the Irish Language*, edited by B. Ó Cuív, Dublin: Stationery Office 70–80: 79.

said that they only succeeded when they returned to 'Irish ways', to the native language.[8] Regardless of the number of native speakers at any given time, the Irish language appears to always play a significant role in the nation's psyche. The loss of Irish as a mother tongue for the majority of the Irish has been well documented. Of importance to this oral tradition was the role of Irish in transferring folklore, history, native law, poetry and song to succeeding generations, and above all a sense of language in which there was 'a keen appreciation of the meaning of words' and a regard for conciseness of expression known in Irish as *cóngar cainte*.[9]

Although Ireland will not return to being Irish-speaking to any great extent, the language continues to be valued. Regardless of the number of native speakers at any given time, the Irish language is always given prominence by the Irish government, in the Constitution, and in its teaching as a compulsory subject in schools. The school child in the Irish Republic learns to read and write Irish while she or he learns to read and write English. Up until the 1960s this meant learning to read and write both scripts, Roman for English and Gaelic for Irish. Irish readers and writers are schooled in the language, and continue to be exposed to this language duality in daily life: street signs, formal documents, names of government departments, and the Irish-language radio and televisions stations Raidió na Gaeltachta and TG4. Most importantly the Irish spelling system that is so different to English orthography is absorbed naturally by the Irish because of its introduction at an early stage. The Irish will as easily read and pronounce bean sí and *banshee*. A press release from Ireland's Central Statistics Office in 2016 outlines the continuing role of Irish in Ireland.[10] Out of a population of 4.77 million at the time of the 2016 Irish census, 1.76 million people were returned as Irish-speaking. Of those, 73,803 spoke the language daily outside of the education system, and 53,217 of those lived outside of the Gaeltacht areas.

---

8   O'Leary, *My Own Story* 48.
9   Ó Danachair, Caoimhín 1969 The Gaeltacht, *A View of the Irish Language*, edited by B. Ó Cuív 112–21: 118.
10   2016 Census of Population, Summary Results, Irish Language, Chapter 7. Dublin: Available at https://bit.ly/32BTC9V.

While English is the language spoken by the majority of Irish people, it is an Irish English dialect, one that carries with it the memory of the native language. The shift from Irish to English in Ireland made use of native language structure and words in creating an English language that was an acceptable form for the Irish people. Isolated Irish words in the English of Ireland continue even into the twenty-first century. Irish writers who use Irish words in their English-language writing are coming from a language duality that demonstrates a continued need to return to the native language for exact expression. The writer may find an equivalent English-language word, but the Irish-language word can carry connotations not available in English.

This essay draws on my collection of Irish-language words used by Irish writers in English-language texts from 1800 to 2016. Irish-language words occurring in English have been the subject of study for lexicographers such as Terence Patrick Dolan and Diarmaid Ó Muirithe whose *A Dictionary of Hiberno-English* (1998) and *A Dictionary of Anglo-Irish* (2000) respectively include both Irish language words occurring in print and oral contributions. None of these dictionaries is based on historical principles as is the case with this collection. The collection documents Irish words as they occur in literature over 216 years, some of which are discussed here.[11] Around 300 Irish words were found to be used by Irish writers writing in English. Some occur in only one text in the study, some in texts separated by decades. Others occur frequently from the nineteenth through to the twenty-first centuries. Four categories of Irish words occurring in English-language texts are apparent: a standard lexis; words confined to the nineteenth century; a lexis that emerged in the twentieth century and that may be classified as a standard lexis; and isolated borrowings from the twentieth century up to 2016.

... it is well known that any kind of emotional stress, favourable or unfavourable, tends to promote a reversion to the primary language. For this reason interjections, ejaculations and oaths, all

---

11   See Appendix for the list of the words

used at moments of emotional stress, are readily transferred from one language to another.[12]

Not surprisingly, the standard lexis includes exclamations, endearments, terms of abuse, and words around death and dying, as well as words from rural life. Words of emotion are the most popular. These can be categorised as interjections, endearments, and terms of abuse:

Words of Emotion

Interjections

Word	Meaning	Time Span
ach	'ah'	1827–2008
ara	'ah'	1827–2015
ochón	'alas'	1830–1967

Endearments

Word	Meaning	Time Span
(a, mo) chara	'oh/my friend'	1830–1934
(a, mo) chroi	'oh my heart'	1830–2010
(a, mo) mhic	'my son/lad'	1830–1964

Two of the most popular words of abuse used by Irish writers are amadán and gaimbín. The glossary entries show a progression from 1830 in the visual presentation of these words and their meaning.

---

12   Bliss, Alan 1969 *Spoken English in Ireland 1600–1749*, Dublin: Dolmen Press 255.

amadán *n.* 'a fool' 1830 *The Denounced* Vol 3, p. 120 'Now, you *omadhaun*'; 1830 *Traits and Stories of the Irish Peasantry* Vol 1, p. 191 'You had betther not be mentioning his name, you *omadhaun*'; 1842 *Handy Andy*, p. 12 'Ride back for your life, you omadhaun'; 1896 *Strangers at Lisconnel*, p. 46 'but Hugh M'Inerney, whom people were apt to call an omadhawn'; 1908 *Further Experiences of an Irish R.M.*, p. 63 'Ye omadhawn'; 1942 *Never no More*, p. 116 'The bad-mouthed omadhaun'; 1967 *Folktales of the Irish Countryside*, p. 21 'for being such an amadan as to lose the fine wish'; *Clancy's Bulba*, p. 4 'There's us daft amadans lyin' on the rock-hard scutterin' floor'; 1984 *Man of the Triple Name*, p. 71 'and you laughing like an ape, you danged amadan'; 2012 *The Boy at the Gate*, p. 108, ' ... ya amadon'; 2015 *An Irish Doctor in Love and at Sea*, p. 147 ' ... a rank *omadahn*'

This word has gradually returned to its correct Irish spelling from the middle of the twentieth century and is one of those words that represents the emergence of a reading population that has been exposed to the word through schooling in Irish. The anglicized form with the 'aun' or 'awn' helps to convey the pronunciation. In correct Irish spelling, this would be served by the *fada* or accent lengthener over the last 'a'. The meaning is a mild form of stupidity, the equivalent, perhaps, of Irish English 'eejit' for idiot. The inclusion of the *fada* would elevate the word, and as a result would be counterproductive in conveying the intended meaning. While the spelling *omadhaun* or its equivalents is unlikely to be used by the modern Irish writer, it is unlikely that we will ever see the correct spelling *amadán* printed as such in an English-language text.

Unlike the word *amadán* that has been de-anglicised in spelling over time, the anglicised spelling 'gombeen' for Ir. *gaimbín* is well entrenched, while its meaning has changed somewhat from being a word for excessive interest to the 2015 example where it indicates stupidity. The word has its origin in Ir. *gamba* 'a lump, hunk, dollop'.

gaimbín *n.* 'usurer' 1896 *Strangers at Lisconnel*, p. 83 and could be described as 'an ould gombeen man'; 1922 *Ulysses*, p. 201 The gombeen woman Eliza Tudor had underlinen enough to vie with her of Sheba; 1937 *Famine*, p. 178 'in order to save the populace from the usury of gombeen-men'; 1950 *After the Wake*, p. 81 Many of them were the sons of gombeen-men; 1979 *Home Before Night*, p. 162 the gombeen men and their wives; 1980 *Apple on the Treetop*, p. 64 I stood outside the remains of some gombeen man's grocery store; 1983 *Clancy's Bulba*, p. 4 'I grant to both ye brainless gombeens that our Bulba could have been sabotaged'; 1985 *Jesus Mary Delahunty*, p. 42 Those sly gombeen, frustrated eyes; 1987 *Under the Eyes of the Clock*, p. 26 Peter and Eddie greeted gaping students' gombeen glances with numbed expletives; 1989 *Unholy Ground*, p. 5 the gombeen sons could have their BMWs; 1999 *A Star Called Henry*, p. 68 'The gombeen men from down the country ... ' 2015 *The Enchanted Isle*, p. 128; 'If I had been spotted, I'd look an even bigger gombeen.'

Recent uses of this word seem to point away from the original meaning of 'usurer' to one more akin to unsophistication. The word in its sense of usury represents a time in Irish history when there were few shops or banks in rural areas and a local moneylending service became the answer to people's financial needs. The 'gombeen men' often charged around forty per cent or more interest.[13]

Irish words of endearment have also been carried over to the English of Ireland but have not endured to the same extent that terms of abuse have.

(a, mo) chroí *n* 'oh my heart'. 1829 *The Collegians*, p. 272 'Say no more, a-chree!'; 1830 *The Denounced* Vol. 2, p. 163 'Phil, ma-chree'; 1830 *Traits and Stories of the Irish Peasantry* Vol. 2, p. 273 'An' weil you'd become them, avourneen machree'; 1842 *Handy Andy*, p. 74 'Take the pail, Oonah, *ma chree*'; 1860 *The Colleen Bawn*, p. 184 'Come, acushla agrah machree'; 1922 *Ulysses*, p. 286 'Ben machree'; 1937 *Famine*, p. 202 'We would and welcome, Kitty a chroidhe'; 2009 *Brooklyn*, p. 90 *Má bhíonn tú liom, a stóirín mo chroí*; 2010 *Ghost Light*, p. 110 'It's Alannah macree and the old sweet song.'

---

13   Miller, Kerby A. 1985 *Emigrants and Exiles*, Oxford University Press 29.

As the 2010 reference shows, this and other endearments have formed part of the lyrics of many popular Irish ballads from the nineteenth century. The 2009 reference in the novel *Brooklyn* presented in correct Irish spelling and in italics avoids the possible comic effect from the overuse of Irish-language endearments in nineteenth-century popular culture and in stage Irishry, but the word in this instance is also part of a sentence. In effect, it is a line from a traditional Irish language or *sean nós song Casadh an tSúgáin*.

Irish words associated with death and dying are also standard in Irish writing in English. The most popular is the bean sí, the 'fairy woman' in its malevolent sense. At the time of language transfer in Ireland the ancient practice of death chanting and fear of the portent of death in the *bean sí* worked alongside the Christian practice of faith and prayer. As with the term 'gombeen', the anglicised spelling is the preferred spelling.

bean sí *n*. 'fairy woman' 1830 *The Denounced* Vol. 2, p. 139 'and a like story ... was told me of a *Banshee* of my own family'; 1830 *Traits and Stories of the Irish Pesantry* Vol. 1, p. 99 'no Banshee ever followed her own family'; 1842 *Handy Andy*, p. 256 it was a Banshee; 1914 *My Lady of the Chimney Corner*, p. 66 'The Banshee is it!'; 1922 *Ulysses*, p. 271 a low incipient note sweet banshee murmured all; 1942 *Never no More*, p. 58 'them sad tunes he plays belong to the banshee'; 1970 *Down All The Days*, p. 48 the ice-cream man rumbled down the street blowing his banshee horn; 1979 *Home Before Night*, p. 30 the one with thick legs beginning to wail like a banshee; 1983 *Holy Pictures* p. 38 waiting for the banshee; 1984 *Man of the Triple Name*, p. 43 'no chimney wind, nor no banshee could howl like this man'; 1985 *Jesus Mary Delahunty*, p. 180 He let loose all the mad banshees of his inbreeding; 1989 *For the Poor and for the Gentry* p. 31 the banshee, who would be heard keening when certain families were going to die; 2012 *The Boy at the Gate*, p. 209 ... mistaking the goal post for a banshee ... ; 2015 *The Little Red Chairs*, p. 47 ... the banshee screams that she had let out; 2015 *The Enchanted Isle*, p. 386 'I think the Banshee lives here.'

Here we can see the word used at times in a non-literal sense. In *Ulysses* 1922 it carries a poetic sense, and in *Jesus Mary Delahunty* 1985 it is used as a metaphor for anguish.

Some Irish words have become so much a part of English in Ireland that they are given as translations of themselves in a dictionary such as Niall Ó Dónaill's[14], often retaining the same meaning and with the original sound expressed in English spelling:

banbh	bonham, piglet
bastún	bosthoon, lout
bóithrín	boreen, country lane
caoin	keen, lament
pincín	pinkeen, minnow
poitín	poteen, home-distilled (illicit) whiskey

We may expect that these words operating in both the Irish and English language equally do so because of their popularity. This is certainly the case for *bóithrín, céilí,* and *poitín*:

Word	Time-Span
bóithrín	1830–2012
céilí	1830–2016
poitín	1812–2014

---

14 Ó Dónaill, Niall 1977 *Foclóir Gaeilge-Béarla,* Baile Átha Cliath: Oifig an tSoláthair.

The word *bóithrín* is usually presented in its anglicised form in an English-language text, usually as 'boreen'.

> **bóithrín** *n.* '**small road**' 1830 *Traits and Stories of the Irish Peasantry* Vol. 2, p. 73 another person made his appearance at the far end of the boreen; 1879 *Knocknagow*, p. 202 they turned off the high road into a narrow 'boreen'; 1896 *Strangers at Lisconnel*, p. 24 in the boreen at the back of the haggard; 1922 *Ulysses*, p. 445 while in the boreens and green lanes the collcens with their swains strolled; 1929 *The Stormy Hills*, p. 14 the rocky passage that led to the bohareen; 1955 *The House on the Shore*, p. 9 The boreen took me to the front door; 1963 *Thy Tears Might Cease*, p. 369 he banged the girl roughly towards the boreen; 1984 *Man of the Triple Name*, p. 34 roving hand in hand one night through the moonlit bohareen; 1985 *The Killeen*, p. 135 he saw that she had gathered on her way up the boreen an armload of dog-daisies and poppies; 1987 *Under the Eye of the Clock*, p. 37 the banks of Dublin's mountain boreens; 1989 *For the Poor and the Gentry*, p. 92 We drove down the Killusty road and up Tullow boreen; 2010, *Ghost Light*, p. 51 … puddled boreens; 2012 *The Spinning Heart*, p. 123 … up a boreen …

In the 1879 novel *Knocknagow* the word is presented in inverted commas. In *The Stormy Hills* 1929 and *Man of the Triple Name* 1984 the spelling is different: there is an interest in conveying the Irish-language pronunciation in the inclusion of the 'h' sound in the spelling *bohareen*.

While the word *boreen* has retained its anglicised spelling in print over the centuries, the word *céilí* has undergone significant changes into the twentieth and twenty-first centuries. This is possibly because Irish people now encounter that word for the first time in some Irish-language settings: in a text, or on a visit to the Irish-speaking areas, and so any form other than the Irish-language one would be strange. The word's primary meaning is a friendly call or visit with secondary meanings of a social evening and an Irish-dancing session. The latter is the primary sense used by modern Irish writers.

céilí *n.* 'visit, dance' 1830 *Traits and Stories of the Irish Peasantry* Vol. 1, p. 53 as he came over on his *Kailyee*; 1948 *Tarry Flynn*, p. 167 when she used to call on her ceilidhe; 1950 *After the Wake*, p. 81 we danced and had a great ceili; 1980 *Apple on the Treetop*, p. 41 there wouldn't be a word out until the night of the ceili; 1987 *Under the Eye of the Clock*, p. 137 the coaches lined up again to bring the Dublin boys and girls to a local dancehall for a nightly ceilidh; 1999 *A Star Called Henry*, p. 178 ... a céilí in full flight ...; 2004 *It's a Long Way from Penny Apples*, p. 264, '... a *céilí* dance in the parish hall'; 2009; *Brooklyn*, p. 128 some céilí tunes; 2016 *Rebel Sisters*, p. 107 'Young women are always welcome along to the Gaelic League and our ceili evenings.'

The Irish language remained in rural areas long into the nineteenth century (and has had an unbroken continuity in the designated *Gaeltacht*, 'Irish-speaking' areas). The city or town child who spends time in the Gaeltacht over the summer becomes familiar with the words *bóithrín* and *céilí*. Another word from rural Ireland is *poitín*. Most tourists will be introduced to Ireland's famous illegally distilled whiskey, *poitín* at some point during their visit. The word is made up of *pota* 'a pot' and *ín*, the diminutive from when the drink was made in 'a little pot'. As with 'boreen', the anglicised form 'poteen' is the norm for *poitín* in Irish writing in English with some exceptions. Again we see how in the early nineteenth century there was an attempt to convey the pronunciation with the spelling *potsheen*.

poitín *n.* 'illicitly distilled whiskey' 1812 *The Absentee*, p. 225 'and across the court came one with a sly jug of *potsheen*'; 1830 *Traits and Stories of the Irish Peasantry* Vol. 1, p. 276 Like most of his brethren he could not live without the *poteen*; 1842 *Handy Andy*, p. 203 'who got the conviction agen the poteen last sishin?'; 1896 *Strangers at Lisconnel*, p. 62 'they'll find that every stone in the walls of it was nothin' else but a crock of poteen'; 1937 *Famine*, p. 16 'if you don't make a pig of yourself with potheen yesterday'; 1958 *The Bitter Glass*, p. 187 Slightly elevated by the poiteen, some of the younger men joined in the next game; 1971 *The Big Chapel*, p. 50 Half drunk already weren't they on wild mountain poteen; 1979 *Translations*, p. 55 'You've seen him drinking that poteen—doesn't know how to handle it'; 1981 *Bogmail*, p. 257 The raids were described by one poteen-maker as the most intensive in the long history of the still; 1983 *Clancy's Bulba*, p. 94 as the poteen continued to flow; 1985 *Jesus Mary Delahunty*, p. 70 stupid from poteen; 1985 *The Trick of the Ga Bolga*, p. 97 'He had to drink a glass of poteen every morning before breakfast to raise an appetite; 2014 *Reluctantly Charmed*, p. 125 … they'd fill his cup with *poitín*.'

The *Reluctantly Charmed* 2014 example is an unusual presentation of the word in its actual Irish spelling, poitín. This writer chooses to elevate the Irish language in doing so. Irish is used in this novel to convey magic and mystery, and so the elevation of the word in its presentation in italics and correctly spelt is in keeping with that function as well as indicating a time when Irish was the vernacular.

Irish writers use Irish-language words in an English text for a variety of reasons. The Irish-language word might not have been replaced with an English word, as with the word *boithrín* instead of 'small road'. The Irish word in this case is specific and succinct. An Irish writer might substitute an Irish-language word for what might be a rude one in English. For example, the Irish word for 'tits' is didí, a softer sound and so one less likely to offend:

> **didí** *n.* 'nipples' 1942 *Never No More*, p. 177 'Sure he was no bigger than a dog's diddy'; 1979 *Home Before Night*, p. 102 Bollicky Biddy had only one diddy; 1983 *Holy Pictures*, p. 16 'Her diddies,' Mary filled in for Nellie's benefit. This word is used in Irish English as slang. A writer can also mitigate the effect of a word by using an Irish-language equivalent even if the word is not used in Irish English. Most Irish readers would encounter the word *liathróid* 'ball' at an early age when learning to read Irish language schoolbooks. Few would read sexual terminology even as adults and so would not be familiar with the word *magarlaí* 'testicles'. What most adult readers would be familiar with, however, is the English slang word for testicles, 'balls'. The Irish writer can make use of the reader's knowledge of basic Irish in

using **liathróid** (**í** 'ball (s) *n.* 2004 *It's a Long Way from Penny Apples*, p. 150 ' … you've got lee-a-rody that's for sure … ', where the phonetic spelling of the word conveys the sound. Another example of choosing an Irish word as a substitute is the word *bundún* for 'bottom': **bundún** *n.* '**bottom**' 1942 *Watergate*, p. 15 'Ah! sit there with your half-hundred of a bundoon'.[15] Other writers use the Irish word along with the English: **rí rá ruaille buaille** *n.* '**commotion**' 1989 *My Dark Rosaleen*, p. 14 'Pandemonium. Ree Raw and rooileh-booileh'. An Irish reader would have heard the phrases *rí rá* and *ruaille buaille* during his or her schooling. The reader unfamiliar with these terms would, nevertheless, understand what was going on because the English word *pandemonium* is presented first. Often individual Irish words are presented along with the English equivalent by way of explanation or as a way of referencing the Irish language as a point of difference such as with the word *bruach* 'a bank': 1985 *The Trick of the Ga Bolga*, p. 154 Then he found the bank, which Salmo called 'the broo'; or the word *brus* 'crumbled bits': 1988 *To School through the Fields*, p. 122 here what we called brus, the broken up sods of turf, formed on the floor; or the words *camán mór* 'big hurley stick': 2004 *It's a Long Way from Penny Apples*, p. 246 his *camán mór*—the big hurley stick.

Some words have become part of Irish English slang, and in this study are first found in *Ulysses*. Three of these are *bacach*, *mile murdar*, and *poc*.

bacach *adj.* '**lame, imperfect**' 1922 *Ulysses*, p. 243 'Poor old bockedy Ben!'; 1985 *Jesus Mary Delahunty*, p. 72 'Christ Bockety'; 1989 *Unholy Ground*, p. 132 a bockety leg; 2014 *The Playground*, p. 9 … a bockety two-ringed hob
mile murdar *ph.* '**blue murder**' 1922 *Ulysses*, p. 327 and he flogs the bloody backside off the poor lad till he yells meila murder; 1964 *The Dalkey Archives*, p. 149 'he'll kick up buggery and melia murder'

---

15 Although this word has been found only once in this study, it appears in Dolan's collection as being used in speech in Kerry, the contributor adding that there was 'no hint of vulgarity in normal usage …'

poc *n.* 'butt from a goat, stroke of a hurley stick' 1922 *Ulysses*, p. 250 'One puck from that fellow would knock you into the middle of next week'; 1925 *The Informer*, p. 83 'Hit him a puck in the jaw'; 1963 *Thy Tears Might Cease*, p. 45 'and if you don't like it I'll give you a puck in the jaw'; 1967 *Folktales of the Irish Countryside*, p. 90 'the cow pucked her and the ram hit her'; 1979 *Home Before Night*, p. 21 She would give a nice and polite woman at a party a puck on the bare back; 1980 *Apple on the Treetop*, p. 135 The boys had a hurley and were pucking stones out into the sea; 2004 *It's a Long Way from Penny Apples*, p. 246 he could puck out the sliotar; 2010 *Ghost Light*, p. 134 Puck him agin, Mister; 2012 *The Spinning Heart*, p. 55 '… and puck the head off of me, though.'

These words would have been part of James Joyce's world as a Dubliner. Joyce was also familiar with Irish. Although Irish was not a compulsory subject for matriculation to the University of Dublin until 1913, eleven years after Joyce graduated with a Bachelor of Arts, he is returned as Irish-speaking in the 1901 census. We also know that he attended Irish classes taught by Patrick Pearse for a few years. Ireland's dual language heritage is very much at play in his writings. As a Dubliner, Joyce's own English would have been peppered with idioms and linguistic constructions taken directly from the Irish language, and English words that had long passed away in England, but that had become ossified in Ireland. As Joyce was writing *A Portrait of the Artist as a Young Man*, and *Ulysses*, the Irish political scene was tumultuous and the Irish literary and language revival was in bloom. The author's language reflects these events.

The Irish language in *Ulysses* can be seen to operate on at least two levels. On one level, Joyce is using Irish as a *language*, especially in scenes with the Citizen. The portrait of the Citizen is based on Michael Cusack, the founder of the Gaelic Athletic Association, a staunchly nationalistic organisation that promotes traditional Irish games. Joyce had met Cusack, but 'liked him little enough to make him the narrow-minded rhetorical Cyclops in *Ulysses*.[16] The italicisation of the Irish-language words and phrases used by the Citizen signals to the

---

16   Ellman, Richard 1983 *James Joyce*, Oxford University Press 61.

reader the act of language switching. Italicisation also lends dignity to these words in print. However, when we examine what the Citizen says when using the language we can see that his longest phrase is spoken to his dog: *Bi i dho husht* 'be quiet'[17], and the second longest is a nationalistic slogan *Sinn Fein. Sinn Fein amhain*.[18] The Citizen uses what is traditionally an Irish language endearment, *a chara*, 'oh friend'. Joyce, as an Irishman, is aware, however, that this greeting has special connotations when used by Irish-speaking nationalists. It is equivalent to the word *comrade* in communist or socialist political settings. It is clear that the Citizen's companions do not share his nationalistic leanings: they are not his comrades, nor is he liked by his companions in the pub, and on both occasions when he uses the term *a chara* it is in the context of being offered a drink—which hospitality we never see him return. The Citizen's use of the Irish language is shown to be false: his companions are not Irish speakers or nationalistic, and the address *a chara* has no true function in this setting. A major part of his communication in Irish is with his dog; the language is not being used as a natural form of communication. The Citizen also makes a fundamental mistake in the language:

> Here says Joe, doing the honours. Here citizen.
> Slan leat, says he.
> Fortune, Joe, says I. Good health citizen.[19]

The correct toast is *sláinte* 'health'. The Citizen, however, has used the term *slan leat* 'goodbye', an error that would not have been made by those with even a rudimentary command of the language. The irony in the mistake is significantly increased because we presume that the Citizen is an Irish speaker. In introducing an error into Cusack's Irish, Joyce puts him down, just as the Citizen had earlier castigated those 'shoneens that can't speak their own language'. [20]

---

17   Joyce, James 1968 *Ulysses*, Harmondsworth: Penguin 297.
18   Joyce, *Ulysses* 304.
19   Joyce, *Ulysses* 313.
20   Joyce, *Ulysses* 309.

Another example of Joyce delighting in the ironies present in the Irish language is in the description of the ceremony of the presentation of 'a silver casket, tastefully executed in the style of ancient Celtic ornamentation, a work which reflects every credit on the makers, Messrs Jacobs *agus* Jacobs'.[21]

Jacobs and Jacobs is the name of a manufacturer of biscuits in Dublin: not known for the making silver caskets. The firm is colloquially known as 'Jacobs'. Joyce has given this firm a title that is incongruous with its usual function in Dublin life, and the irony is further compounded in the use of Irish in the title: the word *agus*, and the fact that *agus*, despite being given a status as a word from another language in being presented in italics, is the simple conjunction 'and'. Joyce is satirising the use of Irish for ceremonial purposes (the *cúpla focal*), but he is also addressing a readership that would have an immediate appreciation of the irony intended – a readership with a passive knowledge of the Irish language. A further use of Irish for the purposes of satire is the scene where Bloom and Stephen are sharing their linguistic heritage in the offering of 'fragments of verse from the ancient Hebrew and ancient Irish languages'.[22] The Irish reader will see at first glance the irony in Stephen's offering of *suil, suil, suil arun, suil go siocair agus, suil go cuin*, because it is a well-known chorus of a bilingual song.[23] Another glance at the Irish phrase by the reader with some command of the language will reveal the mistakes: the word *suil* should read *siúl* and *siocair* should read *socair*. In *Ulysses* the phrase is translated as 'walk, walk, walk your way, walk in safety, walk with care'. However, what Joyce has written translates as 'eye, eye, eye oh my love, eye pretext, and eye quietly'. It is possible, of course, that these are mistakes on Joyce's part, but the irony remains that the 'fragment of verse' chosen is not representative of ancient Irish.

Another example of Joyce enjoying his own inside knowledge of the Irish language is in his use of disguise: a device he was to expand on greatly in *Finnegans Wake*. In *Ulysses*, he presents the following:

---

21 Joyce, *Ulysses* 341.
22 Joyce, *Ulysses* 608.
23 The chorus of this song is usually written anglicised as *as shule, shule shule a roon*, as is its title, 'Shule Aroon'.

Old whatwhat. I called about the poor and water rate, Mr Boylan. You what? The water rate. Mr Boylan. You what-what? That's the bucko that'll organise her, take my tip. 'Twixt me and you Caddereesh.[24]

The final word *Caddereesh* is a mangled form of *cad arís* 'what again' which neatly rounds off the passage that begins with whatwhat and invites a reprise. The passage is about pretence in misunderstanding. The commentator demonstrates his inside knowledge of the pretence by using the disguised Irish-language phrase. He belongs to a community that is close-knit. He knows Boylan for what he is, and demonstrates this by reverting to a secret code. The reader who is capable of deciphering this code at a glance is also a member of this speech community.

The English of Ireland was James Joyce's native language, not the English of England. Joyce's voice was an Irish one, made up of obsolete English words and anglicised Irish words but also the Dublin echoes of a Celtic language that was still in full voice elsewhere in Ireland. He feared the nets involved with the Irish-language revival movement, but he could not possibly have escaped its linguistic influence, nor would he have wanted to. Joyce made full use of all the linguistic possibilities available to him to construct linguistic puzzles and enigmas that continue to keep us all busy.

This study has found almost 300 Irish words in use in English texts by Irish writers (mostly novelists). Irish words in an English text can add variety. If spelled according to the Irish spelling system and presented in italics the words can provide contrast between the Irish and English words on the page. This focus on another language in the text is a reminder that the Irish language in its entirety lies outside of the English text, regardless of the number of native speakers, and that this language duality is part of being Irish and of being an Irish writer.

---

24   Joyce, *Ulysses* 318.

Appendix: glossary of Irish-language words used in English-language writing 1830–2016

Although many of the words in the study appear in an anglicised form in the various texts, they are presented here in the correct spelling.

A

abhaile *n*. 'home' 2015; ach *int*. 'ah' 1830–1983; agus *conj*. 'and' 1922; aguisín *n*. 'addendum' 1984; aililiú *int*. 'good gracious' 1829; ainneseoir *n*. 'miserable person' 1879 and 1984; aird *n*. 'direction' 1914 and 1981; amadán *n*. 'a fool' 1830–2015; anseo *p*. 'here'; aon, dó, trí *phr*. 'one, two, three' 1987; arán *n*. 'bread' 1830; arú *int*. 'alas' 1829–2015; athair *n*. 'father' 1985

B

bacach *n*. 'lame beggar' 1830 and 1842; bacach *adj*. 'lame, imperfect' 1922–2014; baileabhair *v*. 'make a fool of' 1830; báinín *n*. 'woven woollen cloth; jacket' 1937–60; báirín breac *n*. 'speckled loaf' 1963 and 1981; bairneach *n*. 'a limpet' 1985; banbh *n*. 'piglet' 1879–2004; barróg *n*. 'accent' 1829–2014; bastún *n*. 'lout' 1830–1962; beannacht Dé agat *phr*. 'God bless you'; bean sí *n*. 'fairy woman' 1830–2015; bean tí *n*. 'woman of the house' 1830–1987; Béarla *n*. 'the English language' 1922; bior maide *n*. 'wood rod' 1985; bladhm *n*. 'flame' 1967; blas *n*. 'accent' 1963; bleidhre *n*. 'drinking cup' 1964; bó *int*. 'alas' 1829–1942; bodach *n*. 'lout' 1830–1942; bodhrán *n*. 'tambour' 1967–2015; bogán, bogadán *n*. 'a softy' 1830 and 1984; boilg *n*. 'a submerged reef' 1985; bóithrín *n*. 'small road' 1830–2010; bos *n*. 'unit of measurement' 1879; bothán *n*. 'shanty, cabin' 1967 and 1987; bothántaíocht *n*. 'act of visiting' 1984; bróg *n*. 'shoe' 1830–1989; (mo) bhrón *int*. 'alas' 1830; brosna *n*. 'decayed twigs' 1967; bruach *n*. 'bank' 1985; bruachán *n*. 'small person' 1879; brúithleacht *n*. 'uproar'; brúitín *n*. 'mashed potatoes' 1830 and 1937; brus *n*. 'crumbled bits' 1879–1988; buachaill *n*. 'boy' 1830 and 1980; bualadh bata *n*. 'fighting stick' 1830; bulla báisín *n*. 'whirligig' 1879; bundún *n*. 'bottom' 1942

C

cábóg *n*. 'clown' 1950; cadhrán *n*. 'small sod of turf' 1984; cáibín *n*. 'old hat' 1830–1922; cailín *n*. 'girl' 1830–2010; cailleach *n*. 'hag' 1967; cál leannógach *n*. 'green algae' 1981; cam *n*. 'melting–pot' 1830; camán *n*. 'hurling stick' 1916; camán mór 'big hurling stick' 2004; caoin *v*.

'keen, lament' 1829–1989; caoineadh *n.* 'lament' 1830–1982; capaillín *n.* 'pony' 1860 and 1922; (a) chara *n.* 'oh friend' 1830–1934; ceannbhán *n.* 1967 and 1987; céilí *n.* 'visit, dance' 1830–2016; ceis *n.* 'young pig' 1829; cigire n. 'inspector' 2012; ciotóg *n.* 'left-hand' 1830–2012; cipín *n.* 'a little stick' 1830–1989; cis *n.* 'basket' 1830–1962; clab *n.* 'open mouth' 1929–71; clábar *n.* 'mud' 1914 and 1922; clampar *n.* 'commotion' 1988; cliabh *n.* 'creel' 1800; clochán *n.* 'beehive dwelling' 1987 and 2015; clúrachán *n.* 'elf'; cnáimhseáil *n.* '(act of) complaining' 1984; coinín *n.* 'rabbit' 1942; cois *int.* 'shoo!' 1937 and 1958; corp *n.* 'corpse'; cóta mór *n.* 'overcoat' 1830; (a, mo) chroí *n.* 'my darling' 1829–2009; croitín *n.* 'outhouse' 1967; cromleac *n.* 'pre-historic structure' 1922; crónán *n.* '(act of) humming' 1984; crotal *n.* 'lichen' 1985; cruach *n.* 'rick' 1929; crúibín *n.* 'pig's trotter' 1922–1964; crúiscín *n.* 'small jug' 1830–1964; cruit *n.* 'hump' 1830; crupán *n.* 'cramps' 1985; cúb *n.* 'coop' 1829; a cuisle *n.* 'oh darling' 1830–1983; cúl *n.* 'goal' 1916; cumar *n.* 'ravine' 1929; cupán drúchta *n.* 'mushroom'; curach *n.* 'coracle' 1937–87

D

dhera *int.* expression of disbelief or indifference 1908–1984; Dia dhuit, Dia is Muire dhuit *phr.* 'Hello' 2015; diabhal *n.* 'devil' 1830; didí *n.* 'nipples' 1942; doirb *n.* 'water beetle' 1985; doirnín *n.* 'handle'; donn *adj.* 'brown' 1830–1960; droimlin *n.* 'a hill' 2010; dúchas *n.* 'heritage'; duibhean *n.* 'cormorant'; dúidín *n.* 'clay pipe' 1830–1984; duileasc *n.* 'edible seaweed' 1981–2010; duine uasal *n.* 'gentleman' 1830; dúlamán *n.* 'dull-witted person' 1964 and 1979; dún *n.* 'fort' 1922

E

éinín *n.* 'small bird' 1879

F

fáilte *n.* 'welcome' 1830; féar gortach *n.* 'quaking-grass' 1985; fear tí *n.* 'man of the house' 1830; feic *n.* 'a sight, spectacle'; Feis *n.* 'musical festival' 1929–50; fíor Gaeltacht *n.* 'true Irish-speaking district'; fios *n.* 'knowledge' 1985; flaithiúlach *adj.* 'generous' 1922; fleadh *n.* 'music festival' 2015 and 2016; fliúit *n.* 'swig' 1964; forrán *n.* 'attack, assault' 1830; fostúch *n.* derog. 'fellow' 1984; fraochán *n.* 'bilberries' 1987 and 2010; fuilibiliú/pililiú *n.* 'uproar' 1829–1985; fústráil *v.* (act of) 'fussing, fidgeting' 1896–2012

G

Gaeltacht *n.* 'Irish-speaking district'; gailleog *n.* 'mouthful' 1830; gaimbín *n.* 'usurer' 1896–2015; gallán *n.* 'pillarstone' 1987; gammach *n.* 'simpleton', 2012; gan *prep.* 'without' 1922; (mo) ghaol *n.* 'my darling' 1934; gardaí *n.* 'police' 1934–2015; garlach *n.* 'child' 1958; garsún *n.* 'boy' 1800–2012; geansaí *n.* 'guernsey, jersey' 1922–2004; gearrán *n.* 'gelding, drudge' 1830–1896; gearrcaigh *n.* 'fledglings' 1988; geis *n.* 'spell'; 1968 and 1985; geocach *n.* 'vagrant' 1829; gilibín *n.* 'diminutive person' 1963; giobal *n.* 'rag'; gíog *n.* 'cheep' 1980; girseach *n.* 'young girl' 1830– 1971; glaiseach *n.* 'watery bogland' 1988; glas-caorach *n.* 'undyed homespun wool' 1988; glasán *n.* 'coal-fish' 1985; gliobach *n.* 'uproar' 1981; gleoiteog *n.* 'small sailing boat' 1955; go leor *adj.* 'enough, plenty' 1830–1984; gob *n.* 'mouth' 1830–1983; gort *n.* 'field' 1879; grá *n.* 'love, affection' 1830–2015; (a, mo) grá *n.* 'oh, my love' 1860–1985; grámhar *adj.* 'lovable, affectionate' 1908 and 1985; graeipe *n.* 'digging fork' 1948; grianán *n.* 'upper chamber' 1922; griog *v.* 'tease, excite' 1879 and 1922; gríosach *n.* 'hot ashes, embers' 1830 and 1942; guilpín *n.* 'lout' 1985 and 2016

I

íochtar *n.* 'runt' 1984

L

láí *n.* 'spade' 1950; laoch *n.* 'hero' 2014; leaba *n.* 'bed' 1987; leaca *n.* 'slope of the hill' 1929; leannán sí *n.* 'fairy spouse' 1830; (a, mo) leanbh *n.* '(oh, my) darling' 1829–1970; liathróid (í) *n.* 'ball' (s) 2004; lios *n.* 'ring-fort' 1929 and 1985; liúdar *n.* 'large coal-fish' 1985; liúdráil *v.* 'beat' 1830 and 1985; lúdramán *n.* 'lazy person' 1922; longar *n.* 'swaying motion' 1989 and 2016; lugach *n.* 'lobworm' 1953

M

máchail *n.* 'blemish, injury, harm' 1967 and 1984; maide arán *n.* 'bread stick' 1830; maith thú *phr.* 'good on you' 1999; mar dhea *int.* 'forsooth' 1896–1970; margadh mór *n.* 'large market' 1830; masmas *n.* 'nausea' 1967; mé féin *prn.* 'myself' 2014; meadar *n.* 'drinking vessel' 1830 and 1922; mealdar *n.* 'quantity of corn' 1830; meas *n.* 'value' 1985; meascán *n.* 'lump' 1830; meitheal *n.* 'working party' 1985 and 1988; (a) mhaoineach *n.* 'my treasure' 1967; a mhic *n.* 'my son, my lad' 1829–1964; míle *n.* 'great many' 1922 and 1964; mionaerach *n.* 'a type of fever' 1942; mo léir *int.* 'alas' 1958; (a, mo) mhúirnín *n.* '(oh, my) darling' 1829–1922; muise, (a) mhuise *int.* 'well, well' 1829–2010

O

ochón *int.* 'alas' 1830–2010; óinseach *n.* 'foolish woman' 1879–1984; olagón *n.* 'wail, lament' 1929–1979;

P

paidirín *n.* 'Rosary' 1830; páiste *n.* 'child' 1830 and 1985; pincín *n.* 'minnow' 1953; pingin *n.* 'a penny' 2004; piseog *n.* 'superstitious practices' 1829–1958; piteog *n.* 'effeminate person' 1830 and 1922; planc *n.* 'large bite' 1967; pluc *n.* 'rounded cheek' 1922; poc *n.* 'butt from a goat, stroke of a hurley stick' 1922–2012; pocán *n.* 'male goat' 1942; poirse *n.* 'passageway' 1929; póit *n.* 'drinking-bout' 1937–2014; portán *n.* 'crab' 1985; prompa *n.* 'rump' 1934; púca *n.* 'hobgoblin' 1955; púcán *n.* 'open boat' 1896 and 1955; pus *n.* 'protruding mouth' 1922–67

R

raca *n.* 'a rounded hair-comb' 2015; racánaí *n.* 'brawler' 1985; ráiméis *n.* 'nonsense' 1830–1979; ránaí *n.* 'thin person' 1985; rann *n.* 'verse' 1830; rath *n.* 'fairy fort' 1830–2010; rírá *n.* 'uproar' 1962–1989; ropaire *n.* 'rapparee, bandit' 1842 and 1922; rothar *n.* 'bicycle' 1999; ruaille buaille *n.* 'commotion' 1989; (a) rún *n.* ('oh) darling' 1830–1922

S

sagart *n.* 'priest' 1830–1922; Sasanach *n.* 'English person' 1830 and 1922; scailp *n.* 'fissure in the rock' 1937; scalltán *n.* 'fledgling' 1830 and 1942; sceallán *n.* 'small potato' 1988; sceidín *n.* 'small thing' 1981 and 1985; sciathóg *n.* 'shield-shaped basket' 1830; scoil *n.* 1950; scolb *n.* 'looped stick for securing thatch'; scóraíocht *n.* ' social evening' 1950; scraith *n.* 'strip of lea-sod' 1830–1985; seachain *v.* 'beware' 1967; seachrán *n.* 'wandering straying' 1830–1984; sealán *n.* 'ring' 1985; seamróg n. 'trefoil plant' 2008 and 2015; seanchaí *n.* 'storyteller' 1830–1987; seanchas *n.* 'storytelling, chatting' 1879; seilide *n.* 'snail' 1879; seoinín *n.* 'flunkey' 1830 and 1922; síbín *n.* 'speak-easy' 1800–1985; Sinn Féin *n.* name of a political party 1922–1953; siongán *n.* 'ant' 1830; siolú *n.* 'bombast' 1842; síoraí *n.* 'everlasting' 1830; slacht *n.* 'finish, polish' 1958; sláinte *n.* 'health' 1922–2015; slánaitheor *n.* 'saviour' 2014; slán leat *phr.* 'goodbye' 1999; slata mara *n.* 'sea-rods' 1955; sleán *n.* 'turf-spade' 1879–2004; sliabh *n.* 'mountain' 2014; slíbhín *n.* 'sly person' 1896–1979; sliotar *n.* 'a hurley ball' 2004; slog *n.* 'swig'

1830–2004; slópaire *n.* 'absconder' 1908; sliúdrálaí *n.* 'slippery person' 1896 and 1963; smeachán *n.* 'taste, nip' 1964; sonas *n.* 'good luck' 1830; sonuachar *n.* 'spouse' 1829; sop *n.* 'handful of hay' 1879 and 1967; sos beag *phr.* 'a little rest' 2004; spág *n.* 'broad, flat foot' 1922 and 1964; spailpín *n.* 'seasonable labourer, lout' 1830–2015; spideog *n.* 'robin' 1842; spraoi (oiche) *n.* 'night's drinking' 1942 and 2015; spreasán *n.* 'worthless person' 1829; sraimle *n.* 'slovenly person' 1967; staga *n.* 'old nag' 1829; (a) stór *n.* 'oh darling' 1829–2015; strapairlín *n.* 'hussy' 1842; s(t)raoill *n.* 'ragged person, trail' 1830–2010; stuacán *n.* 'surly person' 1896; stuailinn *n.* 'pile of turf' 1984; suanach *adj.* 'lethargic' 1984; súgach *adj.* 'mellow with drink' 1950; súgán *n.* 'straw-rope' 1830–1988; súigh *n.* 'suction' 1830 and 1879

T

Táin *n.* 'list of famous people' 1985; tamall *n.* 'space of time' 1984; taoscán *n.* 'quantity of liquid' 1964; tar isteach *phr.* 'come inside' 1999; (a) théagair *n.* 'oh darling' 1830; teaspach *n.* 'spirit, energy' 1984; Tír na nÓg n. Land of Youth' 2014–16; tomhaisín *n.* 'a cone-shaped paper bag'; tóraí *n.* 'pursuer' 1830; tráithnín *n.* 'dry grass-stalk' 1830–1963; trína chéile *prep.* 'mixed-up' 1879 and 1934; tuathalach *adj.* 'awkward' 1984; tuilleadh *n.* 'addition' 1922 and 1979; turtóg *n.* 'hummock' 1967; turusm *n.* 'pilgrimage' 1965

U

uisce beatha *n.* 'whiskey' 1812–2004

6
Remembering the Celts: Celtic Designs on Modern Coins

John Kennedy

Scholars in the field of Celtic studies are very well aware that what the term 'Celtic' means, and which peoples in ancient and medieval times we should now regard as 'Celts' are very much matters for debate, with linguists, historians, archaeologists, and ethnographers differing across discipline boundaries and amongst themselves as to what the terms signify and how they should be used.[1] But the view that there were Continental Celts during the time when Ancient Greece and Rome flourished, and Insular Celts whose culture reached great heights in Britain and Ireland during the early Middle Ages, remains a widespread one, acknowledged (if sometimes in nuanced terms) in most of the frequently appearing books on the Celts for the 'general reader', and it is likely to be the view of users of modern coins who know anything about the Celts. The approach in this chapter will be to regard as Celtic anything pertaining to the peoples of Iron Age and Roman period Continental Europe widely regarded as being Celtic, and also those of Iron Age, Roman, and early Christian Britain and Ireland, sometimes termed the 'Insular Celts'. However, while this work will note use of Celtic languages in coin inscriptions, it will not regard something as Celtic merely because it is Irish, Scottish, Welsh, etc. Thus, for example,

---

1   For an extensive discussion of the debate see Sims-Williams, Patrick 1998 Celtomania and Celtoscepticism, *Cambrian Medieval Celtic Studies* 36, 1–35.

Irish coins that portray the singer John McCormack or submarine inventor John Philip Holland, and United Kingdom coins portraying the Menai Bridge or honouring Robert Burns will lie outside its scope. It seems logical to begin with the coins of the Irish Free State and Republic, since official Ireland has placed a particular emphasis on what it considers its rich heritage from the centuries before the intrusion from overseas of first Vikings and then Normans—a heritage often designated as Celtic although some in Ireland would probably think of it more as just authentically Irish. It shall then consider the United Kingdom, and then the Isle of Man, famous, if not indeed notorious, as an extremely prolific issuer of coins. Next it will turn to Continental Europe before looking at the use of Celtic motifs by two coin-issuing states outside Europe and without any historical links to Celts of any description.

Ireland

When the Irish Free State came into being in 1922, the coins of the United Kingdom continued to circulate, and would indeed continue to do so throughout Ireland until 1979. But following a vote in the Irish parliament in 1926 a committee was set up to consider designs for a new Irish coinage to circulate beside the British one. Its chair was the poet and Free State senator William Butler Yeats. The poet's former ardour for things Celtic, which had led him to publish *The Celtic Twilight* in 1894, had definitely cooled by this stage, and he urged that models for the new coins be sought in the coinage of ancient Greece. A decision was reached that the new coins should portray the animals and birds of the Irish countryside and farms, and artists were asked to seek inspiration from Greek coins of which they were sent photos.[2] It was also decided to avoid 'hackneyed symbolism' such as 'round towers' and 'shamrocks' and to place the emphasis on achieving the highest possible artistry.[3] The

---

2   Coglan, Edward 2003 *For Want of Good Money,* Bray, Co. Wicklow: Wordwell 177–8.

3   See Cleeve, Brian, editor 1972 *W.B. Yeats and the Designing of Ireland's Coinage: Texts by W.B. Yeats and Others,* New Yeats Papers 3, Dublin: Dolmen Press, especially the essay by Yeats himself, What we Did or Tried to Do, 9–20: 9.

result was that the coins put into circulation in 1928, and continued until decimalisation in 1971 (with a change of inscription from *SAORSTÁT ÉIREANN* to *ÉIRE* following the approval of a new republican constitution in 1937, some very minor design modifications, and the replacement by cupro-nickel of the pure nickel used until 1942 for the threepence and sixpence and the silver used until 1951 for the higher denominations) portrayed pigs, hens, a hare, a wolfhound, etc. (Figure 6.1).[4] They did all feature on their obverse, or main side, the emblem of the Irish state, the so-called Brian Boru Harp, which actually dates to the fourteenth or fifteenth century, and which with one exception has featured on all subsequent Irish coins to this day, but harps on Irish coins were no daring innovation, having very frequently appeared on coins issued by the British for Ireland from the reign of Henry VIII to 1823. The new coins exclusively employed the Irish language in inscriptions—*feoirling* for farthing, *pingin* for penny, etc.—and a version of Insular script, but otherwise there was nothing particularly Celtic about their subject matter.[5] Only one commemorative coin appeared before decimalisation in 1971, the one coin to date without the harp, a ten-shilling silver coin issued in 1966 to mark fifty years since the Easter Rising. Though it did portray the great Irish saga hero Cúchulainn, as well as 1916 leader Pádraig Pearse, the statue of the dead but upright Cúchulainn used as a model surely owes far more to classical antiquity than to anything distinctly Celtic.[6] (Figure 6.2) The Celts were being remembered, but it could hardly be claimed that Ireland's coinage celebrated them in a particularly overt fashion.

Things Celtic did get a bit more attention after Ireland elected to join Britain in going decimal in 1971. The animal designs were retained or reworked for most denominations, but the new halfpenny featured a

---

4   Figures 1–4 and 8 to 15 are based on photographs of coins taken by my friend and relative by marriage, Peter Coombes. Figures 5–7 are based on coin photographs taken by the author. I am very grateful to Peter for his photographic help and for his technical assistance in transferring the photographs into a form which could be used in this chapter.

5   See Coglan, Edward 2000 (March) A Nation Once Again, *Coin News* 37–9: 37–8.

6   See Coglan, Edward 2016 (April) Easter 1916 Remembered: Part 1, *Coin News* 60–1: 61.

Figure 6.1 Republic of Ireland, a selection of pre-decimal coins

stylised bird from a Celtic manuscript in Cologne Cathedral, the penny a detail from the *Book of Kells*, and the two pence a bird detail from the Bible of Charles the Bald in the Bibliothèque Nationale in Paris.[7] (Figure 6.3) However, this was not the unequivocal sign of a new Celtic dawn for Irish coinage that it might at first appear. The abandonment of some of the 1928 animal designs was somewhat unpopular, and writing in a letter to the *Irish Times* the artist Oisín Kelly suggested that this new means of remembering the Celts was extremely inappropriate:

> We have no peculiar right to Celtic art. Celtic art is a 'heavenward leading' art and as such entirely incomprehensible to us. To use these hieratic symbols, which we can no longer read, for our huckstering is not only silly, it is impious.[8]

---

7   Coglan, A Nation Once Again, 38; Coglan, *For Want* 187.
8   Quoted in McLoughlin, Philip 2016 (November) Ireland: Discarded Decimal Designs, and Metcalfe vs. Hayes, *Coin News*, 59–61: 60.

Figure 6.2 Republic of Ireland 1966, ten-scilling coin, showing Padraig Pearse and Cú Chullain

In June 1990 the Irish Minister of Finance announced that two of the animal designs from the old series would replace the Celtic penny and two pence designs, the halfpenny having been demonetised at the beginning of 1985.[9] (By then the predecimal coins had long disappeared from circulation and there was no longer much force in the argument that using designs from the old series on new bronze coins not corresponding in value to any coins in the old series could lead to confusion.)[10] Planning for the new euro coinage, which would feature the Brian Boru harp on the obverse and the standard European designs on the reverse, caused this restoration of old designs to be shelved,[11] but

9   Coglan, A Nation Once Again 39; Coglan, For Want 191.
10   See McLoughlin 60–1.
11   Coglan, For Want 191.

Figure 6.3 Republic of Ireland, a selection of decimal bronze coins

it hardly demonstrates a strong commitment to remembering the Celts and celebrating Celtic art.

In the period from the advent of decimalisation to the switchover to the euro Ireland issued only three commemorative coins, two of them for general circulation and one solely for coin collectors.[12] The circulation fifty pence for the Dublin millennium celebrations in 1988 featured a coat of arms and mayoral regalia and had no Celtic (or

---

12 The number would rise to six if one acknowledged as coins two silver issues and one gold issue from 1990, struck in fairly small numbers to commemorate Ireland's presidency of the European Community. Denominated in ECU (European Currency Units) and featuring a red deer and the Brian Boru harp, these do not find a place either in the standard Krause catalogue or the Coincraft catalogue of Irish coins, though they are listed in Krause's *Unusual World Coins*, a volume largely devoted to fantasy issues; Cuhaj, George S. et al. 2011, *2012 Standard Catalog of World Coins 1901–2000*, Iola WI: Krause; Lobel, Richard, *et al.* 1999 *Coincraft's Standard Catalogue of the Coins of Scotland, Ireland, Channel Islands & Isle of Man*, London: Coincraft; Cuhaj, George *et al.* 2011 *Unusual World Coins*, Iola WI: Krause 367–8. See Coglan, A Nation once again 39.

Figure 6.4 Republic of Ireland 2000, one-punt
coin showing Broighter Boat

Norse) elements, and a large silver pound (or punt) issued for collectors in 1995 featured a dove of peace, a United Nations symbol, and the English words 'Nations united for peace'. More interesting in the present context is a punt (pound) coin issued for circulation in 2000 to mark the millennium. It portrays a Celtic artifact, the fifteen- centimetre gold Broighter Boat held in the National Museum, thought to be about 2000 years old. The design did not win universal acclaim, a reporter for the *Irish Times* irreverently suggesting that the unlabelled object resembled a slice of melon speared by several cocktail sticks![13] (Figure 6.4)

Since the introduction of the euro Ireland has on a modest scale followed the almost universal practice of countries round the world in issuing gold and silver coins minted in limited numbers for coin collectors and sold at prices far in excess of the bullion value of the precious metals they contain. A few of the silver coins have had Celtic

---

13   Coglan, *For Want* 194–5.

Figure 6.5 Republic of Ireland 2007, ten-euro
silver coin, celebrating Celtic influence

themes, notably a rather fussy ten-euro silver coin in 2007, described
by its designer on an accompanying card as 'A Celebration of Ireland's
Celtic Influence in Europe', (Figure 6.5) and a much better 2011 silver
coin said to honour St Brendan the Navigator, though without naming
him on the coin surface. (Figure 6.6) A series of tiny gold coins, eleven
to fourteen millimetres in diameter, have been issued only in numbers
of a few thousand for collectors and *inter alia* feature as subjects Skellig
Michael, a Celtic cross, Irish monastic art, and Brian Boru. But this
homage to the Celtic heritage has not been reflected in the circulating
two-euro commemorative coins. The 2016 centenary of the Easter
Rising saw special coins, including a two-euro for circulation, but again
the subject was classical—a statue of Hibernia from the GPO in Dublin.
(Figure 6.7)

Figure 6.6 Republic of Ireland, ten euro showing
St Brendan

Figure 6.7 Republic of Ireland, two euro
commemorating 1916 Rising

United Kingdom

The coin-issuing program of the United Kingdom's Royal Mint has been vastly more extensive than that of Ireland, but one looks largely in vain for Celtic themes and subjects amongst the great array of commemorative coins for collectors and for circulation, and the bullion issues. There are said to be Celtic elements[14] in the design of the standard United Kingdom two-pound coin, issued for circulation in every year from 1997 to 2015 and intended to celebrate technological development from the Iron Age to the Internet, but they are hardly striking. (Figure 6.8) A better place to look for Celtic influences is in the various one-pound designs which have honoured the four constituent parts of the realm—England, Scotland, Wales, and Northern Ireland (though of course circulating throughout the United Kingdom). With some exceptions these have featured edge inscriptions, in Latin for England, Scotland, and Northern Ireland but in the Welsh language for Wales. The more extensively used *PLEIDOL WYF I'M GWLAD* one can be translated 'I am true to my country'; *Y DDRAIG GOCH DDYRY CYCHWYN* as 'The red dragon leads the way'. But it is the Northern Irish pounds that show the clearest Celtic influence. In 1996 and again in 2001 and to a limited extent in 2008 a design based on a cross from the Broighter hoard, which was in fact found in 1896 in Co. Derry, now in Northern Ireland, was used, providing a link, probably unintentional on both sides, to the Republic's 2000 coin, mentioned previously.[15] (Figure 6.9)

Isle of Man

The Isle of Man, with a population in 2011 of 85,000 people, is an extremely prolific issues or coins—some indication of this can be obtained from the authoritative 2017 Standard Catalog of World Coins 2001–Date,[16] in which its issues occupies over thirty pages, compared

---

14 Cuhaj *2012 Standard Catalog*, 985.
15 Coglan, *For Want* 198.
16 Michael, Thomas, Giedroyc, Richard & Sanders, Kay 2016, *2017 Standard Catalog of World Coins 2001–Date*, Iola WI: Krause. The Isle of Man Treasury

Figure 6.8 United Kingdom 2001, circulation two pounds

with twenty-four for those of the United Kingdom, and three for those of Ireland. Its focus is clearly on the collector market, and very many of its numerous designs have no obvious relationship or particular relevance to Man. But Manx elements, including linguistic ones, are not entirely lacking from coins that circulate on the island. In the late 1980s and early 1990s the Manx name for the territory, ' Ellan Vannin', appeared on several circulating coins, and on one occasion, on a pound appearing in 1987, it appeared without the English equivalent (though the coin possibly shows a Viking warrior rather than a Celt). A two pence issued from 2001 to 2003 features a few words, *CLASHT ROOIN, O HIARN* from a Manx fishermen's evening hymn: they can be translated 'Hear us, O Lord'.

---

recently announced that it planned in future to issue substantially fewer collector coins. See Alexander, Michael 2017 (February) Interview: Business as Usual at Popjoy Mint, *Coin News* 34–36:35.

Figure 6.9 United Kingdom, Northern Ireland one pound

When the Isle of Man went over to decimal currency in 1971 the new penny design, used until 1975, featured a Celtic cross. As has often been the case with Manx coins, the same design was also available to collectors in precious metals, in this case silver and platinum. A two pence issued from 1988 to 1995 has also been identified as having a Celtic design, though perhaps the script used for 'Ellan Vannin' is the most Celtic part of the design. A fifty-pence coin issued 2001 to 2003 as part of a series celebrating Christianity in Man features a pre-Norse cross in the Manx Museum.[17] (Figure 6.10)

Ireland has never honoured its fifth-century patron saint with a coin, but St Patrick, though not named, is the subject of an Isle of Man large crown coin issued for collectors in 2013. The saint is apparently in the act of banishing the snakes from Ireland, in legend at least one of his best-known activities. (Figure 6.11) A five-pound Isle of Man coin in the base metal alloy virenium, issued 2000 to 2003, commemorates 'St Patrick's hymn', and portrays artwork by the Manx designer Archibald Knox (1864–1933), who was inspired by the hymn known as 'St Patrick's Breastplate' or 'The Deer's Cry'.

---

17   Coins of the Manx Pound (Wikipedia).

Figure 6.10 Isle of Man, a selection of coins

Figure 6.11 Isle of Man, St Patrick crown

It should be emphasised that few jurisdictions if any have issued as many different coin designs in the last forty years as the Isle of Man. Its 'Celtic' coins are a very small part of its output of distinctive designs, though they do have some prominence among the coins issued for circulation on the island, a prominence they share with coins featuring Scandinavian subjects, this group also being a part of the island's heritage, and its legacy made central to Manx political culture, which has a focus on the Norse-inspired Tynwald parliament.

Continental Europe

Turning to Continental Europe it is logical to begin with France, famously the land of the Gauls. In 2012 the Gallic hero Vercingetorix was honoured on a ten-euro coin celebrating the Auvergne in a series devoted to French regions and territories. An ancient Celtic coin also figures in the design. (Figure 6.12) In 2000, before the euro, a coin of the ancient Parisii tribe had been reproduced in a series of coins celebrating two millennia of French coinage. But the ancient Celt most honoured by far in French coinage has been the comic-book character Asterix the Gaul. He and his associates were commemorated by seven different gold and silver coins in 2007, and by three different gold and silver coins in 2013. In 2015 twenty-four different Asterix ten-euro coins, and two different Asterix fifty-euro coins appeared, purportedly demonstrating how Asterix and his friends and foes embodied the values of the Republic, Liberty, Equality, and Fraternity. These 2015 coins, made from silver alloys, were indeed intended for collectors, but they were made available in large numbers at a relatively modest face value, and the public was encouraged to mount them in a specially designed album. (Figure 6.13) The coins could be regarded as a tribute to France's Celtic heritage, or perhaps more precisely to *nos ancêtres les Gallois*, but clearly they are far more a tribute to a famous, very popular and very clever series of comic books.

Otherwise Continental Europe offers lean pickings when we look for Celtic themes. From 1993 to 2008 Slovakia placed a coin of the Celtic leader Biatec, issued in the first century BC in Bratislava, on its circulating five-koruna coin; (Figure 6.14) and in 2000 Austria issued a silver hundred schilling commemorative for collectors portraying a Celtic salt miner on one side and an ancient Celtic coin design on the other. In 2007, in a series devoted to European art, Italy displayed the Tara Brooch on a small gold twenty-euro coin, issued in a mintage of only 3500. The brooch, dated to around 700 AD, is one of the treasures in the National Museum of Ireland. A crown from another

Figure 6.12 France, 10 euro, commemorating
Vercingetorix

Figure 6.13 France 2015, featuring Asterix the Gaul

extremely prolific issuer of collector coins, Gibraltar, may perhaps be
added. Dated 2001 and inscribed '21st CENTURY' it was available
in copper-nickel, silver, and tri-metallic (platinum, gold, and silver)
versions and included in a rather crowded design what the relevant

Figure 6.14 Slovakia, circulation five koruna

Krause catalogue[18] identifies as a Celtic cross as well as a Viking ship and artifacts associated with modern technology.

The Rest of the World

Two unlikely countries outside Europe have issued coins with a Celtic theme. In 2010 the Democratic Republic of Congo issued for collectors a set of twelve coins commemorating 'Warriors of the World', and one of these portrayed a Celtic warrior. There is no indication of the Celtic realm or time period he is intended to represent which makes it difficult to comment on the accuracy of the depiction. (Figure 6.15) Fiji in 2016 devoted the second in its series of Mandela Art coins to a design said to reflect 'the Celts' love of geometric decoration'.[19] Bearing a nominal value of $10 this large diameter three-ounce silver coin, adorned with a piece of malachite, does look spectacular, but its price of several hundred dollars would put it beyond the reach of most collectors.

---

18 Michael *et al.* 587.
19 Mandala Art II Celtic 3ox Silver Antique! 2016, *Downies Newsletter*, https://www.downies.com/news

Figure 6.15 Congo Democratic Republic, 100 francs

Conclusion

Some years ago I published a paper looking at medieval Scandinavian or 'Viking' themes on twentieth-century coins.[20] Many European countries have commemorated the Vikings or medieval Scandinavians, and so have the United States, Canada, Benin, the Cook Islands, the Democratic Republic of Congo, Laos, the Marshall Islands, Niue, North Korea, the Saharawi Arab Democratic Republic, the Solomon Islands, Tonga, Tuvalu, and Zambia. The twenty-first century shows no sign of a diminution in the use of such subjects and themes by world mints. But despite the huge numbers of coins that pour annually from the world's mint—there are 1392 large pages in the 2017 version of the standard catalogue of issues from 2001 to date—it is clear that the Celts are not nearly as well remembered numismatically, and arguably not particularly well remembered at all by the world's mints.

An examination of modern 'Viking' coins suggests two major reasons for this. Coin after coin portrays Viking ships. Redolent of

---

20   Kennedy, John 2008 'Viking' Coins of the Twentieth Century, *Vikings and their Enemies: Proceeding of a Symposium Held in Melbourne 24 November 2007*, edited by Katrina L. Burge, Melbourne: Viking Research Network 113–24.

power, grace, and menace these ships are instantly recognisable as Viking artifacts and clearly have captured the popular imagination. They may also be relatively easy to present on the face of a coin. The Celtic peoples produced nothing comparable in fame, and their most renowned art is detailed and intricate (and, as Oisín Kelly suggests) difficult for modern people to appreciate with any level of real understanding. Even more importantly, perhaps, the Vikings (in the sense of Scandinavians living during the period of Viking activity) are the first Europeans with a well-founded claim to have sailed across the Atlantic and discovered the North American continent. Ireland may have honoured its Atlantic explorer St Brendan on a coin, but far more countries, mindful no doubt of the large and wealthy collector market in the United States, have honoured Leifur Eiríksson.

But that the Celts are less famous than the Vikings is not an adequate explanation of why the former has not received more numismatic attention. The relatively restrained coin issuing program of Ireland, the only politically autonomous nation which regards itself as Celtic, may be a factor, and it is worth noting that Ireland normally needs to enlist the aid of foreign mints to produce its precious metal commemorative coins, although it has possessed its own mint at Sandyford near Dublin since 1976. Sadly, perhaps, an even bigger factor is that the numerous other countries of Europe which could claim a Celtic heritage do not see the memory of it as a major part of how they wish to present themselves to their own citizens and the wider world.

7
Scottish Soldiers in Fifteenth-Century France: Remembering an Early Scottish Diaspora

Elizabeth Bonner[1]

This chapter seeks to review and re-evaluate the nature and memories of a late medieval Scottish diaspora, that of Scottish soldiers into France from the early fifteenth century onwards. This account accepts the more extended concept of diaspora that was identified by the Scottish Centre of Diaspora Studies in 2008.[2] Paradoxically, memory of the Scottish diaspora into France in the fifteenth century is best recalled in myth and legend until the eighteenth century onwards. [3] It has received the

---

1   Dr Elizabeth Bonner passed away on 31 May 2020 in the knowledge that this chapter was in press at that time.
2   Created by the grant of £1 million from Alan and Anne Macfarlane to the University of Edinburgh. According to their objectives, these Studies were established to provide 'a supportive environment for research and teaching about issues surrounding migration and diasporas, subjects of great current political, economic, social, and cultural interest both within and beyond the academy'. See: https://bit.ly/3c6aUiz. This view of the diaspora distinguishes it from the original definition of *diaspora* in the *Oxford English Dictionary*: 'noun, the dispersion of the Jews beyond Israel'. Further comment: 'The main diaspora began in the 8th–6th centuries BC, and even before the sack of Jerusalem in AD 70 the number of Jews dispersed by the diaspora was greater than that living in Israel. Thereafter, Jews were dispersed even more widely throughout the Roman world and beyond.'
3   There are numerous publications, but a few examples are: Devine, T. M. 2011 *To the Ends of the Earth: Scotland's Global Diaspora, 1750–2010*, London:

least critical academic analysis. In discussion of the Scottish diaspora on the Web for example, memory of this early diaspora is largely ignored save for its representation on the magnificent Scottish Diaspora Tapestry, where famous fifteenth-century Franco-Scottish historical figures are presented.[4] This does not mean, however, that no significant studies have been made; one thinks of some notable eighteenth- and nineteenth-century antiquarians, as well as others who published Franco-Scottish manuscripts and original documents in the mainly nineteenth-century Scottish History Club publications. Furthermore, there are independent antiquarian publications to consider; the principal ones relevant to this diaspora are: William Forbes Leith's *The Scots Men-at-Arms and Life Guards in France* (1822), Andrew Stuart's *History of the Stewarts* (1798) and Elizabeth Cust's *The Stuarts of Aubigny in France, 1422–1672*, (1891).[5] Therefore, the present study

---

Allen Lane; McCarthy, A. 2012 The Scottish Diaspora since 1815, *The Oxford Handbook of Modern Scottish History*, Oxford University Press; Harper, M. 2009 Transplanted Identities: Remembering and Reinventing Scotland Across the Diaspora, *Ties of Bluid, Kin and Countrie: Scottish Associational Culture in the Diaspora*, Centre for Scottish Studies: University of Guelph; Bueltmann, T. et al. 2013 Diaspora: Defining a Concept, *The Scottish Diaspora*, edited by Tanja Bueltmann, Andrew Hinson and Graeme Morton, Edinburgh University Press 16–33. Recently the diaspora studies have been extended back to the seventeenth century in: McCarthy, A. and MacKenzie, J. M. editors 2017 *Global Migrations, The Scottish Diaspora since 1600*, Edinburgh University Press.

4   For details see, http://www.scottishdiasporatapestry.org/ (accessed 31 March, 2018). The Scottish Diaspora Tapestry (2012–2014) is the creation of the Prestoungrange Arts Festival in Prestonpans, who hold the copyright, and is supported by Barons Courts of Prestoungrange and Dolphinstoun. It was produced by 'hundreds of stitchers and Scotophiles globally, CreativeScotland, the Scottish Government's Diaspora Division, VisitScotland, EventScotland, The University of the West of Scotland, and Bòrd na Gàidhlig'. Since 2014 it has been on constant circulation to global exhibitions.

5   Forbes-Leith, William 1882 *The Scots Men-at-Arms and Life Guards in France, from their Formation until their Final Dissolution AD. MCCCCXVIII–MDCCCXXX [1418–1830]*, 2 vols, Edinburgh: William Patterson; Stuart, Andrew 1798 *Genealogical History of the Stewarts: from the Earliest Period of their Authentic History to the Present Times...*, London: A. Strahan, T. Cadell jun. and W. Davies; Cust, Elizabeth, Lady 1891 *Some Account of the Stuarts of Aubigny in France, 1422–1672*, London: Chiswick Press.

will carry out an historiographical survey in which the limited modern and earlier sources will be examined. Additionally, some observations will be made of how certain French people today remember and memorialise their military 'Auld Alliance' with the Scots, which was waged against their mutual enemy of England.

This general public memory of the Scottish diaspora in the fifteenth century as expressed in the Tapestry identifies very strongly with the entire nineteenth-century view that saw the zenith of a flowering of Scottish culture. This flowering of Scottish culture also extended to the phenomenal European-wide influence of Sir Walter Scott's novels, poetry and ballads portraying a glorified view of what might best be described as 'Tartan History'. Previously, the death in 1788 of 'Bonnie Prince Charlie' the last Stuart Pretender and then the eruption of the French Revolution the following year produced a Scottish review of their 'Auld French Alliance' and its replacement by the more pragmatic one with England and the all-powerful British Empire. It was probably Walter Scott's romanticising of Scottish history through his literary works, whether by design or by accident, that made the vast majority of the Scots acceptable to the vast majority of the English and vice versa, and accomplished the 'Anglicisation' of the Scottish Establishment during the nineteenth century. Of course, there were always dissenters on both sides, but Scott created a *Via Media* on which both sides could amicably travel. Scott had a remarkable relationship with George IV, persuading the king in 1822 to make the first royal visit to Scotland since Charles II was crowned at Scone on New Year's Day in 1651. Indeed, for George's visit Scott dug up the Scottish Royal Regalia of Crown, Sceptre and Sword from a vault in Edinburgh Castle where it had been buried since the official Union with England was signed in 1707. Subsequently, this royal appreciation of Scottish culture was greatly extended during the long reign of Victoria, which also saw the zenith of the European-wide flowering of Scottish culture and the very favourable relationship with England enjoyed by a majority of Scots.

But perhaps the most significant cause of forgetting here is the enormous historiographical influence of the collation, transcription and publication of English State Papers of the Tudor regime in the *Letters and Papers of Henry VII and Henry VIII*, and in the *Calendars of State Papers [CPS], Domestic, Foreign, Scottish, Spanish, Venetian et al;* but crucially the total lack of any editions of a *CPS, French.* Furthermore, there is also to be considered the vast array of other printed Tudor sources, contemporary accounts and chronicles, edited and published mainly during the nineteenth century. The editors and authors of these *Papers* and Tudor sources were mainly Victorian gentlemen who, like the majority of their contemporaries looked back to the supposed glories of the Tudor age, especially under Elizabeth, equating it with the power and prestige of the Empire under Victoria. Thus, their editions and the consequent historiography generally reflect these Victorian imperial attitudes and societal mores.

The old Franco-Scottish relationship had not been entirely forgotten, and at the height of the Belle Époque, when wealthy Britons were enjoying the many pleasures of France, a Franco-Scottish Society was founded in Edinburgh in 1895. This celebrated the 600th anniversary of the signing in Paris of (what has become known as) the 'Auld Alliance' treaty on the 23 October 1295. Then, in 1896, the *Association Franco-Écossaise* was founded in Paris at the time of the 600th anniversary of the Scottish Ratification signed at Dunfermline on 23 February 1296. The original of this document is still held today in the French National Archives in Paris.[6] The Edwardians also embraced this cultural, diplomatic and political alliance with France (for example, the *Entente Cordiale* of 1906) and it was later demonstrated by the support of the now English and Scots allies of France in both the First and Second World Wars. This support was extended as a post-war European-wide peace initiative in the town-twinning movement that started very soon after 1945, with the passionate support of mayors and citizens who vowed that Europe should never again be torn apart by war. For the Scots the natural partner and the most numerous for town-twinning was with France, which recalled memories of the first

---

6   Scottish ratification, Archives Nationales de France, Paris, Trésor des Chartes
     J. 677, No. 1, original, on parchment, sealed with six pendant seals with red
     and green silk ties; copies: National Library of Scotland, Edinburgh [NLS],
     Advocates MSS. 35. 1. 5, fols, 6–14; British Library, London [BL], Harleian
     Collection 1244, fols, 18–26; published: Rymer, Thomas editor 1704–35
     Foedera Conventiones, Litterae et etc..., London: James, John and Paul
     Knapton, *et al...*, 2, 680ff.

Scottish soldiers' diaspora into France in the fifteenth century and of their much older thirteenth-century 'Auld Alliance' treaty. The first Franco-Scottish treaty of which there remains documentary evidence is the one contracted between John Balliol, King of Scots, and Philippe IV (le Bel), which was signed at Paris on 23 October 1295. It was a military defensive–offensive alliance directed against England and the incursions of Edward I, who was pressing his claims to overlordship of the Scots. By the terms of the alliance neither the French nor the Scots would make a separate peace with England. It was further strengthened by the proposed marriage of John Balliol's son Edward to Philippe IV's niece; and also by the French request that the treaty should be ratified not only by King John but also by the Scottish prelates, barons, knights and communities of the towns. Ranald Nicholson says that 'the Scottish burgesses made their entry into high affairs of state when the seals of their six burghs were attached to the Scottish ratification at Dunfermline on 23 February 1296'.[7] Thereafter, it was signed by every French and Scottish monarch (with the exception of Louis XI) until the mid-sixteenth century.

Therefore, it is no great surprise to find one of the earliest twinnings was between the two towns which most exemplified the Scots 'Auld Alliance' with France. Haddington, a town thirty miles east of Edinburgh, was besieged by the English during the wars of Henry VIII's so-called 'Rough Wooing' of the Scots in his effort to force the marriage of his son Edward to Mary Queen of Scots. However, a large contingent of the French king's forces joined the Scots and defeated the English. Mary was then betrothed to Henri II's son, Francis, in 1548 and with Scottish blessings and parliamentary accord she was sent to live and later marry in France. In 1965, Haddington was twinned with the town of Aubigny-sur-Nère, which is situated midway between Orleans and Bourges in central France. It was part of the Lordship of

---

7   The six burghs were: Aberdeen, Perth, Stirling, Edinburgh, Roxburgh and Berwick; Nicholson, Ranald 1978 *Scotland: The Later Middle Ages*, Edinburgh: Oliver and Boyd, 47; cf Thomson, T. and Innes, C. editors 1814–75 *Acts of the Parliaments of Scotland, 1124–1707* [*APS*], 12 vols, London: Great Britain Record Commission I.451–53.

Aubigny granted by Charles VII to Sir John Stewart of Darnley in 1423 in recognition of his military service to the French crown during the Hundred Years' War against England.

In regard to the outcome of this Franco-Scottish relationship, forged at the height of the war, Philippe Contamine presented a paper, 'Scottish Soldiers in the Second Half of the Fifteenth Century: Mercenaries, Immigrants or Frenchmen in the making?', at King's College, Aberdeen in September 1990.[8] Thus Contamine's enquiry concentrates on the thousands of Scottish soldiers (French contemporary sources estimate 15,000 but historians dispute such large numbers) who arrived in France between 1419 and 1424 in response to the Dauphin's (in 1422 Charles VII) pleas for military aid, following the crushing defeat by the English at Agincourt in 1415. The initial victory for the Franco-Scottish force at Baugé in 1421 was followed by disastrous defeats at Cravant in 1423 and, worst of all, at Verneuil in 1424. Contamine comments that despite these losses, at least part of the powerful Scottish expeditionary force 'wished to remain in France for a long period'; the Scots, he claims, represented at one stage 'between one tenth and one fifth of the royal forces on campaign'.[9]

French archival sources show that Scottish soldiers served both in the king's companies of ordnance and in the famous garde écossaise, the French monarchs' personal bodyguard of Scots Guards officially founded by Charles VII in 1445. In the late nineteenth century, Forbes-Leith drew on these sources to identify ninety-one of 'the Estates possessed by the Scots Guards in France',[10] many of whom either came from or were promoted to the seigneurial class. Contamine looks in more depth at one example, that of:

---

8   Contamine, Philippe 1992 Scottish Soldiers in France in the Second Half of the Fifteenth Century: Mercenaries, Immigrants or Frenchmen in the Making? *The Scottish Soldier Abroad, 1247–1967*, edited by Grant Simpson, Edinburgh: John Donald 16–30; see also Contamine, Philippe 1972 *Guerre, état et société à la fin du Moyen Age: études sur les armées des rois de France, 1337–1494*, Paris: La Haye-Mouton.
9   Contamine, Scottish Soldiers 17.
10   Forbes-Leith II.222–6; also see annual Muster Rolls of the *garde écossaise*, Forbes-Leith I and II *passim*.

Walter Stud [Stuart], a companion of Jean Stuart [Sir John Stewart of Darnley][11] Constable of the Scots in France, who [Stud] became captain d'Avallon in 1441; archer of Charles VII's Body Guard, to whom the king granted the lands d'Assay in Gâtinais about 1445. When he died without issue the king granted his lands and titles to his brother, Thomas, also an archer in the *garde écossaise*, from whom descended the family Destutt de Tracy.[12]

From these archival records Contamine also identifies individual Scots serving in the *lances fournies* of the king's ordnance under Charles VII, continued under Louis XI from 1461 and Charles VIII from 1483 until 1498. For the period 1450–1500 he summarises that the figure of 450 to 500 is the minimum with an average of '650–700 Scots over the years in the armies and Royal Household of France'. Contamine continues that

> due to Forbes Leith's exceptional documentation of the *garde écossaise* it is possible to establish that careers spanned from five to 42 years, averaging 23 years, and even those who 'could no longer serve on account of their very great age and debility'.[13]

Therefore, according to Contamine, turnover of Scots was slow and evidence shows that 30 to 40 arrived each year to join the 650–700, attracted and welcomed by relatives and friends already settled in France. There were others who ultimately returned to Scotland,

---

11 Both forms of spelling are correct but *Stewart* is the original Scottish spelling. *Stuart* is the French spelling deriving from the donation by Charles VII of the Lordship of Aubigny to 'Jean Stuart de Darnle' in 1423, AN, Carton des Rois K 168, No. 91. From that time onwards the English appear to have adopted the French form. In this present article the nomination of the spelling *Stewart* or *Stuart* is dependent entirely upon the spelling given in the original manuscript. In references to the family in Scotland however *Stewart* is always used. See *Infra*, Appendix No.1 for a Genealogical Table of the Lennox-Stewart/Stuart family of Darnley and Aubigny.

12 Contamine, *Guerre, état et société* 458, cf. Villenaut, A. de et Flamare, H. de 1900 *Nobiliaire du Nivernais*, 2 vols, Nevers: G. Valière II.542. Also see the muster roll of 24 'Archers du corps du Roy' [Louis XI] 1467: 'Thomas Stut' and 'Gauthier Stut', Forbes-Leith II.40.

13 Contamine, Scottish Soldiers 19, cf, Forbes-Leith II, *passim*.

'nevertheless, numerous statistics suggest that long-term settlement in France occurred'. Contamine gives many examples and asserts that:

> quite soon and in large numbers, the Scots became the owners of houses, lands and fiefs, which they obtained as gifts from king or prince, or by marriage or purchase, especially in certain regions, such as Berry, Touraine, Poitou and Saintonge.[14]

During this period of 1445–94, Contamine notes, 'the foreign captains among whom the Scots were dominant, differed from those of the previous century by establishing themselves in the kingdom'. Among 'the captains of the ordnance' were 'Scots such as Robert Cunningham, whose name was Frenchified to *Conyngham* or *Conigan*, Patrick Folcart, Robin Pettylow, sometimes called *Petit-Loup*, Thomas and William *Stuyer* [Stuart], whose presence explains the traditional friendship of France and Scotland'.[15] In order to elaborate his contention Contamine chose two of these captains from this period, both of whom served as captains in the French kings' ordnance and as captains of the *garde écossaise*, and who best fulfill the criteria of the fifteenth-century 'First Scottish Diaspora': Bérault Stuart 4th seigneur d'Aubigny, one of the so-called 'French Stuarts' who were descended from the Scottish Royal House,[16] and Robert de Conyngham from the well-known and well-connected Scottish Cunningham family. According to Contamine, 'Robert was a captain of the ordnance from 1446 onwards, and, based with his men in upper Auvergne, he took

---

14 Contamine, Scottish Soldiers 21.
15 Contamine, *Guerre, état et société* 419–20; for many other examples of Scottish soldiers, who served either in the French kings' ordnance or *garde écossaise* and who received lands, titles and offices, especially after the accession of Louis XI in 1461 see, Contamine, Scottish Soldiers 20–3.
16 Apart from Contamine's works already cited see also, Contamine, Philippe 1992 *Histore Militaire de la France:* Vol. 1 *Des origines à 1715*, Paris: Presses Universitaires de France; and Contamine, Philippe 1999 Entre France et Écosse: Bérault Stuart, seigneur d'Aubigny (vers 1452–1508), chef de guerre, diplomate, écrivain militaire, *The Auld Alliance: France and Scotland over 700 years*, edited by J. Laidlaw, University of Edinburgh 59–76.

a brilliant role in the recapture of Normandy and Guyenne'. However, continues Contamine,

> in 1455 a plot was discovered which dated back to the siege of Caen [1450]: at the instigation of the duke of Somerset and on a promise of various financial rewards, Robert and his accomplices were to split up from Jean, comte de Dunois, Jacques Coeur, and Jean Bureau, and bring 1,500 Englishmen into the camp of Charles VII.[17]

An investigation and trial followed in the *Parlement de Paris* and on 8 August 1455, Robert was imprisoned but Robyn Campbell, Conyngham's lieutenant, was sentenced to death. Pleas for clemency came the 'following year', continues Contamine, 'from a dozen of Robert's friends and relatives, all of noble birth, and King James II himself intervened from Scotland in his favour'.[18] As a result, says Contamine,

> on 27 June 1456, Conyngham was sentenced to appear before Charles VII before the following 15 August, to 'request his mercy and pardon'. He was stripped of all his offices and forbidden to come within ten miles of the king for a period of three years dating from the day on which he begged the king's mercy.[19]

In the eyes of many, however, evidence of Robert's guilt remained doubtful. For example, Jean Chartier, says Contamine, 'writing in his chronicle after sentence was passed, refers repeatedly and in glowing terms to the deeds of the Scottish captain'. Nevertheless, not until the accession of Louis XI in 1461 was Robert restored to favour at court, 'which was never withdrawn again until his death which probably

---

17 Contamine, Scottish Soldiers 24.
18 *Ibid*, 24; a full transcription of James II's letter appears in Augsbury, Larry A. 2003 (Oct/Nov) Robert de Conyngham, Lord of Cherveux, *The Family Tree*, https://www.electricscotland.com, although no archival or manuscript references are given in this account there are four bibliographical sources and three further websites cited.
19 Contamine, Scottish Soldiers 24, cf. du Fresne de Beaucourt, G. 1882–91 *Histoire de Charles VII*, 6 vols, Paris: Libraire de la société bibliographique VI. 27–9.

occurred in 1479'. During this time he was appointed an 'esquire of the king's stable, councilor and royal chamberlain who was sufficiently well-off to acquire the lordships of Villeneuve and Cherveux', near Niort, where in 1470 he reconstructed the twelfth-century Château de Cherveux[20] into an imposing castle which still stands today. Many Conynghams revolve around Robert; twelve of them were, for example, serving in Robert's company of ordnance or during his tenure of captain in the *garde écossaise*.[21] Robert's son Joachim, seigneur de la Roche, inherited Cherveux as did his son Jacques who 'was a royal master of the household and captain of Niort under Louis XII and Francis I' which, Contamine says, 'is an example of family solidarity and a striking model of service to the French kings'.[22]

An even greater example of family solidarity and service to the French crown was the establishment in France of the Lennox-Stewart/ Stuart family of Darnley in the 1420s. In time they were to become possibly the single most important family involved in the politics and diplomacy of the monarchies and government in the kingdoms of Scotland, France and England during the entire fifteenth and sixteenth centuries. During the late-fifteenth century however it was Bérault Stuart, 4th seigneur d'Aubigny, who became one of the most outstanding soldiers of his age in the service of Charles VIII and Louis XII. He was the grandson of Sir John Stewart of Darnley who, by 1428, had been granted by Charles VII the lordships of Concressault[23] and

---

20 For an archeological survey with numerous illustrations of the Château see Faucherre, Nicolas 2001 Le Château de Cherveux, *Congrès Archéologique de France, Deux-Sèvres*, Paris: Société d'Archéologie française 122–29. Also see Bernage, Georges 2002 Cherveux, château d'un capitaine de la garde écossaise, *Le Moyen Age* 108 (2), 12–27; which briefly summarizes the history of the château and its inhabitants with many illustrations, concentrating on Robert de Conyngham citing mainly the works of Philippe Contamine and Nicolas Faucherre's article.

21 Contamine, Scottish Soldiers 24–5; also see Forbes-Leith, *passim*.

22 Contamine, Scottish Soldiers 25.

23 Anon, Aliénation de la seigneurie de Concressault, donnée par le Roy (*sic*) [Charles VII] en 1521, au connétable [des Ecossais] Jean Stuart, Registre des Aliénations du domaine, Archives départementales du Cher à Bourges C 793, fol. 17v; for a full transcription of the documents, see Anon, 1899 Donation par Charles VII à Jean Stuart, seigneur de Derneley, Connétable de l'armée

Aubigny,[24] the county of Evreux[25] and the title of Constable of the Scottish army in France, and who was also granted by the king the honour of quartering his arms with the royal *fleurs de lys* of France.[26] However, on 12 February 1429 Sir John Stewart was slain at the battle of Rouvray, colloquially known as the battle of the Herrings, when he and his brother Sir William Stewart of Castlemilk, who was also slain, were attempting to relieve the Siege of Orleans. Recent research in the private 'Stuart' archives at the Château de La Verrerie and the departmental archives at Bourges has shown that in 1429 Sir Alan Stewart of Darnley inherited not only his father's Scottish estates but also his father's French offices and titles. In 1437, however, by agreement with Charles VII Alan relinquished these titles to his youngest brother John (Berault's father) who had accompanied his father and uncle to France in 1419. John, 3rd seigneur of Aubigny and Concressault, led a long and successful life in France during which time he was appointed 'Chamberlain to the King, Captain of 100 Scots of the King's Guard, and Chevalier of the Royal Military Order of Saint-Michel'.[27]

Berault's military service to the French crown began, according to Contamine, in 1469 and 1471 where he is found as a man-of-arms in the company of ordnance of Robert Conyngham and in 1475 in his son Joachim's company.[28] By 1483 he had command of 100 Lances in the king's ordnance and had been appointed captain of the château

---

d'Ecosse, des terres de Concressault et d'Aubigny-sur-Nère, 21 avril 1421, 26 mars 1423, et décembre 1425, *Mémoires de la Société Historique, Littéraire et Scientifique du Cher*, Paris et Bourges, 4e série, 14, 21–34.

24 AN, Carton des Rois K 168, No. 91.

25 Concession par Charles VII à Jean Stuart, connétable d'Écosse, du comté d'Évreux (Montluçon, janvier 1427), vidimus (certified copy) au nom de Guillaume Frudct, garde du scel (Keeper of the Seal) de la prévôté de Bourges (Bourges, 14 mars 1427), AN, J 216, No. 20.

26 For a copy and translation of the grant (January 1685), Cust, *Stuarts of Aubigny*, 12–5, cf, The National Archives, London, State Papers, 179, No. 12.

27 Bibliothèque Nationale, Paris [BN], Dossiers Bleus 621, No. 61487, fol. 4, cf. Bonner, Elizabeth 2014 Inheritance, war and antiquarianism: Sir Alan Stewart of Darnley, 2nd seigneur d'Aubigny et de Concressault, 1429–37, *Proceedings of the Society Antiquaries of Scotland* 143, 351.

28 Contamine, Scottish Soldiers, 19.

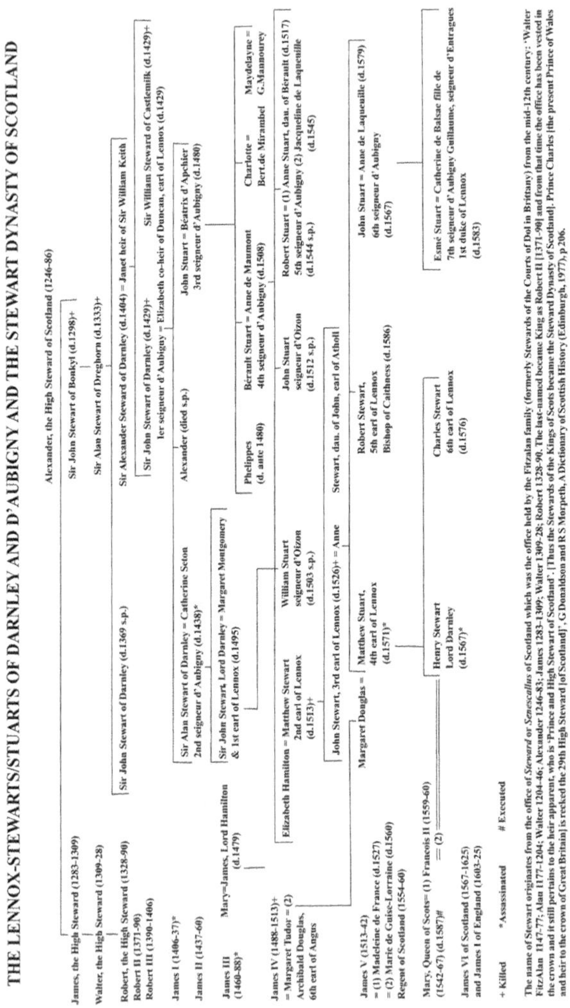

THE LENNOX-STEWARTS/STUARTS OF DARNLEY AND D'AUBIGNY AND THE STEWART DYNASTY OF SCOTLAND

Alexander, the High Steward of Scotland (1246–86)

James, the High Steward (1283–1309)

Walter, the High Steward (1309–28)

Robert, the High Steward (1328–90)
Robert II (1371–90)
Robert III (1390–1406)

James I (1406–37)†

James II (1437–60)

James III (1460–88)*

Mary=James, Lord Hamilton (d.1479)

James IV (1488–1513)†
= Margaret Tudor = (2)
Archibald Douglas,
6th earl of Angus

James V (1513–42)
= (1) Madeleine de France (d.1537)
= (2) Marie de Guise-Lorraine (d.1560)

Mary, Queen of Scots= (1) François II (1559–60)
= (2)

James VI of Scotland (1567–1625)
and James I of England (1603–25)

Sir John Stewart of Bonkyl (d.1298)+

Sir Alan Stewart of Dreghorn (d.1333)+

Sir Alexander Steward of Darnley (d.1404) = Janet heir of Sir William Keith

Sir John Stewart of Darnley (d.1429)+ = Elizabeth co-heir of Duncan, earl of Lennox (d.1429)
ler seigneur d'Aubigny

Sir William Steward of Castlemilk (d.1429)+

Sir John Stewart of Darnley (d.1369 s.p.)

Alexander (died s.p.)

John Stuart = Béatrix d'Apcher,
3rd seigneur d'Aubigny (d.1480)

Sir Alan Stewart of Darnley = Catherine Seton,
2nd seigneur d'Aubigny (d.1438)*

Sir John Stewart, Lord Darnley = Margaret Montgomery
& 1st earl of Lennox (d.1495)

Bérault Stuart = Anne de Maumont,
4th seigneur d'Aubigny (d.1508)

Charlotte =
Bert.de Mirambel

Maydelayne =
G.Maumourey

Phelippes
(d. ante 1480)

William Stuart
seigneur d'Oizon
(d.1503 s.p.)

John Stewart
seigneur d'Oizon
(d.1512 s.p.)

Robert Stuart = (1) Anne Stuart, dau. of Bérault (d.1517)
5th seigneur d'Aubigny (2) Jacqueline de Laqueville
(d.1544 s.p.)
(d.1545)

Elizabeth Hamilton = Matthew Stewart
2nd earl of Lennox
(d.1513)+

John Stewart, 3rd earl of Lennox (d.1526)+ = Anne

Matthew Stuart,
4th earl of Lennox
(d.1571)*

Robert Stewart,
5th earl of Lennox,
Bishop of Caithness (d.1586)

Stewart, dau. of John, earl of Atholl

John Stuart = Anne de Laqueville (d.1579)
6th seigneur d'Aubigny
(d.1567)

Margaret Douglas = Henry Stewart
Lord Darnley
(d.1567)*

Charles Stewart
6th earl of Lennox
(d.1576)

Esmé Stuart = Catherine de Balsac fille de
7th seigneur d'Aubigny Guillaume, seigneur d'Entragues
1st duke of Lennox
(d.1583)

+ Killed   * Assassinated   # Executed

The name of Stewart originates from the office of Steward or Seneschallus of Scotland which was the office held by the FitzAlan family (formerly Stewards of the Courts of Dol in Brittany) from the mid-12th century: 'Walter FitzAlan 1147–77; Alan 1177–1204; Walter 1204–46; Alexander 1246–83; James 1283–1309; Walter 1309–28; Robert II 1371–90] and [from that time the office has been vested in the crown and it still pertains to the heir apparent, who is 'Prince and High Steward of Scotland'. [Thus the Stewards of the Kings of Scots became the Stewart Dynasty of Scotland]. Prince Charles [the present Prince of Wales and heir to the crown of Great Britain] is styled the 29th High Steward [of Scotland]', G Donaldson and R S Morpeth, A Dictionary of Scottish History (Edinburgh, 1977), p.206.

Figure 7.1 Chart of the Lennox-Stewarts/Stuarts of Darnley and d'Aubigny and the Stewart Dynasty of Scotland

du Bois-de-Vincennes on the outskirts of Paris. The following year Charles VIII sent him to Scotland to renew the 'Auld Alliance' treaty with James III, which was signed in Edinburgh on 22 March 1484 and ratified in Paris in July.[29] Also at this time it is claimed that the Scottish king secretly ingratiated himself with Henry Tudor,[30] who had spent the years between 1471 and 1485 in exile, mostly in Brittany, under the protection of the then duke, Francis II, whose mother-in-law was a Scot[31] and whose predecessor had signed a treaty in 1448 with James II, who had proposed a Scottish-Breton alliance.[32] Henry Tudor, moreover, had more substantial reasons to be grateful to the Scots. The invading force with which he landed at Milford Haven included a Scots company under Sir Alexander Bruce of Earlshall, a Fife laird. It was the Scots, according to Pitscottie, who formed the spear-point of Henry's attack against Richard III at Bosworth on 22 August 1485.[33] Whilst Bérault, from this time, had a most remarkable military and diplomatic

---

29 National Records of Scotland [NRS], Treaties with France, No. 16 (Latin) No. 17 (French) No. 18, Ratification by Charles VIII, Paris, 9 July 1484 (Latin) and No. 19 (French).

30 Chrimes, S. B. 1972, repr. 1977 *Henry VII*, London: Eyre Methuen 70, 86–7 & 279; also see Nicholson, *Later Middle Ages* 518.

31 Isabella, the second daughter of James I, was married to the then duke of Brittany in 1442; for precise details regarding the marriage treaty see, Barrow, Lorna 2005 Scottish Princesses go Abroad, *Exile and Homecoming*, edited by Pamela O'Neill, University of Sydney: Celtic Studies Foundation 189.

32 Arch. Dép. de la Loire-Atlantique, Nantes, E. 125; see also Francis's will, 22 January 1450, Arch. Dép., Ille-et-Vilaine, Rennes, 1, E. 10, and a letter from James II to Charles VII, 19 May 1454, concerning the guardianship of his Breton nieces, AN, Carton K. 69, no. 12; also on 22 Oct. 1448 an agreement between James II's ambassadors, William, lord Crichton, chancellor of Scotland, John de Ralston, bishop of Dunkeld, and Nicholas Otterburn, canon of Glasgow; and Isabel and Francis I duke of Brittany, was drawn up at Vannes regarding the right of succession of the duke and duchess to the throne of Scotland, NAS, SP 7/13; see Bonner, Elizabeth 2003 Charles VII's dynastic policy and the 'Auld Alliance': the Marriage of James II and Marie de Gueldres, *Innes Review* 54, 155–7.

33 Pitscottie, Robert Lindesay of, vol. 1, 1899 *The Historie and Cronicles of Scotland* ..., Edinburgh: edited by A.J.G. MacKay, Scottish Text Society 199; Mackie, R.L. 1958 *King James VI of Scotland*, Edinburgh: Oliver and Boyd 27–8; for Bruce of Earlshall see, Griffiths, Ralph A. and Thomas, Roger S. 1985 *The Making of the Tudor Dynasty*, Gloucester: Alan Sutton 131.

career in the service of Charles VIII and Louis XII, predominantly during their Italian campaigns.[34] On 24 October 1480, following his father's death, Bérault had completed the sale of Concressault[35] to 'Guillaume de Monipeny, Chevalier, seigneur Monipeny'.[36] Thus Bérault, who had been brought up at Concressault, was obliged, between military campaigns, to make his residence at 'la maison Jehan Dernle'[37] in Aubigny. In 1493 on 10 September, however, soon after his appointment as captain of the *garde écossaise* by Charles VIII, he paid the 'noble homme Lancelot de Conigant'[38] 13,000 *livres tournois* for the 'seigneuries du Crotet, de Saint-Silvain des Averdines et de Maclou'.[39] Until recently the existence of the Château du Crotet had been lost to historical memory as no reference to it seems to have appeared since the nineteenth century, although the existence of the Stuarts d'Aubigny as the seigneurs du Crotet had been known continuously since the sixteenth century in many historical manuscripts. Indeed, it is

34 Contamine, *Bérault Stuart ... chef de guerre, diplomate* 61–76.
35 Archives privées du château de La Verrerie, Oizon (near Aubigny), papiers de famille, liasse 1, cote XXVIII, original draft on paper.
36 William Monypenny, 1st Lord Monypenny (*c.*1410–*c.*1488), 2004 *Oxford Dictionary of National Biography*, Oxford University Press.
37 Bonner, *Sir Alan Stewart of Darnley*, Appendix No. 2, Transcription of the 'Lettres Patentes d'Amortissement fait par Alan Stewart, 29 avril, 1437', Archives départementales du Cher, Bourges: Chartre 15 H2, No. 35, (Original, on parchment, autograph signature, 3 seals mentioned, all missing) 1.
38 In October 1492 there were fifteen Conighans in the *garde écossaise* under their captain, 'Messire Jean de Conighan, Chevalier, Bailly de Chartres, Conseiller et Chambellan du Roy notre sire et Capitaine des diz hommes d'armes et archiers Escotz de la dite Garde', but in 1493 when 'Messire Bérault Stuart, Chevalier, Seigneur d'Aubigny, Conseiller et Chambellan du Roy notre Sire' succeeded as captain only one Conighan remained in the *garde*, Forbes-Leith II.73–4.
39 Arch. de La Verrerie, Inventaire V, fol. 3. According to A. Buhot de Kersers, 'Lancelot de Conigault [sic] écuyer', was the 'seigneur du Crotet in 1481', 1966 *Histoire et statistique monumentale du département du Cher, Canton de Baugy, Commune de Laverdines*, Paris: 1875 facsimile édition d'original, Bourges, 1, 246–7, I am grateful to Monsieur Jean-Yves Ribault, former director of the archives départementales du Cher at Bourges, for drawing my attention to this reference; references to Lancelot Conyngham appear in the muster rolls of the 'companies des ordonnances du roy' in 1469 and 1475, Contamine, *Scottish Soldiers* 25 and 30.

emblazoned on the large cartoon of Bérault on horseback, presently hanging on the wall of the Renaissance gallery in the courtyard of the Château de La Verrerie:

Monseigneur Bérault Stuart, Lord of Aubigny and of Crotet, Count of Terrenove, Marquis of Girace, Baron of Saint-George, Councillor and Chamberlain of the King our Lord, Knight of the King's Military Order of St. Michael, Captain of the King's Bodyguard [garde écossaise], Grand Constable of Sicily and of Jerusalem and the King's Lieutenant-General of the Kingdom of Naples.

According to Buhot de Kersers, the seigneurie and château du Crotet remained with the Stuarts of Aubigny until Georges Stuart sold it in the year 1642 to François de Durand, seigneur de Thusy.[40]

In order to obtain legal possession of lands, titles, offices, to acquire goods and to grant or bequeath them to their heirs and successors, it was necessary to request official authority from the king. Therefore, French naturalisation of the Scots appears to have devolved from grants to individual Scots by Charles VII and it would seem that what Contamine describes as *libertas testandi* in the fifteenth century was associated with these grants, which were later called letters of naturalisation. French naturalisation was granted not only to individual Scots but also to all Scottish subjects by certain French monarchs from Charles VII to Louis XIV and had its origins in the 'Auld Alliance', and the establishment of the *garde écossaise*. The sixteenth century saw a continuation of Scottish military service to the kings of France as well as a continuation of grants of lands, pensions, titles and privileges accorded by grateful French monarchs to Scottish soldiers in the main, but other Scots as well, many of whom were, and others who became by letters patent of naturalisation, loyal subjects of the King of France.[41]

Contamine also demonstrates that 'many Scots were married in France, to Frenchwomen', not only in the higher ranks which are easier

---

40   Buhot de Kersers, *Histoire et statistique* 246.
41   Contamine, Scottish Soldiers, 22–3; also see Bonner, Elizabeth 1997 French Naturalization of the Scots in the Fifteenth and Sixteenth Centuries, *The Historical Journal* 40 (4) 1085–1115.

to trace in the archives but also at the lower levels, many of whom settled in 'Aubigny-sur-Nère, where apparently an entire Scottish colony existed'.[42] Today, the ancient town of Aubigny-sur-Nère is remarkably well preserved after it was rebuilt in the early sixteenth century in what we would describe as 'Tudor' style. In 1189 the Lordship of Aubigny had been annexed to the royal domain by Phillip-Auguste (1180–1223) who built a small château of earth and wood on a moat and fortified the town. Then, during the Hundred Years War, the town was sacked and set on fire by the English both in 1359 and in 1412. Therefore, following Charles VII's donation of the Lordship in 1423 to Sir John Stewart of Darnley, the first two seigneurs d'Aubigny were obliged to stay in the priory of Aubigny when visiting the devastated town.[43] In the late fifteenth century, however, Bérault Stuart, 4th seigneur d'Aubigny, settled in the area and built a château and magnificent chapel about six kilometres distant at Oizon which he called La Verrerie after the glassworks which had previously stood on the site. Then, in 1512, after another disastrous fire destroyed most of the town, Robert Stuart, 5th seigneur, built the present château d'Aubigny[44] during the general reconstruction. Soon after, Robert engaged builders to enlarge the family's château de La Verrerie, creating a magnificent Renaissance château and chapel in keeping with the French king's (Francis I) building program of Renaissance châteaux in the nearby Loire Valley. Since that time the town, which is still known today as the 'Cité des Stuart', the Stuart châteaux and their private archive have been remarkably well preserved, despite depredations

42 Contamine, Scottish Soldiers, 22, cf. Archives Nationales de France, Paris Trésor des Chartes JJ 198, No. 279.

43 Malnoury, Robert et Jacques, Jean-Claude 1994 Images du Patrimoine: Aubigny-sur-Nère, La Cité des Stuart, Cher, in Inventaire Général des Monuments et des Richesses Artistiques de la France, edited by Bernard Toulier Paris et Tours: Mame Imprimeurs 3 and 12.

44 Daru, Henri 2012 Bérault Stuart d'Aubigny, 1450–1508, Lieutenant général de Charles VIII et Louis XII en Italie: Paris: Copy House, incorrectly claims that Bérault 'construite le château d'Aubigny', whilst decling to give any reference. He also fails to mention Bérault's purchase of the château du Crotet from Lancelot Conyngham, see Supra 8–9 and notes 31–3, and makes a number of other inconsistent statements regarding Bérault's background, even though he is said to have had access to the private 'Stuart' archives at La Vererrie.

suffered elsewhere by the French Revolution (the 'Stuart' archive was hidden in the roof rafters at La Verrerie during this time), the Franco-Prussian War of 1870–71 and two World Wars last century.[45] Thus, the town and the two châteaux are well enough preserved today to give an excellent perception of its state following the general reconstruction under Robert Stuart, 5th seigneur d'Aubigny, who died in 1544. It is therefore fitting that Aubigny-sur-Nére remains the centre for the annual celebrations on 14 July, the French National Day, to remember their 'Auld Alliance' with the Scots.

When we talk of these annual celebrations at Aubigny we come within the purview of the creators of the Scottish Diaspora Tapestry in as much as the fifteenth-century French depictions recorded on the Tapestry are comparable to the themes created for the annual Franco-Scottish pageant which parades through Aubigny: Mary Queen of Scots is a great favourite as is the *garde écossaise*, the 'Auld Alliance', as well as historic figures of the Lennox-Stewart/Stuart family of Aubigny. In 2005 the then Mayor of Aubigny (1989–2012) and present *Deputé* (MP) for Cher, Monsieur Yves Fromion, informed a journalist that

he laments the fact that the rest of France has forgotten about the role of the Scots in the country's history, and inaugurated the Franco-Écossaise festival in Aubigny in 1990 ... Yet now the festival is huge, drawing people from across the surrounding countryside and, of course, from Scotland itself.[46]

However it had already become much grander in 1995 with the celebrations of the 700th anniversary of the signing of the first formal 'Auld Alliance' treaty. A memorial of a traditional Scottish stone cairn, with a massive two-handed Highland Claymore Sword plunged almost

---

45 In 1944, it was at Gien, only 30-odd kilometres from Aubigny that the retreating Germans elected to make their stand against the advancing Americans on the north bank of the Loire, resulting in an almost complete destruction of that town.
46 Stephen Khan, *Independent,* Tuesday, 5 April 2005 23:00 BST; https://bit.ly/35FbKBz.

to the hilt into its heart, was installed outside the Château d'Aubigny and at its base there is a plaque on which is inscribed:

The 'Auld Alliance' is not written on parchment in ink, but engraved on the living flesh of man's skin in blood.[47]

It was unveiled by Monsieur Fromion in 1995, wearing a kilt of the newly created tartan in the colours of Aubigny's arms of three gold buckles on a red background.[48] Prior to 1995 the Haddington Pipe Band was invited to march in the annual festival, but soon after a Scottish bagpipe tutor was employed to give lessons to local musicians, who later formed their own pipe band. Initially they wore the Aubigny tartan but several years later it was decided to adopt the Stuart hunting tartan.[49] Currently, thousands of French and Scottish tourists and pipe bands are attracted each year to the *cité des Stuarts*, to what in 1995 Monsieur Fromion called the *berceau* (cradle) of the 'Auld Alliance'.[50] Indeed, it was he who put paid to academic pedantry, which had developed in the lead-up to the 1995 celebrations. Historians insisted that the original manuscript descriptions of the Franco-Scottish alliance in treaties and official documents of '*les anciennes alliances des royaumens de France et Ecosse*'[51] should stand. Whilst linguists insisted that as '*ancienne*' now generally means 'former' it therefore should be called the '*vieille* (old)

---

47   Alain Chartier, who was a poet at Charles VII's court: my translation, Bonner, Elizabeth 1999 Scotland's 'Auld Alliance' with France, 1295–1560, *History*, Oxford: Blackwell Publishers, 84, 273, 5. For a recent photo of a much diminished stone cairn see: https://bit.ly/35H42GX.
48   The arms were established in the 1420s and derive from the ancient arms of the Stuarts of Aubigny's ancestor, Sir John Stewart of Bonkyl, who died on 22 July 1298 at the battle of Falkirk fighting under the command of Sir William Wallace (Hollywood's *Braveheart*) when the Scots were defeated by an English army under Edward I (known to British history as 'The Hammer of the Scots'). Red and gold were the Scottish monarchs' livery colours in the fifteenth century and continued to be those of the Scottish Royal House.
49   See: https://bit.ly/3hDiToj.
50   Conversation with with M. Fromion at Aubigny, July, 1995.
51   Hands Off Ireland Organisation, Commonwealth Investigation Branch, series B741, item V/26197, National Archives of Australia.

alliance' to create a sense of historic continuity. Indeed, at the time this latter version appeared on many posters, pamphlets and exhibition notices. But it took a politician to sweep aside academic semantics for a practical solution in French of the *'l'auld alliance'*, which has now been accepted in public and in particular academic circles. The benefits of this very pragmatic solution of the French adopting the Scottish word for 'old' is that the spelling and meaning of the 'Auld Alliance' remains exactly the same in both languages, only the pronunciation is different.

Finally, in the conclusion of his article Contamine directs the findings of his research to:

> a specialist in Scottish society of the period concerned, and in particular in its upper classes, [who] would be in a position to broaden the study to other cases, to determine their social and possibly their geographical origins, and to attempt to identify the reasons, not only economic but also political, which regularly led a certain number of Scots into temporary or permanent exile.[52]

This 1992 appeal is as yet unfulfilled. The only relatively recent substantial examination by a professional Scottish historian of Scottish participation in the Hundred Years' War during the fifteenth century is Brian Ditcham's thesis: 'The Employment of Foreign Mercenary Troops in the French Royal Armies, 1414–1470' (1979).[53] Also covering this period a *Colloque d'histoire Médiévale: Jeanne d'Arc, une époque, un rayonnement* was held at Orleans in 1979. Apart from French scholars, included in the published papers are those presented by English historians and others from Brazil, USA, Japan, Italy, Belgium and the then Soviet Union, but no historian of Scottish history is mentioned. Therefore, Scottish participation in the war was presented by Bernard Chevalier of the Université de Tours in 'The Scots in the armies of Charles VII up to the battle of Verneuil [1424]',[54] employing mainly

---

52 Contamine, Scottish Soldiers 25.
53 Ditcham, B. G. H. 1979 The Employment of Foreign Mercenary Troops in the French Royal Armies, 1414–1470, Unpublished PhD Thesis, Edinburgh University.

French sources with the exception of Balfour-Melville's *James I, King of Scots, 1406–1437* (1936) on which he relies exclusively for a Scottish perspective.[55]

Scottish historians, for the most part, have been content to consult not the manuscripts regarding the ancient tripartite relationship of Scotland, France and England but the mainly nineteenth-century published sources, not only the editions of the English State Papers of the Tudor Regime but also those of Scottish Family, Geographical and Institutional Papers published in a similar period;[56] as well as the contributions of the Scottish History Club publications. These latter Scottish publications are rarely mentioned by historians of Tudor history. Indeed, post World-War II, the Scots turned to their own indigenous manuscripts, state papers and muniments held in the Scottish Record Office, and in the national, regional and academic libraries, as well as those held by prominent families in their ancestral homes. A number of the archives of large establishments are managed by their own archivists with whom researchers make their own particular requests. For smaller establishments there are arrangements

---

54 Chevalier, Bernard 1982 *Les Écossais dans les armées de Charles VII jusqu'à la bataille de Verneuil*, Pernoud, Régine (Introduction) *Jeanne d'Arc, une époque, un rayonnement*, Paris: Centre régional de publication de Paris. Éditions du centre national de la recherche scientifique, quai Anatole-France 85–94. Chevalier introduces his article by summarising his opening statement (85) as 'an application of the "vieille alliance" déjà presque centenaire qui liait les deux royaumes', which acknowledges the linguistic preference in 1982 for the 'auld alliance'; see also, Chevalier, Bernard 1999 *Les Alliés Écossais au Service du Roi de France au XVe siécle*, Laidlaw, *The Auld Alliance* 47–58.

55 Balfour-Melville, E. W. M. 1936 *James I, King of Scots, 1406–1437*, London & Aberdeen: Methuen.

56 A few examples of the many: Bain, Joseph editor 1890 *The Hamilton Papers: Letters and Papers illustrating the Political Relations of England and Scotland in the XVIth century*, vol. 1, 1532–1543, Edinburgh: Adam & Charles Black; Ridpath, George 1848 editor, *The Border History of England and Scotland...*, Edinburgh: The Mercat Press; Thomson, T. & Innes, C. 1814–1875 editors, *Acts of the Parliaments of Scotland*, 1124–1707, 12 vols, Edinburgh: Scotland, Great Britain Record Commission, Edinburgh; Maidment, James editor 1834 *Analecta Scotia: Collections Illustrative of the Civil, Ecclesiastical and Literary History of Scotland*, Series I & II, Edinburgh: T. G. Stevenson.

with the Scottish Record Office staff to catalogue and manage their archival holdings and to make them available to researchers for access in the Record Office Search rooms in Edinburgh. In this way historians of Scottish history have had remarkable access to original documents of Scottish history since the post-war years. By the 1970s the publication of this new research began to filter down from the Scottish universities to the general public and educational institutions and changed forever the knowledge and teaching of Scottish history from primary schools to tertiary university levels. Missing on both sides of the border in this period, however, is archival research to any great degree into each other's original documents and manuscripts, which could possibly lead to misinterpretations in their subsequent historiographies. But of much longer duration in both ancient kingdoms is the lack of a critical interrogation of French archival material as regards their ancient tripartite relationship, not only in the archives and libraries of France but also in those held in the national archives and libraries of Scotland and England. Furthermore, a greater dearth of critical interrogation exists in France in this period where there is little evidence or publication that much research by French historians of original documents and manuscripts has taken place in this period into the archives and libraries of Scotland and England.

In the final analysis, therefore, the present memory of the Scottish soldiers' diaspora into France in the fifteenth century would appear to require the application of some academic foresight into the research of original documents and manuscripts, not only in the archives and libraries of all three ancient kingdoms of Scotland, France and England but also into others of interest such as the former Duchy of Brittany.[57] Currently there are, for example, numerous references in the Breton archives and libraries to Scottish-Breton treaties and alliances between the Scottish kings James I and James II and the dukes of Brittany in

---

57   The former Principality of Wales and Duchy of Brittany were not fully integrated into England and France until 1536 under Henry VIII and Francis I; Elton, G. R. second edition 1974 *England Under the Tudors*, Norwich, UK and New York: Methuen 176–79; Guy, John 1988 reprinted 1990 *Tudor England*, Oxford University Press 174–5; Knecht, R. J. 1994 *Renaissance Warrior and Patron: The Reign of Francis I*, Cambridge University Press 349–53.

the mid fifteenth century.[58] A further case in point as regards archival research in this period is that of Henry Tudor, duke of Richmond, who spent fourteen years in exile with his Uncle Jasper, earl of Pembroke, mainly in Brittany but also for about a year in France from 1471 to 1485.[59] This entire period, which ends with Henry claiming the English crown at Bosworth field on 22 August 1485, is an historically confused and contentious chapter in Anglo-Franco-Scottish history deriving from the stories and hearsay of contemporary chronicles to the numerous theories, recreations and hypotheses by secondary sources from the fifteenth to the twentieth centuries. Thus, it would appear that a transnational historical approach is advisable when making an interrogation of the archival holdings of original sources, concerning the ancient tripartite relationship of the kingdoms of Scotland, France and England. This approach should apply particularly during the Scottish 'Auld Military Alliance' with France against England from 1295 to 1560, which could perhaps clarify the Scottish soldiers' diaspora into France in the fifteenth century.

---

58 See *Supra*.
59 Chrimes says that 'Henry was brought up for the first fourteen years of his life (1457–71) in Wales and during these years may not have visited England more than once at most', Chrimes, *Henry VII* 3. This begs the question of how 'English', culturally and linguistically, was Henry Tudor in 1485.

8

Memories of a Celtic Past: Challenges to an Old Culture on the Changing Scottish and Australian Frontiers of Life

James Donaldson

Traditional Celtic culture after the year of 1746 was always vulnerable to change. When the underpinning patterns of Highland life lived under the system of clanship were destroyed and their cultural and political influences upon social and economic life left fractured and outmoded, the way was open for a flood of increased change and transformation. The extraordinary speed and intensity of economic growth emanating from England and Lowland Scotland, especially following the middle years of the eighteenth century, were little short of astonishing. The Highland regions were quickly drawn into the orbit of this expansion and commercial influence, yet many elements of the processes of transformation were initiated before 1745, as part of wider and prolonged English-speaking cultural imperialism over various parts of the British Isles.

Eric Cregeen has drawn attention to the radically altered conditions between the old Highlands and those of the new Highlands of the end of the eighteenth century:

> It is commonly held that the old highlands died on the field of Culloden in 1746, and that the subsequent statutes abolishing hereditary jurisdictions, military followings, highland dress, and the rest, destroyed the clan system. This is a naive and superficial view. What destroyed the old highland social and political

structure was its growing involvement in the general cultural influence of neighbours to the south, England and Scotland lowlands. This influence, expressed in speech, manners, religion, political sympathy and activity, trade, seasonal migration, and so on, was at work in the highlands a long time before 1745, and reached its climax considerably after.[1]

For many living at the time, the revolutionary process in the Highlands that took place during these decades was to be found in the belief that progress lay in the exploitation of the natural environment; and in the creation of income earnings through trade and commercial enterprises. This 'progress' was achieved through such innovations as the widespread production of seaweed kelping on the coastal sea shores; by the introduction of extensive sheep farming, with the consequent evictions of surplus local population; by changes made to the traditional methods of farm husbandry; by altering the attitudes to the economics of estate management; by the establishment of rent-paying crofters; by the development of coastal areas; and by the redirected use of the resident Highland people as the labour workforce. Creegan notes that:

> The economy of the highlands changed radically, so that its near-independence was transformed into almost total subordination to the demands of local industry. By the early nineteenth century the supply of cattle and sheep, wool, kelp and labour to the southern towns had become the specialised function of the west highlands.[2]

New patterns of relationships ensued, with the traditional ties between landed proprietors and their tenants becoming more commercially based on financial considerations, thus destroying a previous sense of community identity and belonging. Such changes impacted daily upon the people, their environment and their Gaelic culture, which

---

1   Cregeen, Eric 1970 The Changing Role of the House of Argyll in the Scottish Highlands, *Scotland in the Age of Improvement,* edited by N. T. Philipson and R. Micheson, Edinburgh University Press 5–23: 8.

2   Cregeen 9.

inevitably drew the Gaelic-speaking people living in the Highlands into the mainstream of contemporary English/Scottish ways of life and ultimately into a crisis of their Celtic identity.

Eric Richards aptly draws attention to the fact that

> Behind these large anonymous shifts in social and economic existence were the lives of individuals, the immigrant experience in reality. Consequently there is a tension in the juxtaposition of the broad forces of history with the biographies of particular, perhaps representative, Scottish emigrants.[3]

Significantly, the first complement of immigrant passengers to be selected by Dr David Boyter RN as part of the government migration scheme of 1837–1840, to sail for New South Wales on the ship *John Barry* of 524 tons, was not ready to sail from Dundee until 15 March 1837, more than nine months after Boyter's appointment had been verified in Britain. The backgrounds and origins of those on board reveal the fluid nature of movement of people in Scotland at this time and reflect very personal cultural influences. Many of the married adult migrants had a spouse who had been born at a distance from their own particular home location, while the children of these marriages were often born in cities other than those associated with their parental origins, such as Edinburgh, Glasgow, or Dundee. Of interest is the fact that the Counties of Banffshire, Perthshire, Forfarshire, Aberdeenshire, Sutherland-shire, Inverness-shire and Caithness-shire are represented among the emigrants from the Highlands on board this ship's passenger listing.

These facts reflect the uncertainty and volatility that abounded in Scotland at this time and gives weight to the theory that once Highland

---

3   Richards, Eric 1985 *Varieties of Scottish Emigration in the Nineteenth Century, Historical Studies* 21, 473–94: 475. See also: Richards, Eric 1982 *A History of the Highland Clearances; Agrarian Transformation and the Evictions 1746–1886*, London: Croom Helm. The work of Don Watson competently interweaves the tension in the juxtaposition of the broad forces of history with the biographies of particular, perhaps representative, Scottish emigrants and their interface relationships with the Aboriginals on the Gippsland frontier of Port Phillip District: Watson Don 1984 *Caledonia Australis,* Sydney: Collins.

people were subjected to enforced change, they became disconnected from their traditional roots. Their lives made barren by having fewer traditional Celtic attachments, they were more likely to seek relocation elsewhere, even to the extent of settling themselves permanently overseas.

Periodically, the economic and social conditions were so bleak in the Highlands that the actual choice to move away seemed to be the best of possible alternatives. While leaving their traditional origins would have presented a physically difficult transition for them, in terms of changing their geographical locations, and their partings from their former surroundings would have affected their lives, mentally and emotionally, in terms of the adaptation of their lives to new contexts and cultural transformation, the view of Linda Colley that Highlanders were sometimes poorly viewed by others living in other parts of Lowland Scotland surely would have added more stress to such movements of Gaelic-speaking people.

This patronising view of attitudes held within Britain itself of the Gaelic-speaking Highlanders living in Scotland is cited in a study of British identity:

> Even in the early 1800s for example, and despite the enormous impact of Sir Walter Scott's heroic evocation of the lochs and glens of the North, some Lowland Scots still automatically referred to their Highland neighbours as savages or as aborigines.[4]

This attitude, however, may essentially have been caused by these Highlanders not being able to speak or write the English language. This single factor adversely affected the occupations they could then occupy in the cities. It also conveys the intolerance of those living in the Lowlands towards others speaking a different language from their own, and a narrow-mindedness in their attitude against those Highlanders from the north not sharing their same culture. Differences such as these between peoples often contribute to suspicion, ill-considered

---

4   Colley, Linda 1992 British and Europeanness: Who are the British Anyway? *Journal of British Studies* 31 (4), 309–29. See also Colley, Linda 1992 *The Britons: Forging the Nation 1707–1837*, New Haven CT: Yale, for an interesting perspective upon the subject.

judgment and discrimination. It is often expressed in language as well as in behaviour.

Many men from the Highlands moved to the larger cities of Scotland such as Edinburgh, Glasgow, Aberdeen, Dundee and Paisley where they found jobs at the lower levels of employment. This was probably because many of them spoke only Gaelic, or had been previously employed as agricultural labourers and lacked formal education. Contemporary writers, at the end of the eighteenth century, make mention of such folk. T. Newte in 1791 wrote:

> As the offices of drudgery, and of labour, that require not any skill, are generally performed in London by Irishmen, and Welsh people of both sexes, so all such inferior departments are filled in Edinburgh by the Highlanders ... There is a constant influx of stout healthy men from the mountainous country into Edinburgh, as well as into other cities of note in Scotland to supply the places of porters, barrowmen, chairmen and such like.[5]

T. M. Devine presents a number of factors, which help to explain the continued use of Highlanders in the agriculture of the Lowlands despite the presence of Irish migrants.[6] He cites that the farmers in the Lowland belt between Ayrshire and the Lothians were slow to abandon the use of the Highlands as their source of tried, traditional and secure supply of labour. Secondly, although the Irish scythe-hook later did displace the Highland toothed-sickle as the predominant harvesting implement in this central harvesting belt, it also increased the need for more female workers. Significantly, most of the Irish migrants were male. Thirdly, Devine points to the fact that the Irish were to be found more in the districts in the western Lowlands and the south-east, while much of the rest was traditionally harvested by those from the Highland regions.

The economic conditions, if they were sufficient to move a significant number of people to Australia, when they were most

---

5   Newte, T. 1791 *Prospects and Observations on a Tour of England and Scotland*, London: G. G. J. and J. Robinson 362.
6   Devine, T. M 1979 Temporary Migration and the Scottish Highlands in the Nineteenth Century, *Economic History Review* 32, 344–59: 349.

reluctant to move to the Scottish mainland, even on a temporary basis, must have been challenging indeed. The 'push' factors in Scotland to emigrate must have far outweighed the 'pull' influences from Australia. This language element and an uncertainty of mind, of how they may have been received in the new country, may also offer a reason why these Highland passengers, such as those on board the ship *Midlothian*, were reluctant to separate from each other following their arrival in New South Wales. Many other families also sought to be engaged in employment by the same pastoral proprietor in the one location as such employment would offer them security and reassurance. This community togetherness and extended kinship represents another factor in their wishing to remain together following their arrival. It might also reflect an unwillingness to alter traditional patterns and familiar ways, and an awareness of the benefits of being close to others who shared their culture and their values.

Marjory Harper emphasises, what is in fact certainly true, that most Highlanders travelled in family groups, often with whole villages and neighbourhoods migrated together, filling single ships with emigrating families and neighbours, as they sought a new home.[7] This may have been because of the ongoing persistence of clan associations, or religious togetherness such as the Catholic Macdonalds of Glengarry, or the Gaelic language, which engendered separateness, while for those with it, a sense of extended community.

Interestingly, there is a contemporary reference to this very problem of isolation from one's roots, in a testimonial given in Scotland by the Rev. William Campbell of Coull, to the Rev. Colin Stewart, who became the chaplain to one of the later Highland emigrant ships to Australia, the *Boyne*, in late 1838. Stewart was subsequently appointed as the Presbyterian minister of Bowenfels in country New South Wales. In commending Stewart for service in the Colonial Ministry of the Church, Campbell stated on 16 June 1838, in his letter of commendation:

---

7   Harper, Marjory 1988 *Emigration from North East Scotland: Willing Exiles*, Aberdeen University Press 3.

In a testimonial bearing on Mr. Stewart's qualifications for forming and taking charge of a Gaelic congregation, I consider it my duty to state that a body of young highlanders from Loch Broom, Skye, etc. having during the great scarcity of last year, come in search of employment into this quarter, and resided for about two months in this parish, Mr. Stewart finding that they did not understand English, convened them in the parish church on the Sabbath evenings and preached to them in Gaelic, his own native language as well as theirs.[8]

It is clearly apparent, from the evidence available, that so many other Gaelic-speaking Highlanders immigrating from Scotland, in the period between the years 1837 and 1840 had already broken some of their traditional allegiances to the long-standing culture in the Highlands and were in a state of personal upheaval and transformation caused by the changes to their economic circumstances and social structures. These disruptive breaks with their culture were variously caused or influenced as a result of the following: an involvement with the kelping industry; years of temporary migration to the coastal regions to find jobs in the fishing industry; by moving to the lowlands for harvest employment; through young women accepting domestic service tasks in English-speaking households; young men making military commitments; as the result of marriage to non-Highlanders; the loss of Celtic culture and language within their local neighbourhoods; and the contrived loosening of their traditional connections to the soil resulting from the policies of landed estate owners. The *New Statistical Account* for the parish of Glenorchy and Inishail puts the situation of the changes to Highlanders caused by the introduction of sheep:

The introduction of sheep constitutes an era of great importance in the history of this, as of almost every other Highland parish. It effected everywhere in the Highlands, a complete revolution in the

---

condition of the population. It snapped the tie which bound the occupant to the owner of the soil ... the anticipated result followed. [9]

Those few Highlanders or English-speaking workers who continued to live upon these lonely sheep-walk estates did so in locations that had formerly been the scene of a vibrant Highland life that had virtually disappeared with the coming of sheep. These innovations meant that many small hamlets disappeared, especially in remote regions, and the people resident in them were dispersed to other places. This planned procedure of change thus created a human supply of labour that was socially and geographically divorced from its original communal economy. Community and culture were fractured. For the old, their traditional lifestyle became the stuff of memory, while the young embraced the new opportunities of a changed situation. Eric Richards has noted that

> Much of the development effort in the Highlands was directed towards the separation of the common people from their dependence on the old communal runrig/pastoral economy. The creation of villages and the settlement of small plots of coastal land was intended to replace the old agriculture. [10]

The process of change caused by such revolutionary transformations was irreversible, and its outcomes, although resisted, remained final and decisive. The psychological break with the land, once begun, caused the solidarity of traditional life and culture in the glens and straths to fade with it.

James Hunter properly draws attention to the loosening of traditional ties with the land brought about by crofting and kelping:

> For proprietors to thus encourage, in fact compel, an essentially agricultural people to become dependent for their livelihood on

---

9   *New Statistical Account,* Parish of Glenorchy and Inishail VII.93. See note 14 below for full publication details.
10   Richards, *A History* 129.

non-agricultural pursuits ... whether kelping or fishing ... was a recipe for ultimate catastrophe.[11]

Each of the elements which loosened traditional ties to the land and traditional life contributed significantly to the decline of the traditional Celtic culture, and particularly to the decline in the use of the Gaelic language, especially among the young. Such diversions and changes acted as a means of breaking the bond from the land, both psychologically as well as materially, thus making it easier for Highlanders to move elsewhere when circumstances pressured them to do so. This, of course, is what happened with the decline of the kelping manufacture, following the Napoleonic wars, and was the cause of economic devastation for both landlord and tenant alike. In order to compensate for a lack of monies with which to pay the rentals on their crofts, the surplus Highland peasantry resorted to temporary migration as a means of earning an income with which to pay their rents.[12]

The periodic absences of members of the family engaged in temporary migration enabled the meagre supplies of food resources to last longer among the members of the family who remained at home, yet their absences meant a loss of relationship and community; longer hours and harder toil for those who were left behind; a neglected croft; and a greater absenteeism of children from their schools due to their being required to accomplish crofting tasks at home. Time spent away from family, community and church involvements was a negative factor in the sustenance and maintenance of a Gaelic culture. Altered attitudes of younger people to the old culture broke the links with generations of the past.[13] It fostered a break-up of Celtic identity. It became a part of the regular rhythm of a fracturing Highland life, yet, each of the elements within it loosened their ties to their heritage, and contributed significantly to the decline and erosion of the traditional

---

11   Hunter, James 1976 *The Making of the Crofting Community*, Edinburgh: John Donald 31.
12   Gray, Malcolm 1957 *The Highland Economy 1750–1850*, Edinburgh: Oliver and Boyd.
13   For this aspect, see Bil, Albert 1990 *The Shieling 1600–1840: The Case of the Central Scottish Highlands*, Edinburgh: John Donald.

Celtic culture, and particularly to the decline in the use of the Gaelic language. The older traditional speakers of Gaelic could do little to prevent its passing. The same trends are readily evident in the records of the Gaelic-speaking Highland migrants in Australia.

Decline of the Gaelic Language

Between the late seventeenth century and the beginning of the nineteenth century, there is substantial evidence that a change and loss in language had occurred, both in the spatial sense of territory within the Highlands, particularly in the east-central Highlands, in central Perth-shire and in parts of the south-west Highlands, and in the prominence of the Gaelic language to be found in daily living and culture. The geographical area within which Gaelic-speaking was predominant continued to shrink under this general cultural influence during the first half of the nineteenth century, as a comparison of the *Old Statistical Account* (1791–1799) with the *New Statistical Account* (1834–1845) clearly shows.[14] There are many existent contemporary illustrations to be found within the pages of the *New Statistical Account* of the decline of the Gaelic language in local parishes over the period.

The Rev. Murdo Cameron, minister of the Parish of Creich in Sutherland-shire, wrote: 'The Gaelic language is spoken in the parish but the English has now gained so much ground that it may be said to be spoken by the greater number of the inhabitants.'[15] This is typical of many parish reports, and indicates a wide transformation taking place across many districts. Church parishes like Edinkillie and Knockando[16] in Moray, which had used Gaelic as a medium of devotion in worship and preaching in the mid-seventeenth century no longer did so, ninety years later.[17] The *New Statistical Account* for Knockando signified that

---

14 *Old Statistical Account of Scotland 1791–1799,* edited by John Sinclair, 21 vols, Edinburgh: William Creech; *New Statistical Account of Scotland 1834–1845,* edited by John Gordon, 15 vols, Edinburgh: Blackwood.
15 *New Statistical Account,* Parish of Creich, XV.19.
16 *New Statistical Account,* Parish of Knockando, XIII.60.
17 A study of the Gaelic-speaking areas of Scotland, known in the language as the '*Gaelhealtachd*' has been made by Withers, Charles, W. J. 1981 The

although Gaelic had been spoken in the parish 'not very long ago', there were 'now not above a dozen individuals who understood it and not half of these were natives'.[18] Although still designated a 'Highland Parish', Knockando was a parish where the memories of a Gaelic past were now fast fading into distant recollection.

The District Presbytery of Caithness (a regional synod of Presbyterian Church government) by the year of 1840 had come to the crucial decision to discontinue the practice of preaching the sermons in the Gaelic language, within the bounds of the mission station of Bruan, a small settlement area in the eastern district of the Parish of Latheron. This Highland Presbytery took the unprecedented step of appointing a missionary there who could not speak the Gaelic tongue. Thus, not only would the language of worship and preaching be displaced from the gathered spiritual life of the congregation with its consequent loss of shared community values, but the capacity of the new minister to counsel and advise the Highland people in pastoral situations would be rendered impossible to the congregation in their native language. This appointment represented not only a loss of language but inevitably a loss of being and culture. For Highlanders whose whole tradition of worship and spirituality had relied upon the Gaelic language as the medium of thought and reflection, and as a means of developing their growth in piousness and prayer, this step must have been almost ruinous to their way of life.[19] That parish's *Statistical Account* report indicates that had it not been for the fact that several small communities of Gaelic-speaking Highlanders had been forcibly removed from the district around

---

Geographical Extent of Gaelic in Scotland 1698–1806, *Scottish Geographical Magazine* 97 (3), 130–39; Withers, Charles W. J. 1982 Gaelic Speaking in a Highland Parish: Port of Monteith, *Scottish Geographical Magazine* 98, 16–23; and Withers, Charles W. J. 1984 *Gaelic in Scotland 1698–1981: the Geographical History of a Language Region*, Edinburgh: John Donald.

18 *New Statistical Account*, Parish of Knockando, XIII.72.

19 This would certainly have been the case for the people living within the boundaries of the Parish of Ardchattan, County of Argyle, described in the *New Statistical Account*, where it is recorded that, 'More than nine-tenths of the people prefer religious instruction in the Gaelic, while a majority can receive such instruction through the medium of that language: *New Statistical Account*, Parish of Ardchattan, VII.502.

Kildonan (a small village in Strath Ullie, in Sutherland-shire) as a result of the territorial expansion of sheep runs, and had been relocated within the jurisdiction of the Latheron Parish, the loss of the Gaelic language and the encroachment of the English language would have been more extensive and rapid. Significantly, even this influx of Gaelic speakers into the parish had not been sufficient to delay the appointment of an English-speaking minister without the Gaelic tongue, nor the influential expansion of the English language into the parish. The changing tide was obviously coming in quickly upon the shores of the Gaelic language. The old Gaelic tradition was dying out with the passing of the older people while the younger generation chose to adhere to the new paradigm of life.

There are many existent contemporary illustrations of the decline of the Gaelic language in local parishes. The causes of the fast decline of the Gaelic language in the county of Sutherland in the forty years prior to 1840 were attributed by Golspie's minister, the Rev. Alexander Macpherson, to better education and the residence of 'persons from the south country'.[20] Significantly, the period of the forty years being referred to was precisely the same forty years that had seen the development of sheep runs in the district, and the occupation of the land in large farms, operated and managed by people other than the traditional Highland peasantry, and whose primary language was not Gaelic but English, and whose presence and behaviour were also to add culturally in its decline as a medium of social interaction.

Charles W. J. Withers has shown that that Highland rural communities were bilingual along the fringe lines of Highland margins, while Albert Bil was unable to find any known records written in Gaelic being used in Perthshire during both the seventeenth and eighteenth centuries.[21] Bil concluded that the lack of Gaelic writing in these districts reflected an ascendency of English and Lowland Scots as the medium of written business, although many Perthshire landowners continued to understand the spoken Gaelic language. There was a preference for English in its written forms, probably because the language as a vehicle of commerce and trade was more universally understood. Many Gaelic speakers in Perthshire could not read their own Gaelic language nor

---

20 *New Statistical Account,* Parish of Golspie, XV.35.
21 Withers, Gaelic Speaking in a Highland Parish; Bil 35.

indeed write it. Thus, on this very boundary of changing culture within Scotland itself, where the Gaelic language was becoming lost and the Celtic culture placed into severe decline, the place of memory and shared recollection between those Highland Celtic people left behind by the moving frontiers of change must have remained as only the sad, almost forgotten, remnants of an altered pattern of life.

In many places, while Gaelic continued to be spoken in the home, it was the English language that had become the language of trade and commercial life. Many Highlanders, especially those men who were engaged in commercial business dealings, also spoke English; whereas women, who were more inclined to be involved with home and family, were less likely to be fluent in the use of English. This scenario was also true of life on the Australian frontiers. This necessity of learning and practising English in order to participate in commerce, or to earn a living, beyond the Gaelic frontiers was a powerful influence in the breaking down of the Gaelic language. Progressively, as time passed, English became more and more necessary. Catherine Sinclair, writing in 1840, noted the growing necessity in her journal:

> Not all persons in the Highlands are now so accomplished as to speak two languages fluently. Those who are born to use the Gaelic tongue only, often start for Glasgow, the instant they have realised the necessary funds, to 'get English'.[22]

Memories of a Highland Past in New South Wales

The consequential results for the Highland Gaelic-speakers in making their new homes in Australia were far more drastic than any mere theory of disruption or process of language decline. For them, it was a matter of being gradually dispossessed from their traditional language, their core of culture, their living heritage and their past way of life. It is both an actual and a symbolic example of the process of disorientation. The reality of the change had many emotional repercussions and

---

22 Sinclair, Catherine 1840 *Scotland and the Scotch or Western Circuit*, Edinburgh: Wm Whyte and Coy 228.

psychologically related effects upon the Gaelic-speaking Highlanders who were caught up in it.

The plight of Gaelic-speaking migrants who made the long journey by ship to New South Wales in the years 1837 to 1840 can be readily appreciated. 'In the ships that Dr Boyter is sending from the Hebrides, it may be presumed that the majority of the passengers will be Presbyterian and speak little else but Gaelic';[23] indeed, many of the Highland immigrants, especially those from the more isolated and rugged parts of the Highlands, were completely unable to speak any English. The clash of cultures started for many Gaelic-speaking women, and especially for those who were pregnant, as soon as they boarded the Highland ships, which had been chartered by the Royal Navy for the use of the Highland migrant voyages.

It must have been something of a surprise to have discovered, as those men and women on board the first ship, the *William Nichol* from Skye, certainly did, that the Medical Officer on board the ship was an Officer of the Royal Navy, who did not speak the Gaelic language. His expertise in obstetrics was likely to have been limited, as experience of assisting women at childbirth was not normally gained from working among the sailors of the Royal Navy.[24]

Women especially, whose lives had been more sheltered from English speech and outside culture, were often completely unable to speak, write, or to understand English. The *Sydney Gazette* of 19 December 1837, published only days after the disembarkation of the *Midlothian* passengers, noted that a

large majority (of them were) ignorant of any other language than that of the ancient Gael, and that even those who speak English were much too imperfectly acquainted with it to worship God after the manner of their fathers in that language.[25]

---

23   Mr T. F. Elliot to Under Secretary Stephen, Enclosure No. 3 Glenelg to Bourke, 28 June 1837, *Historical Records of Australia* XIX.29.
24   This difficulty was phased out in the later Highland ships where native Gaelic-speaking surgeons were appointed.
25   Apart from the obvious meaning of the newspaper report, the message relating to the inability of the Highlanders to worship God in any other language than in the Gaelic language may also be a part of the proposal,

No worse experience could be imagined for a Gaelic-speaking woman than that of Christina Gillies, who sailed on the ship *Midlothian* from the Isle of Skye and who possessed no English whatsoever. After her husband, John Gillies, had died in February 1838, his wife Christina became ill in body and mind and was placed in the Benevolent Asylum. The record of her plight, dated 9 March 1838, included a report of her situation: 'Colonial Office—Christina Gillies with youngest child could be received into Benevolent Society—imbecile state of body and mind.' Christina had been one of those suffering from the effects of scurvy, and no doubt was one of those women described in the Sydney papers as being in 'a very delicate state of health' on her arrival of the *Midlothian*.[26] What a predicament for Mrs Christina Gillies to have found herself in within three months of landing in Australia. She had experienced a husband dying on arrival in Sydney; she was the grieving mother of three dead children, with her other surviving children in the orphanage, while she was still suffering from the effects of scurvy, and being temporary delicate in mind, having been placed in an asylum. She was isolated in the asylum from her Highland friends, and was unable to speak any words of English, but converse only in her native Gaelic language. She later recorded, that 'Some of the poor Highland Emigrants got me out of it on account of having no English.'[27]

The total incapacity of many of these people in English reflects that their life on Skye must have remained largely isolated, even from those on Skye who were bilingual. Fortunately, after her release, Christina Gillies lived to a grand old age, dying on 14 September 1892 and was later buried at the Maclean Cemetery on the Clarence River. There she rests with other Highland emigrants from the *Midlothian*.

---

encouraged by Dr John Dunmore Lang, for them to remain together by settling in the one geographical location as a body.

26 The fact that many of the female passengers on board the *Midlothian* were in a 'very delicate state of health' on disembarkation was noted in both the *Sydney Gazette* and the *Sydney Herald* in the week following the landing of the *Midlothian* on 20 December 1837.

27 Petition of Christina Gillies 20 December 1842 to the Colonial Secretary, received 27 December 1842. The petition was rejected by the Governor, Sir G. Gipps, 30 December 1842.

In fact, many resident settlers living in the Colony could not tell the difference between those speaking in broad Scots or Scotch and those newcomers speaking in Gaelic. This comment from the *Commercial Journal* (18 July 1838) clearly illustrates:

> We were very much surprised when passing by the immigrants quarters on Monday morning last about the hour of seven o'clock, to observe a man (who on enquiry turned out to be an emigrant by the *Duncan*) entering the gate of that establishment in a state of beastly intoxication, supported by two women (one of them his wife) also in a state of mental oblivion; and with barely sufficient animation to squeak out with a purely Gaelic accent, 'We'll gang nae mair to Scotland dear.' Mr Bell very properly cut short their music and sent them about their business.[28]

Here obviously is an illustration of a newly arrived Scottish immigrant, suffering the sadness of homesickness and loss of his culture, but whose broad Scotch language could not be recognised by his Sydney listeners and misidentified it for the Gaelic tongue.

In later years, the *Maitland Mercury* newspaper offered several illustrations, relating to several of these very same Gaelic-speaking Highlanders who could neither speak nor write fluently in the English language. At the end of an article published in the *Sydney Morning Herald* (28 August 1841), written to the Sydney editor by a group of Highland tenant farmers from the 'Dunmore' Estate, several made 'X' marks rather than signing their own names. Significantly, no less than fourteen of these 'Dunmore' men were unable to write their own names. Many of these were the Gaelic-speaking *Midlothian* migrants from Skye.

Some like John McSwan and Angus Beaton had no comments recorded against their names on arrival. Some of the co-signers, such

---

28 The comment concerning the 'Duncan' migrants speaking in a broad Scotch accent, brought to mind the humorous remark contained in the pages of the *South Australian Colonist* 25 August 1840: 'Excellent Whiskey'—'A friend of ours had some excellent whiskey of such superlatively excellent quality, that one tumbler makes a man talk broad Scotch, and three glasses, pure Gaelic.'

as Donald Munro, had stated incorrectly that they were able to read and write, but had made an 'X' mark. Exceptions to this group of tenant signatories were other *Midlothian* passengers from Skye, who could write their names, such as William McLeod, Lachlan Grant and Fergus Ferguson, the former schoolmaster, and who were obviously more clearly literate in English than some of their fellow tenants.

The *Maitland Mercury* (29 April 1843) carried a story about a Highlander who had a very imperfect knowledge of English, and whose evidence in court was given through the medium of an interpreter. He had sold a quantity of potatoes to a lady in Morpeth, and had received change for a one-pound note instead of a ten-pound note. This Highlander was the same *Midlothian* passenger, Angus Bethune or Angus Beaton. It is not so strange that someone will try to defraud another, but rather to discover that Angus as a Scot, did not know his local currency, even after living five years in Australia. The fact that he, like others, had not learned the English language more fluently in the years following his coming to Australia illustrates that he probably spent most of his life and time on the Paterson only in the midst of other Gaelic speakers.

Following the arrival of the third Highland ship, the *Brilliant*, in late January 1838, which brought the total number of Highland immigrants to about one thousand people who had sailed from the Isle of Skye and Isle of Mull and adjacent mainland locations in a short period of only three months, the *Sydney Morning Herald* (5 March 1838) reported that '[v]ery few of these persons can speak English which is a great drawback to their usefulness as labourers'. Thus, a lack of capacity to speak English not only hindered their ability to find work in Scotland, but with Australian country proprietors or Sydney companies. Being impelled by circumstances to accept employment as shepherds or country labourers in isolated New South Wales almost certainly meant becoming geographically separated from other Gaelic speakers and having to rely upon other family members for the preservation and use of their native language. Their incapacity to communicate with any person that they came into contact with, and to make themselves understood in everyday situations without any English, must have been a serious disadvantage to both themselves and to others. This is the reason why so many of the Highland immigrants chose to seek employment in districts such as the Hunter River, and later in the Manning River settlements where there was a significant presence of other Gaelic speakers, living in scattered communities along the rivers.

Alexander MacKillop, one of the two young men aboard the ship *Brilliant* who acted as teachers for the Highland children on the voyage (and later to become the father of Mother Mary MacKillop, the first Roman Catholic Saint in Australia), stated in the first of his three letters to the Colonial Secretary, Mr Deas Thomson, written in Sydney on 1 February 1838, that he had 'acted as interpreter between them [namely, the Highlanders] and the gentlemen who came to engage them, and to acquaint them with the character of the latter previous to their final agreement'.[29]

Thus, for these brave Gaelic shepherds from the Highland ships, the *William Nichol*, the *Midlothian* and the *Brilliant*, their placement on isolated sheep runs in the frontier areas of New South Wales with their families put their Gaelic culture under severe threat. The Gaelic-speaking minister Colin Stewart, who had arrived as chaplain on board the ship *Boyne*, was an important support in sustaining these Gaelic speakers, by continuing to have an ongoing relationship with them over many years while he was resident at the Vale of Clwyd. To do this he was obliged to travel many miles from his home parish. For such families, generally isolated from other Gaelic-speaking families, working as shepherd servants, the visit of a Gaelic-speaking minister must have provided a refreshing and welcoming uplift.[30] It was virtually

---

29   Correspondence from Alexander MacKillop to Deas Thomson, Colonial Secretary Correspondence Reel 38/1114, NSW State Archives. MacKillop probably means that he acquainted the prospective employers with the characters of the *Brilliant* immigrants that he knew through his involvement with them on the voyage rather than the background character of the proprietors that he did not know. The spelling of his name is taken from his signature at the foot of his letters.

30   It was common practice for Presbyterian ministers living in small township communities of the colonies of NSW and Victoria where they were located to make extended journeys on horseback into the countryside to make contact with Scottish settlers and shepherds and their families in order to maintain links with the Presbyterian Church and their adherents. At the time it was common for ministers to conduct services and baptise children. This practice

the only means of Celtic encouragement, apart from the occasional Highland neighbour or family member with whom they could converse in their own tongue. Without this opportunity, it was easy to imagine how quickly their cultural background could quickly become lost living on these frontiers, sustained by few supports if any, to their former past existence. Their memories of the Celtic past must have remained precious reminders of a far and distant lifestyle.

Stewart's Church Register shows that he regularly ministered to these Scottish shepherd migrant families on his visitations to isolated locations such as Cullen Bullen, where on no less than three separate occasions during the 1840s he baptised the children of Allan Kennedy, on the very same day as the children of Archibald Cameron; and once on the same day as Archibald McVicar's child.[31] He also conducted separate baptismal services for McVicar, and for another Highlanders: Peter McPhee and his wife Jane McMaster from Kilmalee in Argyllshire, who had four children baptised in three different locations in the 1840s; William McMillan also from Kilmalee, at Dubbo; and Donald McPhail from Mull. McVicar's niece Catherine, the daughter of his brother Norman, was married in Stewart's home in 1842. Catherine continued having children until 1867, and at least one of them was baptised by Stewart before the Pound family moved to Carcoar in the Lachlan District in 1850.

In contrast, other Scottish shepherds, being ministered to by the Reverend Colin Stewart, the *Boyne* passengers, Allan McDonald at Delegate in the Maneroo (Monaro), and James Campbell and Catherine McMaster, shepherds in the service of Sir Frances Forbes at

---

can be illustrated from the Diary of William Hamilton (National Library of Australia Manuscript Library); and by Rev. Peter Gunn, who was associated with the Campbellfield Presbyterian Church, and who came to Melbourne on 25 February 1824. Because he was known to have the Gaelic he was commissioned to minister to the Gaelic-speaking Highlanders. See also, Robert Hamilton, 1888 *A Jubilee History of the Presbyterian Church of Victoria*, Melbourne: 27; Robert J Wilson, 1975 *The Apostle in the Saddle; the Life of the Central West of New South Wales in the Nineteenth Century*, Carcoar NSW: Carcoar Village Society.

31 Parish Records for Vale of Clwyd, Presbyterian Church, Ferguson Library Archives, Sydney.

Queanbeyan in 1839, had to rely upon Anglican priests, the Reverend E. G. Pryor and the pioneer priest in the Canberra district, the Reverend Edward Smith for the baptism of their children.[32] Another *Boyne* passenger, Donald Cameron, a shepherd, and his wife Anne McPhee, who had been engaged by the Macarthurs at Camden before moving to Palmerville in the Ginnindera district in 1840, also had a child named Charles (after Charles Campbell) baptised by the Reverend Edward Smith in 1842.

Many immigrants who found work as shepherds or overseers of sheep runs were employed in the outer districts where the Presbyterian Church had no settled minister. Many were employed by landed proprietors who were Anglicans, and who were regularly visited by priests of their own denomination. They, like their fellow Scots living in the margin counties of Scotland who became open to the powerful influence of the English-speaking commercial imperialism, were made most vulnerable by their situation, and left helpless to preserve the future of their Gaelic culture around them.

Some Highlanders from the *Midlothian*, like Donald McLean and his wife Catherine, went much further northwards to the Upper Hunter than the 'Dunmore group', and they worked as labourers and shepherds in more remote locations, like Skellator near Muswellbrook. In 1838, these districts were the lonely frontiers of settlement, isolated from neighbours, medical help and supplies, and often subjected to attacks from the Aboriginals, trying to stem the expansion of the pastoralists upon their traditional lands. The McLean parents had their children baptised by Anglican priests because the Presbyterians had not established themselves there in the Upper Hunter at that time. There, on 29 March 1840, the Rev. John Morse, chaplain to the Australian Agricultural Company, baptised their son, Donald, on the same day as Alexander McLennan from the *William Nichol* and his wife Mary,

---

32 The Campbells, however, later moved to Webber's Creek near Tocal on Paterson River in 1841 and had three children baptised by the Gaelic-speaking minister William Ross, who was the minister at Paterson during the 1840s. The James Campbell family later joined with many of their Highland companions to settle in Dingo Creek, where their daughter Sarah was married in 1857, by the Rev. James Carter to a Scottish immigrant shipwright from Fyfe.

who had gone to Invermein, had their child baptised.[33] These Gaelic-speaking Highlanders living on the frontiers were placed in the sad situation of losing their traditional identity and culture, simply because the underpinning supports of their Celtic culture and life had been lost by them.

The Commercial Journal (5 October 1839) included a tale of a traveller who hurt himself twelve miles from Cudgelong, and being in agony and in need of friendly help found a ready refuge and the sensitive care he required in the rustic cottage of a Highlander named Kennedy who had a wife and six children. None of these children could speak any language but Gaelic: 'While I lay in agony, it was pleasing to hear the little children chaunting their Gaelic songs as it were a soothing lullaby to a hapless traveller.' This may well have been Charles Kennedy and his family from Lochaber, in Inverness-shire, passengers on the *Boyne*, bravely keeping their Celtic tradition alive in their children, through the happy remembrances of singing their Gaelic songs.

In the later year of 1843, the first elections were held in New South Wales. Dr John Dunmore Lang was a candidate. At the small township of Paterson on 15 July 1843, a riot took place and a young man named Duncan McGillivray, a Highlander from Ardnamurchan in Argyle-shire, an emigrant per the *George Fyfe*, was injured and killed. During the trial of the two prisoners, great difficulty would have been experienced by the court and by the jury, from the fact that several of the witnesses being Highlanders had a very limited knowledge of English, had not the services of an interpreter been obtained. At the trial Duncan McIntyre, and Hector McDonald from the *Brilliant*, gave evidence through an interpreter in the Gaelic language.[34] That instance is probably one of the only murder trials held in Australia where the Gaelic language was

33 Parish Records for Vale of Clwyd.
34 Hector was married at Bracadale on the Isle of Skye in 1825. His wife Ann died on the passage to Australia. McDonald was a farmer residing on Mr Eales's land and had known the accused prisoner Kelly for four years. See *Maitland Mercury* 19 September 1843. The minister of the Church who wrote his character reference was the Rev. Roderick McLeod, minister of Snizort, who was ordained in 1823, and died on 23 March 1868. He was a Disruption minister of 1843. He was the son-in-law of the Rev. Donald McQueen from Kilmuir, the erudite minister who met James Boswell.

used as the language of legal justice. While the result of the trial is not of importance in this instance, the fact that it could only be conducted effectively with the help of a Gaelic interpreter, then a police constable, who had sailed on board the *Brilliant*, certainly is.

Many of the *Brilliant* passengers gave indications that they were of a higher educational standard than some of the Skye migrants, being able to both read and write. The very large and extended family of James McLaurin, from Dunoon, were clearly able to speak and write in English. Such comments as 'Can read and write well'; 'Reads Gaelic', and 'Can read and write English' are common. These immigrants had obviously come from locations where the English-speaking influence upon their Gaelic culture had been tempered by their capacity to receive an adequate knowledge in English literacy. Obvious among many of the records of the *Brilliant* passengers are comments such as, 'Can read and write a little'; 'Cannot read nor write'; 'Neither reads nor writes'; 'Reads a little', and 'Can read but cannot write'.[35] These literary comments made on arrival in Sydney would indicate that the Gaelic language was spoken in many of the homes associated with the Isles of Mull, Coll and Tiree and mainland Morven in Argyle-shire, but that the capacity to write in Gaelic or read in English was not always present. Years after her arrival, the wife of Lachlan McKay living in the Bathurst district was still unable to converse in the English language: 'She hasna yae a word o'English, puir auld crature and now am prood to say that she has mair coos than she kens what to do wi'.[36] Gaelic remained orally strong and flourished amongst those orders of rural Highland society who had received little formal education.

This adherence to the Gaelic language remained strongly amongst such people, notwithstanding the fact that their native language from

---

35   The literacy questions asked of the Highlanders upon arrival in Sydney make no reference to the emigrants' capacity to read, speak and communicate in Gaelic. The answers given by the emigrants and written down by the English-speaking emigration clerk probably refers only to abilities in English(Disembarkation Records for Ship *Brilliant* on arrival January 1838, NSW State Archives). The literacy comments relating to other immigrants from the Highlands and Islands are similar in other ships such as the *Midlothian, British King, Hero* and the *James Moran* arriving in the same time period.
36   Hood, John, 1843 *Australia and the Far East* John Murray: London 132.

the 1820s was being constantly corrupted by the intrusion of the English tongue into the very heart of their community life. The writer of the *New Statistical Account* for the Isles of Coll and Tiree stated in his Parish report that this had occurred, 'in consequence of their frequent intercourse with the low country',[37] an opinion that was again recorded in the 'Parish Report of Strath in Skye', where it was noted: 'but of late, in consequence of the constant intercourse held by the natives with the low country, it is very much corrupted with a mixture of English words and phrases'.[38] This phenomenon might be understood as an illustration of the finality of their plight as one of the traditional and fundamental aspects of their Highland life, namely their native language, crumbled around them. When the undergirding ultimates in life fell away, one by one, the culture collapsed, or was largely displaced.[39] Those who could not, or would not, make the necessary cultural adjustments to become fluent in English continued to live and die within their Gaelic paradigm, as did Mrs McKay in Australia.

The *Australian*, 8 May 1839, commented, that 'the women and children are frequently unable to speak or even understand, a single word of English'. A return from the ship *James Moran*, which sailed from Loch Inver in Ross-shire and which arrived in Sydney on 11 February 1839, confirms this statement. Many married couples such, as the 38-year-old Alexander McLeod and his 38-year-old wife Ann McLeod are listed as 'Cannot read nor write'; and 37-year-old Donald McDonald and his 29-year-old wife Kate McDonald listed as 'Neither reads nor writes'; and 50-year-old Roderick McKenzie and his 46-year-old wife, Barbara McKenzie, 'Neither reads nor writes.' Being illiterate, Roderick did not know when he was born.[40] Thus, these older migrants qualifying for a free passage to Australia from rural Ross-shire, and speaking only Gaelic, were completely illiterate in reading and writing in their own language. Some others, such as Alexander Bain and his wife Catherine, could only read, as could

---

37 *New Statistical Account,* Parish of Coll and Tiree, VIII.220
38 *New Statistical Account,* Parish of Strath, XIV.380
39 Withers, *Gaelic Scotland 1698–1981* 236
40 Disembarkation Records for Ship *James Moran,* February 1839, NSW State Archives.

Duncan Ferguson and his wife Mary Ferguson, but clearly could not write. Hugh Morrison, a 28-year-old from the Parish of Eddrachilles in Sutherland-shire, could read and write a little while his 26-year-old wife Barbara from the same place could neither read nor write. Most of the other ninety-seven adults on board could read and write, even imperfectly. Most of the younger unmarried men and women on the *James Moran* possessed some degree of literacy, although some did not know the month in which they were born. The men especially were able to read and write. Two women, Mary McKay from Assynt and Catherine McKay from Erribol in Sutherland-shire, were able to read in Gaelic. While three of these couples went to the Hunter River to the one proprietor, and thus could stay in close touch with each other, many of the others went separately to the frontiers of the Colony and took up pastoral life in isolated parts of New South Wales. There their Gaelic heritage was placed at risk of becoming only a memory.

The elements of isolation in the interior of the Colony; the intermarrying of these immigrants into non-Gaelic speaking families; the cultural influence of their pastoral proprietors who employed them; the ongoing involvement with Anglicanism for baptisms and marriages; the lack of Gaelic-speaking parish ministers for social encouragement and administration of the Sacraments; the declining strength of Gaelic-speaking congregations; the lack of Gaelic speech among their own children; the passage of time; the death of parents, and the deeper involvement of these immigrants in the day-to-day activities of ordinary Australian life, each contributed to the fading of the Gaelic culture and language. This, despite revivals from time to time could never have regained the former tradition as it once was in Scotland. These elements, together with a lack of sufficient, gathered numbers of Gaelic-speaking families in frontier Australia made the continuance of their Gaelic culture and language in the face of an alien English-speaking Colonial society even more difficult than it had been for those living in marginal counties in many parts of Scotland.

Even when these Gaelic-speaking Highlanders settled together in close proximity to each other, the ultimate maintenance of the language was not to be assured in the midst of variant and powerful Colonial cultural factors operating against its continuation. The observation made in the pages of the *Sydney Gazette* (27 January 1838) regarding the future of the Gaelic language spoken among migrants from the ship *Midlothian* who went to settle together as a community at 'Dunmore' on the Hunter River sadly did not endure. The *Gazette* states that

> Twenty-three families consisting in all of upwards of one hundred and twenty individuals compose the germ of this new highland settlement where it is probable the language of the Gael may form the medium of general communication for ages to come.

The reference to the Gaelic language being spoken 'for ages to come' is an intriguing one. As long as these migrants remained together, there were attempts made by the various branches of the Presbyterian churches in New South Wales to gain their allegiance.[41] Without this critical mass of families who continued to speak Gaelic, the language over the years sadly fell into a rapid decline.

Early in March 1838, soon after their arrival on the Hunter River, many of the *Midlothian* emigrants signed a 'call' inviting the Rev. Robert Blain to undertake the pastoral charge of Scot's Church in the Maitland parish of the Presbyterian Church. The names of these Highlanders comprised a significant proportion of the 134 adults who subscribed to the invitation. Interestingly, there is no record whatsoever that the chosen minister, the Rev. Robert Blain, spoke any Gaelic at all, and would therefore not have been an obvious first choice for most of those Highlanders, as many of them spoke only that language. Robert Blain was, however, an ordained minister of the Church of Scotland, and Presbyterian, a bond, which he and the Highlanders shared in common; and significantly, was a minister in favour with the Rev.

---

41 For a more detailed consideration of this intriguing topic of Presbyterian church influence upon the Highlanders in the Hunter; and the part played by the Rev. Dr John Dunmore Lang in the migration and settlement of these Highlanders on his brother's property at 'Dunmore', see my book *Farewell to the Heather*, privately published 2004 and its subsequent revisions and reprints until 2015.

Dr John Dunmore Lang, whose support, and favourable persuasion, probably facilitated the 'call to the parish'.[42]

Later in the same year, in October 1838, the Sacrament of Communion, known among Presbyterians as The Lord's Supper, was dispensed for the first time at the new Scot's Church, with the Minister Robert Blain being assisted by the Rev. William McIntyre, the former chaplain on board the *Midlothian*. The report in the *Colonist* (3 October 1838) stated that thirty-six people were present: 'Mr McIntyre preached on the Saturday at Maitland in the English language and in Gaelic, both on the Saturday and Sabbath evenings in the new schoolhouse at Dunmore.' Presumably, the Highlanders did not attend the Communion service in English at Maitland, as the small numbers indicate, but waited until the minister, Mr McIntyre, visited the schoolhouse at 'Dunmore', their home estate, where he would preach and conduct the worship service in the Gaelic language. In later months, McIntyre made periodic visits to Maitland to preach to the Highlanders in their native Gaelic tongue, and presumably to maintain relationships with, and perhaps even to develop an influence over, those Highland emigrants from the *Midlothian*.

Whereas an ability to speak the Gaelic language was not considered to be essential for a minister at Maitland in March 1838, it very soon after became a key to gaining the allegiance of the Highlanders. The *Colonist* announced on the 17 November 1838 that

> The Colonial Presbyterian Church received an accession to its strength on Thursday in the person of the Rev. William Ross from Sutherland-shire in the North of Scotland, who could preach, both in English and in Gaelic.

However, with the arrival of the Rev. William Ross in the vicinity of the Hunter River, the rivalry and bad feeling between Dr Lang and the other Gaelic-speaking ministers in the district came to a head. Lang was afraid of the other ministers having too much influence among

---

42   The full text of the wording of the Call to the Rev. Robert Blain, and the complete listing of the members of the congregation inviting him to become their minister, is found in the *Colonist*, 3 March 1838.

the Gaelic-speaking Highlanders at 'Dunmore', a province which he considered to be his own.

The manipulation of Church influence under Lang became apparent in the organisation of the congregation to cater for the language requirements of the Highlanders. The *Maitland Mercury* (16 February 1850) reported that as the Rev. C. Eipper, the ordained Minister of the Paterson Charge, had 'demitted' or resigned from the pastoral care of the congregation, that a suitable replacement be found who could meet the

> peculiar condition of the people: 'a large number speaking the Gaelic tongue' and would benefit from having a minister, qualified to converse with them in their native tongue, and preach to them in their own language.

This step was not taken on the personal free-will decision of the Minister to leave, but was the result of a tactical plot engineered by the district Presbytery to remove Mr Eipper and replace him with a Gaelic speaker.

Significantly, only two years later in 1852, the Rev. James Brotherton Laughton, a non-Gaelic speaker, was admitted to the pastoral responsibility of the same Scot's Church, at Paterson. However, by this time, the number of native Gaelic speakers had been reduced through death or by resettlement to other places, and was in decline within the families of Highlanders, especially among the young, and the district being settled by a wider range of other non-Gaelic-speaking settlers. Gaelic speakers within the Paterson district were then provided for in an alternative manner, by having Gaelic-speaking ministers preach in the homes of parishioners. For example, the *Maitland Mercury* (16 February 1850), announced that the Rev. William McIntyre would preach in Gaelic at Lewinsbrook at the farm of Donald McLeod, his fellow passenger on the *Midlothian*.

Thus, the capacity to keep these Gaelic-speaking family communities together as occurred in the Hunter, Manning and Clarence River settlements over the years was the main factor in providing an ongoing Celtic culture and a living Gaelic language in northern New South Wales for many years after their arrival. In a style not unlike their life in Scotland, many of them lived in clusters of Highland tenants, maintaining relationships, and working together in a close harmony of life, where intermarriage between families and shared dates for marriages and baptisms were common. The Gaelic language lasted there while the people remained. The lack of Gaelic speakers to converse with; the deaths of those who did; the ongoing influence of non-Celtic life around them and the necessity of using English in general intercourse with others each contributed to the general passing of the language, apart from a very small number of families who persisted in its ongoing use, chiefly at home or for family devotional worship.

These Highland communities fostered relationships and mutual support. The opening up of further tracts of land in the northern rivers districts of the Manning, Clarence and Richmond in the late 1850s, coupled with unusually severe floods in the Hunter, were the main reasons that so many people left the Hunter and 'Dunmore' to move northwards, and this movement accounts for the decrease of Gaelic-speaking tradition in that Hunter area. Those who moved northwards took their Highland ways and language with them, with the last remaining children of their original migration families dying at the end of the nineteenth and early decades of the twentieth century.[43] Local reminiscences in Woodford Island recalled their capacity to speak the Gaelic language.[44] Their Celtic memories among their families and communities moreover continued long after the language ceased to be spoken. Their Gaelic bibles remained treasured long after they ceased to read them. The ships in which they had sailed to Australia were proudly remembered by name.[45] Their contribution to the welfare of local districts is fondly remembered wherever they went.

---

43   The *Clarence and Richmond Examiner* 12 November 1898, gave notice of the visit of the Rev. Mr Isaac McKay to the Manning River where he intended to hold special services, some in the Gaelic language for members of the Presbyterian Church of Eastern Australia. It is also recorded by that newspaper on 14 February 1899 that he preached in Gaelic at the Second Synod of that denomination in early February 1899.

44   *Richmond River Herald* 31 October 1911.

45   *Clarence and Richmond Examiner* records the deaths of Mrs M. Macleod on 10 March 1900 and Alex Munro on 18 September 1894.

9
'To the Land of My Praise': Memories of Hugh Boyd Laing

Katherine Spadaro

Immigration to Australia, along with the regulations which, rightly or wrongly, have surrounded it, is a subject of enduring and controversial interest; even those of us who are not historians have some vague familiarity with the landmark moments in its evolution. There are probably two highly productive streams of primary sources in relation to immigration: the documents produced to frame and support official policy, and the written and spoken output, in its multivarious forms, of the hundreds of thousands of individuals who experienced the process of immigration. The intention of this paper is to bring to light a source which runs outside these two streams: the account of a community leader at the time who, having no official connection to customs or immigration, was brought in to implement one of the instruments of immigration law. His account was written not in English but in Scottish Gaelic, and it appears in a short volume of poetry, story and reminiscence published by the *Stornoway Gazette*, a major newspaper of the Scottish Highlands and Islands. The instrument in question is the Dictation Test,[1] the writer is Hugh

---

1   The *Immigration Restriction Act* of 1901 allowed for the operation of a Dictation Test to filter out unacceptable immigrants. The test was to comprise fifty words in any European language (or in any language

Boyd Laing and the volume is entitled *Gu Tir Mo Luaidh* (To the Land of My Praise).[2]

Laing was born in 1889 in South Uist, an island of the Scottish Hebrides, where Gaelic was widely spoken. He was educated at Kingussie on the mainland and went on to study Arts and Divinity at the University of Glasgow. He began his teaching career in Scotland and after emigrating to Western Australia taught at several schools, including Scotch College, Goldfields High School, Kalgoorlie and Bunbury High School, where he eventually became Principal. He also served as Principal of Northam and Albany High Schools and Superintendent of schools in the state. (His attempts to enlist for military service during the First World War were rejected because of his flat feet).[3]

Laing's entry in the *Australian Dictionary of Biography* emphasises his dedication both to his subject and to his role as an educator:

> Laing was an outstanding, talented teacher, with a logical approach and a quizzical sense of humour; he took a keen interest in his students and had a strong influence on many of them. The nicknames he was given, 'Whizz-Bang' and 'Whizzy', stemmed from his Gaelic Christian name, Uisdean. His rather craggy appearance and unusual accent made him a butt of student humour, which he took in good part. Laing's greatest strengths were his knowledge of language and the pleasure he took in it, particularly the teaching and appreciation of English literature.

When the demands of school subsided and time allowed, as Laing says in the Foreword to his volume, he returned to his first love—Gaelic poetry. He translated in both directions: verses of poets such as Hopkins, Rossetti, Shakespeare and Donne into Gaelic, and Gaelic

---

selected by the Customs Officer, after 1905) which the potential immigrant was required to transcribe correctly.

2   Laing, Hugh B. 1964 *Gu Tir Mo Luaidh*, Stornoway Gazette.
3   Medcalf, M. 2000 Laing, Hugh Boyd (1889–1974), *Australian Dictionary of Biography*, National Centre of Biography, Australian National University, http://adb.anu.edu.au/laing-hugh-boyd-10772.

poetry into English. He also wrote original Gaelic verse which was very well received: with his work *Am Fiabhras Nach Faigh Bàs* 'The Fever that Will Not Die' he won the poetry section of the Gaelic Mòd and was awarded the title of National Bard for Scotland in 1965–66. He was the subject of an article in the *Australian Women's Weekly* of January 1970 which describes his being the 'uncrowned' bard, uncrowned because of an illness which kept him from travelling the thousands of miles to the ceremony.[4] A warm endorsement at the beginning of his volume, entitled *Facal bho Charaid* 'A Word from a Friend', was contributed by no less a figure than Derick Thomson.[5]

Laing's involvement in the Dictation Test occurred during his time in Bunbury when a South African ship, the *Apolda*, docked there in 1927. In an attempt to stay in Australia three Africans jumped ship. The local customs official resorted to the Dictation Test as a mechanism of ensuring that they would not succeed, and asked Laing to deliver the test in a suitably obscure language.[6] The passage which follows is my translation of Laing's recollection of the experience as it appears in *Gu Tìr Mo Luaidh*.[7]

GAELIC IN AUSTRALIAN LAW COURTS
The Judgement of the Dictation

When I was a schoolmaster in Bunbury High School in Western Australia in the year 1927, boats from South Africa used to come to the port from time to time for hardwoods which were needed for the South African railways. One day the steamship *S.S. Apolda* came to the quay at Bunbury and started to load timber as usual. The work had not progressed very far before the

---

4   'This former Bard is in love with Gaelic', *Australian Women's Weekly*, 7 January 1970.
5   Thomson was Professor of Celtic at the University of Glasgow for many years and a poet, writer editor, critic, publisher and advocate of all matters Gaelic.
6   It should be evident that the Dictation Test was designed to be failed.
7   I am most grateful to Mrs Katie Graham, as well as to participants at the Ninth Australian Conference of Celtic Studies, for helpful comments on the translation, remaining flaws being my own. I also greatly appreciate comments from the late Professor Anders Ahlqvist and Dr Pamela O'Neill on the subject matter of the presentation.

captain noticed that three sailors, black people, were missing, and, although he searched every corner of the boat and the quay, they could not be found.

So he had to go to the police station in the hope that they would find the Africans in the town of Bunbury, or in the little townships in the Bunbury area, or hiding in the bush. If the Captain left Bunbury without all the Africans who were on board when the ship arrived, he would have to pay £100 to Australian Customs for each one who was missing. The police caught the three men in a small town thirty miles from Bunbury three days after they absconded, and they took the men to the prison in Bunbury because they refused to return to the *Apolda*. The customs officer sent word to the Australian capital, Canberra, that he had three black Africans in Bunbury who refused to return to their own country, and he quickly received the firm order that he had to send them out of Australia without delay, because it was against the law and against the will of the populace for black people from other countries to live in the land.

At that time there was only one way to return them to their own country—the 'dictation', a dictation in languages that were used in any country in Europe. But what language would he choose, and who would prepare and read the dictation? He knew that there were plenty of Europeans within ten miles north of the town—Italians, Greek, Macedonians and Slavs—people who had between them many uncommon languages, but although they were skilled in growing potatoes and vegetables they had very little education and they were not used to reading 'dictations' according to the rules of the Department of Trade and Customs of Australia. He needed somebody who had more education than they had.

While he was in this doubtful state, he left the office and took a walk up the street where he met a shopkeeper he knew, and asked him where he could find a person who would read a dictation in some European language for the Africans who had left the *Apolda*. His friend told him there was a Scotsman in the High School who knew four or five European languages well. The customs officer didn't listen to any further talk. In six minutes he was at the door of the High School, looking for the Scotsman with the languages!

When he told me who he was and what he needed, he asked if I could give a dictation to the Africans in Latin. I answered that I could, but in my opinion a dictation in Latin was not lawful, for there was no population in Europe which used Latin as their common language. Ancient Greek was no better, and Hebrew or Arabic would not work either, as they were not European languages. I told him there was a female scholar at the High School who was very knowledgeable and fluent in German and French, and perhaps these would do the trick. He said they would not. The German language was still similar to the Dutch language which a number of the people of South Africa used, and, if we gave a dictation in German, there was a risk the Africans might not fail. As well as that, he knew that one of them had spent three years in Mauritius where French was spoken.

As we were losing hope of finding a language that would be suitable, he asked if I knew another European language, and I told him I thought I could read Scottish Gaelic, although I had not spoken it for over fourteen years. He knew very little about Gaelic, and he asked where the people were who spoke it, and whether it was a kind of English, like the funny English he heard people from Glasgow speaking, or like the English of Harry Lauder's songs!

I told him that 1. It was not a sort of English, 2. That it was spoken in the west and north of Scotland, and in eastern Canada, 3. That it was the common language of a hundred thousand people in these two countries, and 4. That it was in my opinion lawful and according to the Immigration Act to give the dictation to the Africans in Gaelic, for the reason that Gaelic was spoken at that time by a people in Europe. He agreed that we needed to set the dictation in Gaelic as there was no other language to be found, and that Gaelic was 'safer'[8] than the other languages that had been suggested.

That's how it happened in the history of Australia that Scottish Gaelic was included in the languages which kept the country white.

---

8   Quotations marks as in the original.

The poor (black) men were given the dictation in Gaelic that very night at seven o'clock, and needless to say the three of them failed it, and the morning of the next day they were tried in the Courthouse in Bunbury, because they were breaking Australian law by staying in the country without invitation. One of them—the one who had been in Mauritius—was quite talkative in court, and he was totally against returning to Africa. About the dictation he told the judge that he had never heard of such a language anywhere, 'and if it is a language,' he said, 'it's a devil of a language!'

'Silence, silence!' replied the judge quickly. 'That sort of language is not allowed in this court.'

They were convicted, and the judge ordered that the three of them be put back on board the *Apolda* at 4 o'clock in the afternoon. That's how the captain saved £300 and Gaelic made it possible for the Department of Trade and Customs in Australia to keep the country white until the law regarding the 'dictation' changed in 1932 and in 1958.

The Gaelic dictation was very beneficial to me. I got time off from school without loss of pay, £1 as a paid witness and £2 for being educated in Gaelic dictation. I also became more famous (or infamous) from that dictation than I did for over twenty years of work in schools. People stopped me in the street day after day to say, 'Don't you think, Mr Laing, that it's a shameful thing to be throwing poor people out of Australia just because they don't know Gaelic? Will Customs try and throw me out since I don't know Gaelic?' There was only one way to answer questions like that: 'I don't know what Customs have in mind, but if I were in your place, I wouldn't say anything about being ignorant of Gaelic, but I'd start to learn it right away. If you're in need of a teacher, I can find you one, and I think he'll only charge fifteen shillings for a lesson!'

Although the purpose of this paper is simply to bring to light an account with intrinsic interest, a few comments might be made. Clearly, Laing takes a humorous approach to the telling of his story: he has no intention to present a considered evaluation of immigration law as it stood. The customs official was operating within both the letter and the spirit of the law, and although Laing feels some sympathy for the absconders, he does not present them as victims of injustice. He clearly appreciates the absurdity of knowledge of Gaelic, a language known by so few Australians, being the criterion used for such a test.[9] At the same time, he is pleased to highlight the profile of Gaelic within his community. The oddity of the situation clearly appealed to Laing's sense of humour, and yet he may have become increasingly uncomfortable with this sort of exploitation of Gaelic. His interview with Winfred Bisset for the *Women's Weekly*, cited earlier, indicates this (and particularly after the Kisch case): 'As a linguist and a patriot, Mr Laing did not approve of this use of his native tongue. "It was a trick," he said, "used for political purposes"'.

Appendix

Below is a transcript of the Gaelic text of the passage from *Gu Tir Mo Luaidh* translated above:

A' GHÀIDHLIG ANN AN CÙIRTEAN-LAGHA ASTRÀILIA[10]
Breith an Deachdaidh
An uair a bha mi 'nam mhaighstir-sgoile ann an Ard-sgoil Bhunbury ann an Astràilia-an-Iar anns a' bhliadhna 1927, bha e 'na chleachdadh aig bàtaichean á Africa-a-Deas a bhith a' tighinn gu port o àm gu àm air son fiodh chruaidh air an robh feum ann an rathaidean-iarainn ann an Africa. Latha de na làithean thàinig am bàta-smùide, S.S. *Apolda*, chun a' chidhe ann am Bunbury agus thòisich i air luchd-achadh fiodha mar a b'àbhaist dhi. Cha robh an obair seo fad air adhart an uair a mhothaich an Caiptin gu robh e as aonais triùir de na seòladairean—daoine dubha—agus,

9   *Gu Tir Mo Luaidh* contains a second article on Gaelic and the Dictation Test with a focus on the famous Egon Kisch case. This event, which took place in Sydney and did not involve Laing directly, is described by him in a manner best described as scathing. I hope to treat this second article in a future paper.
10   Although some minor changes in Gaelic orthography have been made in intervening years, this transcription reflects the article as originally published by Laing.

ged a rannsaich e gach cùil anns a' bhàta agus air a' chidhe, cha d'fhuaradh iad.

Mar sin b'fheudar dha a dhol dh'ionnsaigh Oifig nam Maor-sìthe ann an dòchas gun deanadh iadsan gréim air na daoine dubha ann am baile Bhunbury, no anns na bailtean beaga a bha làmh ri Bunbury, no air am falach anns a' choille. Mur toireadh an Caiptin air ais leis á Bunbury gach duine dubh a bha aige air bòrd an uair a ràinig e am baile, dh'fheumadh e ceud not (£100) a phàidheah do Bhòrd a' Chuspainn an Astràilia air son gach fear a bha air chall. Ghalc na maoir an triùir ann am baile beag deich mìle fichead a mach á Bunbury trì làithean an déidh dhaibh teicheadh, agus thug iad air ais iad chun a' phrìosain ann am Bunbury a chionn gun do dhiùlt iad a dhol air bòrd na h-*Apolda* a rìs. Chuir oifigeach a' Chuspainn brath gu ceanna-bhaile Astràilia, Canberra, gu robh triùir dhaoine dubha aige ann am Bunbury a bha a' diùltadh tilleadh d'an dùthaich fhéin, agus fhuair e òrdugh cruaidh agus aithghearr gum feumadh e an cur a mach á Astràilia gun dàil, oir bha e an aghaidh an lagh agus toil an t-sluaigh daoine dubha á dùthchannan eile a bhith a' còmhnaidh anns an dùthaich.

Aig an ám sin cha robh ach aon dòigh air an tilleadh d'an dùthaich fhéin—is e sin, le "dictation" no deachdeadh ann an cànain a bha sluagh sam bith anns an Roinn-Eòrpa a' gnathachadh. Ach dé an cànan a thaghadh e, agus cò a dheasaicheadh agus a leughadh an deachdadh? Bha fios aige gu robh Eòrpaich gu leòr mu dheich mìle tuath air a' bhaile—Eadailtich, Greugaich, Macedonaich, agus Slabhaich—daoine aig an robh eatorra móran chànan neo-chumanta, ach, ged a bha iad làn de sgil ann an tuathanachas bhuntàta agus mheasan, cha robh ach glé bheag fòghluim aca agus cha robh iad cleachdte ri "dictations" a leughadh a réir riaghailtean Bòrd a' Chuspainn ann an Astràilia. Dh'fheumadh e cuid-eigin eile fhaighinn aig an robh tuilleadh fòghluim na bha acasan.

An uair a bha e anns an staid theagmhaich seo, dh'fhàg e an oifig agus thug e cuairt suas an t-sràid far an do choinnich e marsanta air an robh e eòlach, agus dh'fhaighnich e dheth càit am faigheadh e duine a leughadh deachdadh ann an cainnt Eòrpach air chor-eigin do na h-Africanaich a theich as an *Apolda*. Thuirt a charaid ris gu robh Albannach anns an Ard-sgoil aig an robh deagh eòlas air ceithir no cóig de chànainean Eòrpach. Cha do dh'èisd fear a' Chuspainn ri tuilleadh còmhraidh. Ann an sia mionaidean bha e aig dorus na h-Ard-sgoile, ag iarraidh Albannaich nan cànan!

An uair a dh'innis e dhomh có e agus dé a bha a dhìth air, dh'fhaighnich e am b'urrainn dhomh deachdadh a thoirt do na daoine dubha ann an Laidinn. Fhreagair mi gum b'urrainn, ach b'e mo bheachd nach robh dcachdadh ann an Laidinn laghail, oir cha robh sluagh sam bith anns an Roinn-Eòrpa a' cleachdadh Laidinn mar chainnt chumanta. Cha robh seann Ghreugais dad na bu fhreagarraiche, agus cha deanadh Eabhra no Arabaig a' chùis, oir cha b'e cànain Eòrpach a bha annta. Thuirt mi ris gu robh ban-sgoilear anns an Ard-sgoil a bha fìor-ionnsaichte agus fileanta ann an cainnt nan Gearmailteach agus nam Frangach, agus theagamh gun deanadh iadsan an gnothach. Thubhairt e nach deanadh. Bha cainnt nan Gearmailteach tuilleadh is coltach ris a' chainnt Dhùitsich a bha cuid de shluagh Africa-a-deas a'cleachdadh, agus, nan cuireadh sinn deachdadh ann an Gearmailtis, bha eagal air nach fàilinneadh na h-Africanaich. A bharrachd air sin, bha fios aige gun de chuir aon dhiubh trì bliadhna seachad ann am Mauritius far an robh Frangais 'ga labhairt.

An uair a bha sinn a'call dòchais gum faigheadh sinn cànan sam bith a bhiodh freagarrach, dh'fhaighnich e am b'aithne dhomh cànan Eòrphach eile, agus dh'innis mi dha gu robh mi a' smaointinn gum b'urrainn dhomh Gàidhlig Albannach a' leughadh, ged a bha còrr is ceithir bliadhna deug o nach do labhair mi i. Cha robh ach glé bheag eòlais aige air Gàidhlig, agus dh'fheòraich e càit an robh an sluagh 'ga bruidhinn, agus an e seòrsa de Bheurla a bha innte coltach ris a' Bheurla neònach a chual e daoine á Glaschu a' labhairt no coltach ris a' Bheurla anns na h-òrain aig Harry Lauder!

Thubhairt mi ris (1) nach e seòrsa de Bheurla a bha innte, (2) gu robh i air a labhairt ann an Alba an Iar agus Tuath agus

ann an Canada an Ear, (3) gu robh i 'na cainnt chumanta aig
còrr is ceud mìle sluaigh anns an dà dhùthaich sin, agus (4)
gu robh e 'nam bheachd-sa laghail agus a réir Achd-pàrlamaid
nan Coigreach deachdadh a thoirt do na daoine dubha ann an
Gàidhlig, do bhrìgh gu robh Gàidhlig 'ga labhairt aig an ám sin le
sluagh anns an Roinn-Eòrpa. Dh'aontaich e gum feumadh sinn an
deachdadh a chur ann an Gàidhlig a chionn nach robh cànan eile
ri fhaotainn, agus bha a' Ghàidlig na bu 'shàbhailte' na na cànain
eile a chaidh ainmeachadh.

Sin mar a thachair e ann an eachdraidh Astràilia gun deach
Gàidhlig Albannach a chur ann an àireamh nan cànan a bha a'
cumail na dùthcha geal.

Fhuair na daoine bochda (agus dubha) an deachdadh ann
an Gàidhlig an oidhche sin fhéin aig seachd uairean feasgar, agus
cha leigear a leas innse gun do dh'fhàilinn an triùir aca, agus
anns a' mhadainn an ath latha chaidh am feuchainn ann an
Tigh-na-cùirte ann am Bunbury, a chionn gu robh iad a' briseadh
lagh Astràilia ann a bhith a' fuireach anns an dùthaich gun
fhiathachadh. Bha fear dhiubh—am fear a bha ann am
Mauritius—gu math cabach anns a' chùirt, agus bha e a mach
agus a mach an aghaidh tilleadh do dh'Africa. Mu dheighinn na
'dictation' thubhairt e ris a' bhreitheamh nach cual esan gu robh a
leithid de chànan an àit sam bith, 'agus ma's e cànan a tha innte,'
ars esan, ''s e diabhal de chànan a tha innte!'

'Bi sàmhach, bi sàmhach,' fhreagair am breitheamh gu
h-aithghearr, 'chan 'eil cainnt de'n t-seòrsa sin ceadaichte anns a'
chùirt seo.'

Chaidh an dìteadh, agus dh'òrdaich am breitheamh an trùir
dhiubh a chur air bòrd na h-*Apolda* aig ceithir uairean feasgar.
Is ann mar sin a shàbhail an Caiptin trì cheud not agus a rinn
a'Ghàidhlig e comasach do Bhòrd a' Chuspainn an Astràilia an
dùthaich a chumail geal gus an d'atharraicheadh an lagh mu
dheighinn 'dictation' ann an 1932 agus 1958.

Bha an deachdadh ann an Gàidhlig 'na bhuannachd
thlachdmhoir dhòmhsa. Fhuair mi saorsa o'n sgoil gun chall
tuarasdail, aon not mar phàidheadh fianais, agus dà not a chionn
gu robh mi fòghluimte ann an deachdadh ann an Gàidhlig. Fhuair

mi cuideachd barrachd cliù (no mì-chliù) as an deachdadh na fhuair mi á obair nan sgoiltean ré suas ri fichead bliadhna. Bha daoine 'gam stad air an t-sràid là as déidh là, ag ràdh, "Nach saoil sibh féin, a Mhaighstir Laing, nach e gnothach maslach a th'ann a bhith a' tilgeil dhaoine bochda a mach á Astràilia a chionn nach aithne dhaibh Gàidhlig? Am fiach Bòrd a' Chuspainn ri mise a chaitheamh a mach a chionn nach eil Gàidhlig agam?' Cha robh ach aon dòigh air freagairt cheistean de 'n t-seòrsa sin. 'Chan 'eil fios agam dé a tha ann an inntinn Bòrd a' Chuspainn, ach, nam bithinn-sa 'nur n-àite-se, cha chanainn guth mu dheighinn a bhith aineolach air Gàidhlig, ach thòisichinn air a h-ionnsachadh gun dàil. Ma tha fear-teagaisg a dhìth oirbh, tha e comasach dhomh fhaighinn, agus cha chreid mi gum bi e ag iarraidh ach cóig tasdain deug gach leasan!'

10
Nicholas O'Donnell on the Origins of Munster O'Donnells

Val Noone

Adelaide Attack on Backsliders

In April 1909, when the leaders of the United Irish League (UIL) in Adelaide, South Australia, found out that Nicholas O'Donnell, Melbourne-based leader of the Australian UIL, was in town, they hastily arranged an evening at the Criterion Hotel in King William Street for members to hear him speak on 'the Irish situation'. After Patrick Healy, the local president, welcomed Nicholas as 'the leader of the Irish people in Australia', their guest spoke at length and knowledgeably about the state of the Home Rule campaign and its Australian support. Songs were sung, recitations given and, after Mr O'Leary played the violin, Nicholas took up the instrument and played 'The Blackbird'. All joined in singing 'God Save Ireland'.[1]

Healy expressed a high opinion of O'Donnell: 'There is no man so loved, honoured and respected by Irishmen throughout Australia.'

---

1   United Irish League, Welcome to Dr O'Donnell, a Great Irish Night: Review of the Irish Situation by the Guest, *Southern Cross* 23 April 1909. Nicholas O'Donnell's press cuttings about his 1909 Adelaide visit can be found in the first of two of his scrapbooks which were digitised in 2016 by Newman College Melbourne: see https://www.snac.unimelb.edu.au/collections.

Half a dozen historians have endorsed Healy's view. Born in 1862 at Bullengarook, near Gisborne in central Victoria, son of Michael O'Donnell from Camas, near Bruff, and Johanna Barry from Liskennett near Croom, he graduated in medicine from the University of Melbourne. Husband of Molly Bruen, father of nine, a Gaelic scholar, a founder of the Celtic Club, and for more than two decades leader of Australian support for Irish Home Rule, he was, as Chris McConville said, 'a towering figure', evoking both his tall stature and his prominence in public life.[2] His pre-eminence would come to an end in 1916, after he endorsed enlistment in World War I and criticised the Easter Rising as 'ingratitude of fanatics', supplanted by Archbishop Daniel Mannix as spokesman for majority Irish Australia. Because there are a number of O'Donnells in this article, I will refer to him henceforth as Nicholas.

At the Criterion, in some closing remarks, one of the speakers (unnamed in press reports) urged vehemently that Nicholas, their guest, must surely be descended from Red Hugh and the Donegal O'Donnells. In his reply, Nicholas attacked some unnamed contemporary O'Donnells as 'perverts, backsliders and unionists'. As a journalist noted, this was 'a statement somewhat reflecting on the present descendants of the great northern O'Donnells'. Thinking it over, Nicholas wanted to amend his remarks. In consequence the *Southern Cross* published an explanation by Nicholas:

> There is just one correction I would like to make. I said without consideration that the lineal descendants of Red Hugh, as far as they can be traced, were perverts, backsliders, Unionists, etc. That is not correct or accurate.

---

2   Noone, Val editor 2017, *Nicholas O'Donnell's Autobiography*, Ballarat Heritage Services; O'Farrell Patrick 2000 *The Irish in Australia*, Sydney, University of NSW Press 178–9; McConville, Chris 1988, O'Donnell, Nicholas Michael (1862–1920), *Australian Dictionary of Biography, Volume 11*, Melbourne University Press 60–1; O'Neill, Jonathan 2012 Language, Heritage and Authenticity: Nicholas Michael O'Donnell and the Construction of Irishness in Australia, *Journal of Irish and Scottish Studies* 5 (2), 39–55; Geary, Laurence 2016 Nicholas O'Donnell (1862–1920): A Melbourne Medical Life, *Australasian Journal of Irish Studies* 16, 13–29.

Figure 10.1 Nicholas O'Donnell

The direct line of 'Sir' Hugh (who took the English title of Earl)—Red Hugh's father—is extinct in the male line. The descendants of his sons, Red Hugh, Roderick, Caffir, and Manus have died out. Their only sister Nuala (the subject of Mangan's translation from the Irish, 'O Woman of the Weeping Wail'), married her cousin, Niall Garv, and had children whose descendants exist.[3]

In this explanation Nicholas did not retract his harsh description of certain O'Donnell contemporaries but he denied them any right to claim descent from Red Hugh and other famous Ulster patriots. Most of his audience were familiar with the tales about Red Hugh O'Donnell (1571–1602) of Donegal, a military leader against the Elizabethan invaders, famous for his escape from prison. Red Hugh had some successes during the Nine Years War, notably alongside Hugh O'Neill in the Battle of Yellow Ford, but he was defeated at the Battle of Kinsale in County Cork in 1601. In song he is commemorated by the perennial 'O'Donnell Abu', which was popularised by the Clancy Brothers during the folk revival of the 1960s.

Who were the 'perverts, backsliders and Unionists' of 1909 whom Nicholas had in mind? Pervert at that time could mean sexual pervert but more likely it meant one who had perverted the cause of Home Rule. Elizabeth Malcolm has suggested that one contender was Francis Hugh O'Donnell (1848–1916), who claimed to be descended from the O'Donnell chiefs (a claim O'Donnell rejected), once a prominent Home Ruler, regarded by many nationalists as one who had sold out to the Unionists. William Butler Yeats described him as a 'mad rogue'.[4]

Another contender was Bishop (later Cardinal) Patrick O'Donnell of Raphoe, who had that year drawn the anger of Irish-language activists for opposing the campaign to make Irish a necessary prerequisite for entry to the new national university. In his anonymous, hard-hitting pamphlet Father Michael O'Hickey, Professor of Irish at Maynooth seminary (soon to be sacked), had described Bishop O'Donnell as a 'degenerate bearer of a great name'.[5] O'Hickey's use of

---

3 The O'Donnells of Donegal: Interesting Letter from Dr O'Donnell of Melbourne, *Southern Cross* 7 May 1909.
4 Personal communication, Elizabeth Malcolm 26 September 2016.
5 Maume, Patrick 2009 O'Hickey, Michael (Ó Hiceadha, Micheál), *Dictionary of Irish Biography*, edited by James McGuire and James Quinn, Cambridge University Press & Royal Irish Academy VII.557. On O'Hickey, see Noone, Val 2014 Daniel Mannix, Michael O'Hickey and the Irish language: beyond stereotypes, *Australian Celtic Journal* 12, 51–69.

the word 'degenerate' was echoed by Nicholas. After suggesting that descendants of exiled O'Donnells in Spain and Austria, descended from Red Hugh's elder brother Calvagh, remained patriotic, Nicholas returned to unnamed O'Donnells who remained in Ireland as 'wretched degenerates in comparison'. His next sentence said: 'Bishop O'Donnell of Raphoe belongs to the northern clan, though he does not spring in direct line from the nobles of the clan, so far as can be traced.' Without speaking directly against Bishop O'Donnell, Nicholas's sequence of thought was open to interpretation as an indirect attack on him. If perchance in 1909 Nicholas had the bishop in mind, three years later he made amends. When forwarding to Ireland funds collected for the Home Rule cause, Nicholas wrote a fulsome public letter of praise in Irish to Bishop O'Donnell, who was at the time one of the trustees along with John Redmond and John Fitzgibbon of the funds of the United Irish League.[6]

Whoever his target was, at the close of a jovial evening, with betrayal of the Home Rule movement in mind, Nicholas had abandoned his usual diplomacy and courtesy in public discourse. However, within a couple of weeks, Nicholas returned to the question in more measured tones. He wrote for the Adelaide *Southern Cross* and the Melbourne *Tribune,* Irish Australian weeklies, a full-page article on his researches into whether or not his Limerick O'Donnells were descended from the famous sixteenth-century O'Donnells of Donegal.[7] His article was long and dense but clear and well reasoned. He also corresponded with scholars in Ireland about the genealogical and historical issues involved. What follows is an outline of how Nicholas's views developed.

---

6   The Home Rule fund: £3000 sent from Victoria, *Advocate* 13 January 1913.
7   O'Donnell, Dr N. M. 1909 The O'Donnells of Munster, *Southern Cross* 14 May 313. Reprinted as O'Donnells of Donegal and Munster, *Tribune* 5 June 1909.

Family Tradition re Ulster Heroes

Initially, Nicholas seems to have shared the inclination of others with the surname O'Donnell to identify as descendants of a chain of national figures from Ulster. In those years, and to this day, a common view was that the O'Donnells of Munster were descended from stragglers of the retreating army of Red Hugh following the disaster at Kinsale. That Nicholas once held that or a similar position is indicated by the names of two of his sons. In 1896, he and his wife, Molly, named their second son Hugh, evoking the memory of Red Hugh. Four years later Aunt Kate Shinnors née O'Donnell wrote from Ireland:

> I think you were right to call your little son Hugh. Poor father used always boast that his O'Donnells belonged to the old race. We used to call him the real Milesian.[8]

Prior to receiving this letter from Aunt Kate, Nicholas had uncles living in Victoria who were in a position to transmit the same family folklore. Nicholas's father, Michael, had died at thirty as a result of a riding accident when Nicholas was three but Nicholas lived with his paternal uncle Nicholas for many years and questioned, on several occasions, James, the other paternal uncle living in Victoria. Thus, when Nicholas wrote that 'my grandfather ... used to claim that he sprung from the 'rale ould O'Donnells', one can conclude that he was quoting his emigrant uncles as well as Aunt Kate; and that the 'rale ould O'Donnells' meant Red Hugh and his clan.[9] In 1900 Nicholas and Molly called their youngest son Manus, the name of a Renaissance O'Donnell chieftain who, in addition to military, government and diplomatic activities, in 1532 compiled *Beatha Colaim Chille, The Life of Columcille*.[10]

However, by 1909 when Hugh and Manus were teenagers, Nicholas came to doubt the opinion of his elders, writing that evidence was

---

8   *Nicholas O'Donnell's Autobiography* 78.
9   *Nicholas O'Donnell's Autobiography* 325.
10 Bradshaw, Brendan 1979 'Manus the Magnificent': O'Donnell as Renaissance Prince, *Studies in Irish History presented to R. Dudley Edwards*, edited by Art Cosgrove and Donal McCartney, Dublin: University College Dublin 15–36.

lacking to support his grandfather's view. He decided that there was 'no warrant' for the theory about O'Donnells of Munster as remnants of the stragglers from Kinsale, and he rejected the idea that the Limerick O'Donnells sprang from the famous Donegal clan.

Study and Letter Writing

In pursuing this matter, Nicholas carried out his own assiduous library research as well as corresponding with scholars in Ireland. Among the authors he studied were Geraldus Cambrensis, *Annals of the Four Masters*, William Betham, Roger O'Farrell, John O'Donovan, Patrick Woulfe and John O'Hart.[11] Later he drew on the newly initiated *Archivium Hibernicum*. In reaching his conclusion that the possible northern origin of some Munster O'Donnells was an open question, Nicholas followed Patrick Woulfe, John O'Hart, *The Annals of the Four Masters* and *Cambrensis Eversus,* and reluctantly disagreed with John O'Donovan.

The scholars he corresponded with were Patrick Dinneen, Richard Foley, (Risteard Ó Foghludha, Fiachra Éilgeach), and J. J. O'Farrelly (Seán Ó Fearchallaigh).[12] Dinneen, the famous lexicographer and a ground-breaking editor of Irish-language poets, encouraged Nicholas and also wrote to genealogist Patrick Woulfe on Nicholas's

---

11 Betham, William *Irish Antiquarian Researches,* Dublin: W Curry & Co. 1826–27; Connellan, Owen (ed.), *The Annals of the Four Masters,* Dublin: B Geraghty, 1846; O'Donovan, John 1856 *Annala Rioghachta Eireanan, Annals of the Kingdom of Ireland, by the Four Masters, from the earlierst period to the year 1616,* Dublin: Hodges Smith & Co; O'Farrrell, Roger *Linea Antiqua: a Collection of Irish Genealogies* (which he seems to have quoted from a secondary source); O'Hart, John 1876/1887 *Irish Pedigrees: the Origin and Stem of the Irish Nation,* Dublin: James Duffy & Sons; Woulfe, Patrick 1906 *Sloinnte Gaedheal is Gall: Irish Names and Surnames,* Dubin: M. H. Gill.

12 In November Mary Doyle and I found one letter from Nicholas to Richard Foley and four to J. J. O'Farrelly in the National Library of Ireland, Dublin. They are held in 'Seventy-seven letters to J. J. O'Farrelly, genealogist and record searcher, 1910–1930' in 'Séamas Ó Casaide papers 1877–1943', Ms. 10,683. The letters are reproduced as Appendix B to *Nicholas O'Donnell's Autobiography.*

behalf—Woulfe's views formed the core of Nicholas's published articles. Dinneen's influence on Nicholas will be discussed further below. Foley from Cork, who wrote under the pen-name of Fiachra Éilgeach, ten years younger than Nicholas, a lexicographer and place-name expert, for many years earned his living selling typewriters—in a revolutionary era he became Dublin manager for Underwood's, and he was an authority on compiling shorthand—but is remembered as an outstanding author, editor and teacher.[13] Foley had an unusual link to Melbourne by correspondence not only with Nicholas, but also with Thomas F. Culhane continuing into the 1950s. O'Farrelly, seventeen years older than Nicholas, was reported to be the last person employed officially in Trinity College Dublin and in the Royal Irish Academy on the transcription of documents in the Irish language, that is, one of the last of the scribes from the manuscript tradition, which was for centuries central in the transmission of Irish literature.[14]

By 1913 Nicholas's findings led him to disagree with O'Farrelly, telling him to stop looking for a Donegal link. He noted that pursuits of noble blood extending back several centuries can lack meaning in biological terms:

About ten generations have come and gone since the period of Red Hugh's mundane existence, and it has been stated somewhere recently that the proportion of the original blood of an ancestor of ten generations back that flows in the veins of his descendant today is about 1025th [1024th?] part—for the infusion of the wife's blood in the successive generations has to be taken into account. Thus even if a man could actually trace his descent back to the admirable hero and warrior of the Cinel Conaill, the fraction of Red Hugh's nature he would inherit would be too small to warrant airs of arrogance.

13 Ní Mhunghaille, Lesa 2009 Ó Foghludha, Risteard (Richard Foley)
    (1871–1957), *Dictionary of Irish Biography*, VII.478–9.
14 Ó Faircheallaigh, Seán Seosamh (c.1845–1927), <ainm.ie>, accessed online
    24 July 2014.

Thus, Nicholas, who had come to reject any family descent from Red Hugh and others, sensed that O'Farrelly had misunderstood his request for assistance:

> ... I don't think that following up the present line of enquiry is likely to lead to anything definite. You are beginning at the wrong end.
> If anything is to be discovered of my ancestry it will only be by working backwards, and not from the remote past to the present. My people were small farmers with no pretensions to high lineage, wealth and influence.[15]

In this firm statement of his mature view, Nicholas rejected descent from Red Hugh and others. Nonetheless, as we shall see, he found evidence that his Munster-based O'Donnell 'small farmers' had patriotic forbears.

Medieval O'Donnells of Munster

Drawing on the sources noted earlier, Nicholas found evidence of two distinct O'Donnell families in Munster, the Corca Bhaiscim (Corcabaskin) in southwest County Clare and the Corca Luighdhe (Corcu Loídge) in County Cork. The latter had since died out but he gave particular attention to the O'Donnells who were the chiefs of Corca Bhaiscim in at least 1013.

Alongside that, Nicholas tabled John O'Donovan's 'bold assertion' that the O'Donnells of Limerick and Tipperary 'are descended from Shane Luirg, one of the sons of Turlough of the Wine, prince of Tir Connell, banished to Munster in the beginning of the fifteenth century'. He found O'Donovan's view shared by earlier writers such as Roger O'Farrell and William Betham. However, such O'Donnells were of an earlier era than Red Hugh O'Donnell.

In his acclaimed reference work, *Irish Families: Their Names, Arms and Origins*, Edward MacLysaght emphasised that the O'Donnells are 'chiefly associated with Tirconnaill [Donegal], the habitat of the largest

---

15   *Nicholas O'Donnell's Autobiography* 325.

and best known O'Donnell sept, but he affirmed the existence of 'quite distinct septs [of O'Donnells] in other parts of the country'. MacLysaght recorded, for instance, the importance of the Corca Bhaiscim sept of Clare, whose medieval role Nicholas had noted.

The four-hundredth anniversaries of the Battle of Kinsale in 2001 and of the Flight of the Earls in 2007 catalysed valuable new works on the Ulster O'Donnells. Relevant to our discussion of how Nicholas's views developed is Bernadette Cunningham's analysis of *The Annals of the Four Masters*.[16] Nicholas was influenced by the *Annals*, quoting both Owen Connellan's and John O'Donovan's translations. Cunningham celebrates the achievements of the Four Masters but argues that because of their links to the O'Donnells, the *Annals* are biased in favour of the O'Donnells, emphasising their victories and playing down their defeats. Indeed, she assesses the descriptions of the O'Donnell exploits in the *Annals* as 'longer and more complex' and 'more vivid' than older entries. Nicholas would also be interested to read Brian Lacy's argument that 'neither Cenél nEógain nor the Cenél Conaill came into Donegal from outside at all' and that almost certainly the eponymous founders of those dynasties 'had no blood connection whatsoever with the allegedly Tara-based Niall Noígiallach. Instead they probably descended from the range of peoples whose origins lay in Ulster itself'.[17] While such findings intersect with Nicholas's overview of the O'Donnells, discussion of the Munster O'Donnells and their possible links to Ulster was outside the scope of these works. A thorough study of contemporary research on the origins of the Munster O'Donnells is a task for another day.

---

16 Cunningham, Bernadette 2007 *O'Donnell Histories: Donegal and the Annals of the Four Masters*, Rathmullan & District Historical Society.

17 Brian Lacey 2010 Facts and Fabrications: the Earls and their Ulster Ancestry, *Flight of the Earls: Imeacht na nIarlaí*, edited by David Finnegan, Éamonn Ó Ciardha and Marie-Claire Peters, Derry: Guildhall Press 94–103: 99.

Modern Munster O'Donnell Patriots

From the publications of Patrick Dinneen, and aided by correspondence with him, Nicholas found family links to other famous patriotic O'Donnells, not in Donegal but in Limerick. In the poems of Seán Clárach Mac Domhnaill (1691–1754, famous as the author of *Mo Ghile Mear*, the rousing lament for Bonnie Prince Charlie) edited by Dinneen he found a beautiful elegy for a patriotic James O'Donnell who was murdered in 1725 near Ardpatrick—not far from Nicholas's parents' birthplaces—by two men named Collins and Cunningham. Although he had a print copy of this poem Nicholas also appreciated the gift from O'Farrelly of a personally prepared manuscript copy.[18] Nicholas was moved to learn that Seán Clárach Mac Domhnaill came from Athlacca, some seven kilometres south of Camas, from where his late father came. He wrote to Richard Foley that 'geographically Athlacca seems very close to Camas and there is a possibility of family connection.'[19]

At the same time, in addition to the beauty of its lament, this poem interested Nicholas because, as the scholar Eugene O'Curry remarked:

> This is a valuable poem as it preserves an account of the existence in Munster of a line of the great O'Donnell family of Donegal of which we have no other historical memorial, namely the line of Shane of Lurg, the son of Torlough of the Wine, O'Donnell.

18   Pádraig Ua Duinnín 1902, *Amhrain Sheaghain Chlaraigh Mhic Dhomhnaill: priomh-olamh na Mumhan le n-a linn*, Baile Átha Cliath: Conradh na Gaedhilge; J. J. O'Farrelly, 'Marbhna Shéamuis Uí Dhomhnaill' by Seán Clárach Mac Domhnaill, manuscript copy in Irish with English translation, signed 6 May 1913, in an untitled envelope, Irish Studies Library, Newman College, University of Melbourne—the latter was uncovered by Miriam Uí Dhonnabháin at Newman College in 2014.
19   Nicholas O'Donnell to Richard Foley 9 September 1912, in *Nicholas O'Donnell's Autobiography* 316; Ua Duinnín, *Amhráin Sheaghain Chlaraigh Mhic Dhomhnaill*; compare Ó hÓgáin, Dáithí 2001 (eag.), *Binsín Luachra: Gearrscéalta agus Seanchas le Prionsias de Róiste*, Baile Átha Cliath: An Clóchomhar Tta.

As mentioned, this line is said to have moved to Munster in the fifteenth century, and did not descend from Red Hugh. Against that Nicholas took account of O'Hart's arguments 'that Shane of Lurg was not the eldest son of Turlough of the Wine, that he was not even legitimate' and that 'the name O'Donnell came into use in West Munster and other parts, as well as in Donegal, without any affinity of common origin'. Despite ridiculing O'Hart for tracing the pedigree of Queen Victoria back to Adam, Nicholas respected his laborious research on ancient records and took seriously his rejection of the theory of a northern origin.

Adding to his pride in the James O'Donnell story, Nicholas discovered a poet-priest of eighteenth-century Limerick who had the same name as himself, Nicholas O'Donnell of Adare (c.1700–c.1759) of the Franciscan order.[20] Father Nicholas wrote a well-known poem, 'Caoineadh ar a chapall', about his grief at the death of his horse. Dinneen wrote in the preface to his book, *Filidhe na Máighe,* that Nicholas was 'probably a kinsman of Fr Nicolas O'Donnell'. Furthermore, Uncle James O'Donnell spoke to Nicholas of family folklore linking this poet to the family tree.

Thus from 1908 when Nicholas began writing his family history he chose to concentrate on the details of his Limerick ancestors and did not claim descent from Red Hugh O'Donnell. As he told Foley in 1912, he had concluded that his O'Donnells 'seem to have been nomads … spread over Munster with no fixed habitation or territory like the settled clans'.[21]

Return to Possible Ulster Link

Although he held the belief 'that we are not of a northern origin', nonetheless, in 1916 after reading the fourth volume of *Archivium Hibernicum,* and referring back to the first volume of 1912, Nicholas concluded that his family's use of the Christian name Nicholas could

---

20   O'Duinnín, Padraig, Irish exiles and the Irish language, *Advocate* 23 February 1907.
21   *Nicholas O'Donnell's Autobiography* 317.

be an indication of their connection to an older branch of the Ulster O'Donnells. He wrote:

> At page 247 there are given the names in Latin from some old document of those who escaped with the Earls O'Neill and O'Donnell in 1607 from Lough Swilly. Here are some: Comer de Tyrcinel, Baro de Donagal agus filius, Caffer O'Donnell frater comitis cum mac agus filio, Fionnuala O'Donel soror dictu comitis, Nicolaus O'Donncl etc.[22]
> [Comer de Tyrcinel, Baro de Donagal and his son, Caffer O'Donnell a friend's brother with son and daughter, Fionnuala O'Donel sister of the aforementioned friend, Nicolaus O'Donnel etc.]
> This latter Nicholas was probably translated from a Niall O'Donnell, a name quite common in the great O'Donnell family as Niall Garbh. This dissertation tends to prove two things: 1) that Nicholas may have had its origin in history as an Irish Christian name, and 2) that our Camas O'Donnells were really connected with the northern O'Donnells for we are the only Limerick O'Donnells in which the name Nicholas is traditional as a Christian name.[23]

Nicholas wrote this and further comments on a sheet of foolscap paper, which he entitled, 'Theory of the origins of the Christian name Nicholas among the O'Donnells and some other Irish families'. He then pasted the sheet into his autobiographical manuscript, one of the last additions he made to that document. In this way, Nicholas, who had firmly decided not to be 'easily led ... by claims of former grandeur' nonetheless maintained an interest in a possible link of the Munster O'Donnells with Ulster although not to Red Hugh.

---

22   Hagan, J. 1915 Miscellanea Vaticano-Hibernica, 1420–1631, *Archivium Hibernicum* 4, 215–318. Nicholas was quoting 'Ex litteris scriptis ex Anglia. 18 Xbris 1607', p 247.
23   *Nicholas O'Donnell's Autobiography* 73.

Scholar and Home Ruler

This discussion of the origins of the Munster O'Donnells throws new light on the role of Nicholas O'Donnell as scholar and community leader in early twentieth-century Irish Australia. As the leader of the Home Rule support movement Nicholas wished to cultivate a sense of pride and loyalty in Irish heritage. His off-the-cuff and atypical comment in Adelaide about 'perverts, backsliders and Unionists'—whose identity needs further investigation—can best be understood in this context. He hastened to shift the public debate to encouraging his audience in the Australian Irish press to care

> not so much about tracing his descent to a great ancestor as proving by his life for Ireland and the race that he has endeavoured to be worthy of the patriots of the past, and to emulate their high aspirations, cheerful sacrifices, and noble deeds.[24]

Although he and his wife had named two sons Hugh and Manus after famous Ulster O'Donnells, by 1909 Nicholas stood for a critical handling of evidence:

> I am not easily led by the claims of our people (Irish people generally) to a former grandeur, aristocracy cultivation, civilization for which in many instances there is not real basis of truth. The exaggeration or twist in the evidence is not deliberate untruth: it has grown in accretions 'by little and little'—imperceptibly small but extending with the generations—poets adding to it—until in the end an unrecognisable story is put forward that one would not know beside the original truth if they could be placed side by side.[25]

Following these principles he found, firstly, a family tradition that his father's Limerick people were descended from the famous Ulster

---

24 *Southern Cross* 14 May 1909.
25 *Nicholas O'Donnell's Autobiography* 324.

O'Donnells; second, no evidence for the widely held view that the O'Donnells of Munster were descended from stragglers of the retreating army of Red Hugh following the disaster at Kinsale; third, scholarly evidence for the presence of O'Donnells in Munster from medieval times; fourth, that the possible northern origin of some Munster O'Donnells was an open question, with the possibility of a fifteenth-century movement south; and fifth, the likelihood that his family were small farmers and somewhat nomadic. For him the history of the O'Donnells in Limerick was by no means settled and he foresaw years more of investigation but was hopeful that 'with the new light that has been kindled in Ireland by the Gaelic League, men are being prepared and equipped with the training to grapple successfully with such abstruse and knotty themes'. The evidence presented here shows that Nicholas O'Donnell, working in Melbourne in the first decades of the twentieth century, was well read and up to date in his scholarship of the origins of his father's clan. Such a qualification would not, however, enable him to retain his leadership in the post-1916 world.

11

'Dark and rude and strange ...': Cardinal Patrick Francis Moran and the St Mary's 1904 Fair

Richard Reid

A large and most remarkable steam barge, freshly painted a flaring green, and flying an enormous Irish flag, made a circuit of the Liguria, while a strong-chested cornet performer, pedestalled in the centre of the deck, played 'Killarney' and 'The Harp that Once'.[1]

Soon this barge the *Azelea* was joined by a host of others, one even with a band on board playing 'Garryowen' and 'St Patrick's Day'. And so the day proceeded with a welcome by the Colony's leading Catholic politician, Sir Patrick Jennings, at the quayside; a short ride in a state coach provided by the Governor of New South Wales through a crowd estimated at 100,000 overall with some 10,000 at Circular Quay and another 20,000 behind them in the vicinity; an endless pealing of bells from St Mary's Cathedral; and the arrival at the cathedral door where, as Moran appeared, the 'cheering was deafening'. As he swept into the building the assembled congregation, allegedly 5000 of them, rose like a 'great wave of the sea' to acknowledge the Archbishop and receive his passing blessings.[2]

---

1   Anon 1902 The Welcome in Sydney, *His Eminence: Australia's First Cardinal Prince of the Church and Public Man*, edited by James T. Donovan, Sydney and Brisbane: William Brooks & Company 31.

2   The Welcome to Sydney 31.

This prominent element of spectacle in his reception in Sydney was undoubtedly not lost on Moran himself. My interest in Moran comes from an involvement in putting together the National Museum of Australia's 'Not Just Ned' exhibition on the Irish in Australia from 1788 to what was then the present, 2011. The search for objects led, at one point, to the Sydney Catholic diocesan collection housed in the basement of the church's administration building beside St Mary's Cathedral. There, and in working cathedral collections of processional crosses etc., was a treasure trove of what we might call 'Moranalia'. Similar amazing objects were to be found in Catholic collections all over Australia. Feeling apprehensive about whether we had amassed enough stuff for a reasonable exhibition, one of my assistant curators responded with words to the effect: 'Stop worrying, we have loads of "bling"'. And an important part of that 'bling' came from Catholic collections relating to big figures like Cardinal Moran.

This exhibition research pointed to something that book- and manuscript-oriented historians of the church possibly take a bit for granted and waste little time describing—the showmanship of it all, the presentation of the faith, in many forms, to the faithful using objects with powerful narratives.[3] Moran, in particular, from some of the great occasions in which he participated, or himself organised, was a master showman and aware how carefully staged presentations were a powerful technique with which to drive home the ways in which he wanted Australian Catholics to think about their past, an Irish and a Catholic past he approved of and spent some energy constructing for them. While Moran's publications in this area are well-known to historians, Moran's construction of public spectacle is rarely touched on except for the fact that he took over the running of St Patrick's Day in Sydney in 1896, a story that still calls for some investigation.[4]

---

3   For excellent overviews of Moran's time as Archbishop of Sydney see O'Farrell, Patrick 1977 *The Catholic Church and Community in Australia*, ch. 4, Melbourne: Thomas Nelson; Campion, Edmund 1987 *Australian Catholics*, Ch. 2, Ringwood: Penguin Books; and the entry for Moran by Anthony Cahill in the *Australian Dictionary of Biography*, http://adb.anu.edu.au/ biography/moran-patrick-francis-7648.

4   Historians such as O'Farrell and Campion certainly mention this St Patrick's Day takeover by Moran but provide only limited descriptions of what he put

Let us look at three splendid occasions where 'His Eminence', the title given Moran by that lavish 1902 hagiographical publication which described his 1884 arrival in Sydney,[5] was the central focus or organiser—the dedication, or opening, on Sunday 31 October 1897 of St Patrick's Cathedral, Melbourne; the 1901 St Patrick's Day procession (note the word 'procession', not 'parade') in Sydney; and the central presentation at the great St Mary's Cathedral Fair of September 1904.

It is Sunday 31 October 1897; imagine for a moment you are Thomas Lord Brassey, Governor of the Colony of Victoria by appointment from Her Majesty Queen Victoria, educated at Rugby and Oxford and undoubtedly, at least in public, a fully committed member of the Anglican Church.[6] As Governor you have been invited, along with Lady Brassey, to the opening of the great cathedral of St Patrick's. Shortly before 11 am, dressed, perhaps, in the full uniform of a Viceroy of Empire, and with your considerable entourage, you enter St Patrick's through the great doors of the main entrance. When you appear the assembled congregation of more than 4000 souls rises to its feet while you walk to the front, and seat yourself facing the altar.[7]

A significant entry, but at 11 am totally outshone by a long procession of robed Catholic prelates, bishops, monsignori, priests and other religious men coming down the aisle to the strains from the organ, orchestra and choir of the 'Ecce Sacerdos Magnus'—'Behold the great priest'. On this occasion there is no doubt who is the great priest, the man leading the procession in the scarlet robes of a Prince of the Catholic Church, Cardinal Patrick Francis Moran, Archbishop of Australia's premier Catholic see, Sydney. During the first part of the ceremony, a Pontifical High Mass, the Cardinal sits above the Governor

---

in place of the old activities. Similarly, Mike Cronin and Daryl Adair in their comprehensive account of the history of St Patrick's Day worldwide—2002 *The Wearing of the Green: A History of St Patrick's Day*, London and New York: Routledge 93—describe the takeover but say little about precisely what Moran did in reorganisation of the day's events.

5   Donovan, *His Eminence*.
6   Thomas Brassey, 1836–1918, *Australian Dictionary of Biography*, http://adb.anu.edu.au/biography/brassey-thomas-5339.
7   The following account of the opening of St Patrick's Cathedral, Melbourne, is from the *Advocate* (Melbourne) 6 November 1897.

on his archbishop's throne on the elevated dais around the altar. It is a
lush ceremony punctuated by moments from Beethoven's sonorous and
expansive Mass in C sung by a choir of 250 and accompanied by an
orchestra of twenty-five musicians. Apart from the splendour of it all
one might think there is nothing unusual here.

Mass over it is Moran's turn and it is his performance that widens
this straightforward cathedral dedication into an occasion to impress
upon this significant assembly the achievements of what historians such
as Colin Barr have called the 'Imperium in Imperio', the Irish Catholic
episcopal empire of the nineteenth century.[8]

For forty-five, perhaps even fifty minutes of this
two-and-a-half-hour ceremony, Moran from the pulpit delivered what
was referred to, and published as, 'A Discourse' on the 'Apostolate of St
Patrick'. An innocuous enough title but careful listeners that morning
might have been alerted to what was to come from the Cardinal's
opening words from Psalm 67:

> Let God arise and let his enemies be scattered and let them that hate
> Him flee before His face. God is wonderful in his Saints; the God of
> Israel is he who will give power and strength to his people.[9]

Nobody in the cathedral including the small Jewish contingent, led on
this occasion by Isaac Isaacs, Victorian Attorney General and destined
to become Australia's first native-born Governor-General, would have
been in any doubt by the time Moran ended that 'his people', the
chosen people, were none other than the Catholic Irish. The Irish had
received Patrick, accepted his message and in Moran's words, the 'Isle
was transformed into a hive of learning and sanctity'. And who
benefited greatly from this? Why the Anglo-Saxons who, according
to the nineteenth-century French Ultramontanist historian Charles de

---

8   Barr, Colin 2008 *Imperium in Imperio*: Irish Episcopal Imperialism in the
      Nineteenth Century, *English Historical Review* 502, 611–50.
9   Moran, Patrick 1897 *The Apostolate of St Patrick, Discourse of Cardinal Moran,
      Archbishop of Sydney, at the Consecration of St Patrick's Cathedral, Melbourne,
      31st of October, 1897*, Sydney: F. Cunninghame & Co. 3.

Montalembert, quoted approvingly by Moran, flocked to the Christian monasteries and abbeys of this blessed isle:

The Irish schools opened their doors with admirable generosity to strangers from every country ... above all to those who came from the neighbouring island, England.[10]

And how was this generosity repaid? For at least the final quarter of his discourse Moran took English Governor Lord Brassey and everyone else in the cathedral through the centuries of persecution visited on the Catholic Irish after the Protestant Reformation in England:

For three hundred years all the terrors and cruelty of the ten general persecutions were renewed through the length and breadth of Ireland. To the sword of Henry VIII, and Elizabeth, succeeded the confiscations under the Stuarts, and then came the deluge of desolation and destruction under the Puritan Commonwealth. An eye witness of the sufferings of Ireland in those days cries out: 'All the cruelty inflicted on the city of Rome by Nero and Attila, by the Greeks on Troy, by the Moors on Spain, by Vespasian on Jerusalem, all has been inflicted on Ireland by the Puritans'.[11]

Moran continued the narrative through the period of the Penal Laws down to the Great Famine and accounts of the efforts of proselytising Protestants and proclaimed that, despite all of this, the Irish remained 'ineradically Catholic', the roots of the shamrock being nourished 'by the blood of Martyrs and it has been well said that the very dust on which you tread in Holy Ireland is the dust of Saints'.[12] Who knows what thoughts went through Brassey's mind, or what remarks were passed at afternoon tea later that day at Government House. Moran cleverly finished by extolling the virtues of that Anglo-Celtic empire in which they all now lived although if the English language was not simply the language of heresy then that was due to the 'Sons of Erin':

---

10   Moran 12.
11   Moran 20–1.
12   Moran 22 and 24.

Wheresoever the English language holds sway, thither through
the Celtic Soldiers of the Cross, the Catholic Church extends
her conquests.[13]

Moran's discourse was reported in full not only in Melbourne's Catholic
paper, *The Advocate*, but also in the main metropolitan papers, *The
Argus* and *The Age*.[14] While *Advocate* readers might have nodded at
the Cardinal's interpretations of history, neither *The Age* nor *The Argus*
made any comment but there may have been some interesting reactions
in the Protestant evangelical papers. In Moran's dramatic 'discourse',
delivered in that cathedral built largely by Irish immigrant and native
Australian Catholic donations, and in front of the English Governor,
the claims of the Irish spiritual empire were on full public display. Set
high on a hill above central Melbourne stood this Catholic cathedral,
the embodiment of the expansion of the Irish 'Imperium in Imperio',
with, as Moran said in triumph, the name of St Patrick 'emblazoned on
its portals'.[15]

Another major piece of Moran's Irish Catholic imperial theatre was
the Sydney St Patrick's Day procession of 1901. Before describing this
some context is necessary. In 1898 the Cardinal was upstaged in Sydney
by his own people when a distinguished group of Irish Australians,
prominent among them Moran's own physician, Dr Charles McCarthy
from Tipperary, organised the disinterment of that most famous of
early Irish/Australian rebel exiles, the Wicklow Chief, Michael Dwyer,
and his wife, 'Mary of the Mountains', and their reburial at Waverley
Cemetery.[16] There it was proposed to erect a great monument over
their graves dedicated to the rebellion of 1798. The procession of the
coffins to Waverley was one of the most massively attended of Irish

---

13 Moran 28.
14 *Argus* 1 November 1897: *The Age* 1 November 1897.
15 Moran, *The Apostolate* 4.
16 For Moran's initial opposition to the Dwyer reinterment see O'Farrell, Patrick
    2000 *The Irish in Australia*, Sydney: University of NSW Press 238/240 and
    O'Donnell, Ruán 2007 Irish Australia and the 1798 Centenary in Sydney,
    Echoes of Irish Australia: Rebellion to Republic, edited by Cheryl Mongan, Jeff
    Brownrigg and Richard Reid, Galong NSW: St Clement's Retreat and
    Conference Centre 7-8.

Australian events ever and this emphasis on an Irish rebel past was not one approved of by Moran. Eventually, however, so great was the pressure from his flock that he was forced to accept it and he allowed the coffins to rest in St Mary's Cathedral before the reburial where he even gave a eulogy.

How many have read this eulogy? By comparison with Moran's efforts the previous year at St Patrick's it was cursory and would have taken all of a couple of minutes to deliver. He began as he intended to go on by saying he had no intention of detaining the large congregation, knowing that 'further proceedings awaited them'. Dwyer, Moran conceded, was a patriot who had loved Ireland, and Australia needed patriots, like Dwyer, who would be true in their love of country and no less true in their love of religion.[17] He did not accompany the entourage to Waverley nor did he attend the unveiling of the 1798 Memorial there in April 1900. Patrick O'Farrell writes of all this in *The Irish in Australia* and is well across the whole idea of the so-called Irish empire in Australia with Moran as its high priest. What neither O'Farrell, or anyone else I have read, mentions is Moran's reaction to the Dwyer funeral or at least that's how it could be interpreted.

In 1901, the year of Federation, St Patrick's Day fell on a Sunday. Having taken over the organisation of the day in the mid-1890s Moran could now do as he wished with it and on this occasion he staged his own significant disinterment and paraded not just two but four coffins through the main thoroughfares of central Sydney from St Benedict's on Broadway to St Mary's Cathedral.[18] The large procession was led by key Catholic organisations such as the Australian Holy Catholic Guild, the Hibernian Australasian Catholic Benefit Society and a large contingent of religious. Musical mood was created by the Royal Artillery Brass Band and the band of the Irish Rifles, while the Cardinal rode in front of the four coffins. One estimate put the crowd at 250,000 which, if anywhere near accurate, was a greater number than the estimated 100,000 who

---

17 Moran's eulogy reported in: Who Fears to Speak of 98? *Freeman's Journal* (Sydney) 28 May 1898.

18 My account of the 1901 procession is based on the description in: The Irish National Festival, How it was spent in Sydney; A Unique Celebration, Honouring the Pioneers of Australian Catholicity, *Freeman's Journal*, 23 March 1901.

witnessed the Dwyer procession.[19] The *Freeman's Journal's* explanation for this was that many non-Catholics turned out to pay tribute to those in the coffins, men considered in the public mind to be as much pioneer citizens of Sydney as what they had also been in life, leading Catholic priests and prelates. In the coffins were the remains of Englishman Archbishop Bede Polding, Sydney's first Catholic Archbishop appointed in 1835 and three Irishmen—Archpriest John Joseph Therry, one of the first two official Catholic priests appointed to the Colony of NSW in 1819, Father Daniel Power, who arrived in 1826 and died in 1830 and the Venerable Archdeacon John McEncroe, perhaps the most prominent Irish priest in the colony from his arrival in 1832 until his death in 1868. Irish rebellion generated two coffins for the semi-pageant of 1898; for this manifestation of the 'Imperium in Imperio' of the Hiberno-Roman church in Australia Moran produced four, and a bigger crowd. The *Freeman's Journal* reporter on the spot gives a good sense of the spectacle:

> Soon after the procession arrived, the front doors of the cathedral were thrown open and in a short time every seat was occupied. Thousands of people fought to gain an entrance. The strains of the bands could be heard in the distance, whilst overhead the cathedral bells rang out their peals changed only to the mournful wailing of the 'Funeral march' by the band of the Permanent Artillery. The members took their respective places in the cathedral allotted to them. The clergy on arriving walked through the lines, and took their places on the sanctuary, which was tastefully draped in white and black. His Eminence was the last to arrive, and having vested, accompanied by the clergy, and the students of St. Patrick's College, Manly, proceeded to the main door in College Street, and received the remains, which were borne upon the shoulders of the bearers, and deposited upon four pedestals in front of the altar rails, where the acolytes placed six

---

19 Estimates for the attendance at these two events vary considerably. O'Farrell has the figure of 100,000 for the Dwyer procession to Waverley; O'Donnell quotes that the *Freeman's Journal* gave the figure at 200,000. The *Freeman's* certainly gives a figure of 250,000 for the reburial procession of the Catholic prelates.

lighted candles. The Dies Irae and Benedictus were then chanted by the students.

His Eminence, having upstaged 'rebel Ireland', had found another suitable occasion to illustrate his preferred interpretation of their Irish heritage to his by now largely Australian-born Catholic flock. Arguably Moran's greatest Irish/Australian spectacle was his contribution to the 1904 St Mary's Cathedral Fair. The Fair, held in September/October 1904, had three clearly articulated purposes: to clear the cathedral debt and allow extension of the building; to mark the fiftieth anniversary of the Papal declaration of the definition of the dogma of the Immaculate Conception; and to celebrate Moran's own fifty years as a priest.[20] To whip up enthusiasm for the occasion Moran visited and spoke to every Catholic parish in the Sydney area and encouraged them to set up a committee to arrange a stall at the fair where a special annexe to the existing Cardinal's Hall was built to house these parish stalls.[21]

The spiritual centre of the Fair was devised by Moran—an exhibition of objects from his own and the cathedral's collections depicting glimpses of the history of Catholicism both in Ireland and, to a more limited extent, in Australia.[22] This was perhaps the first exhibition of its kind ever attempted by a transplanted European faith in Australia and at the centre of his display the Cardinal placed a large object, 5.8 metres high, which, in the words of the *Catholic Press*, became the site at the Fair where 'people most do congregate'.[23] A description of exhibition objects was a feature of the Fair's souvenir handbook along with essays on the history of the building of the cathedral, Moran's sacerdotal jubilee, the meaning of the Fair and a poem by well-known Catholic poet Roderic Quinn.

---

20 O'Farrell, Patrick editor 1971, *St Mary's Cathedral Sydney 1821–1971*, Sydney: Devonshire Press 52 and 219; *Freeman's Journal*, 23 January 1904.
21 For example see: St Mary's Jubilee Fair, Meeting in Balmain, *Catholic Press*, 18 February 1904.
22 *St Mary's Jubilee Fair, 1904*. This very rare item, in the Special Collections of the National Library of Australia, is the souvenir booklet produced for the Fair. A list of items in Moran's display is on 50–1.
23 Around the Stalls by 'Eblana', *Catholic Press*, 8 September 1904.

The extensive exhibition section of the handbook divided the objects into four types: smaller personal historical objects called 'Mementos and Curios'; larger objects being three replicas of Irish Celtic shrines—St Patrick's bell, the Lough Erne shrine and the Ardagh chalice; photographic facsimiles from the Book of Kells (accompanied by a lengthy piece on the art of Celtic illumination); and the large central 5.8-metre-high object.[24] The 'Mementos and Curios' cabinet contained some remarkable pieces. Moran made a small bow towards rebellion by including two pike heads from the battlefield of Vinegar Hill in 1798 given to him by Archbishop Croke of Cashel. These rebels, at least the Catholic ones, in Moran's eyes had fought to defend the faith, not for the United Irish aim of an Irish republic. More unusual for the Sydney audience would have been the two bullets fired by the Catholic defenders of Athlone under siege in 1691, bullets fired at Dutchman Ginkel's army of Protestant heretics. An Australian object that illustrated old stories of official opposition to Catholicism in early colonial times was the silken cover of the Pyx in which the remnants of the Blessed Sacrament, left behind by the deported priest Father O'Flynn, was hidden by Irish rebel transportee William Davies. Two other objects added flavour to these years of colonial persecution that persisted supposedly until the arrival of Father John Therry in 1819—a watercolour of O'Flynn with a caption describing him as having been 'sent home a prisoner in 1818', and the original writ for the transportation of one of the priests transported after the 1798 rebellion, Father James Harold. The Fair booklet listed thirty-seven 'Mementos and Curios', among them miscellaneous items such as a paper knife made for Archdeacon John McEncroe by convicts on Norfolk Island, a Bible printed in Venice in 1511 and a prayer book that once belonged to Mary Queen of Scots. There was no particular theme around which this material was organised, but eighteen of the thirty-seven objects can be associated, sometimes a bit loosely, with Catholic persecution either in Ireland or Australia.

---

24   *St Mary's Jubilee Fair, 1904*: Three Celtic Shrines, 34–45; The Art of Illumination 46–8.

The piece de resistance of the whole show, the object around which the *Catholic Press* asserted 'people most do congregate', was a life-size replica of the great ninth/tenth-century Irish high cross from the Monasterboice monastic site in County Louth, Muiradach's cross.[25] Moran's biographer, Philip Ayres, describes Moran's 1902 trip to Europe when he spent three and a half months in Ireland. During that time Ayres states that Moran made an extensive trip to Drogheda and it is surely certain that he went out to Monasterboice a short journey north of the town.[26] Staying in Dublin Moran would have been able to view the replicas of ten Irish high crosses commissioned in 1898 by the director of the forerunner of the National Museum of Ireland, the Dublin Museum of Science and Art, Colonel G. T. Plunkett, and indeed the Monasterboice cross was the first of these replicas to be completed. Plunkett also commissioned replicas of other early Irish Christian objects such as the Ardagh chalice.[27] In 1903 Moran placed an order for the Monsasterboice cross and undoubtedly for the other three replicas, which he had in his exhibition in 1904.[28]

The cross at the Fair generated little press interest. Only the *Catholic Press* produced a special article about this colossus that towered over every stall and exhibit, calling it 'One of the World's Wonders' and, in a passage that could almost have been written by Moran, exclaimed:

And the more the materials of Ireland's history are investigated the more reason do we find to deplore the prejudice or indifference which have tended so long to veil, if not to blot

---

25 Around the Stalls by 'Eblana', *Catholic Press* 8 September 1904.
26 Ayres, Philip 2007 *Prince of the Church, Patrick Francis Moran, 1830–1911*, Melbourne: Miegunyah Press 239.
27 Battersby, Eileen, Ancient art in high crosses, *The Irish Times* 27 October 2007.
28 I have yet to sight actual documents relating to Moran's order for these objects, but in a Facebook article entitled Irish Medieval Art is a reference to Moran placing an order for the Monasterboice Cross with the firm of John Deghini & Son and that the object was shipped to Sydney for £46 and 10 shillings. https://bit.ly/3lFtMbE

Figure 11.1 Replica of the Monasterboice high cross, County Louth, on display in the St Mary's Fair, Sydney, 1904 (*St Mary's Jubilee Fair* program, National Library of Australia).

away, those memories which should form the noblest part of the inheritance of all who have a drop of Irish blood in their veins.[29]

Aware that the cross needed some explanation Moran produced an essay in the Fair souvenir handbook detailing what was to be seen on the four faces of the cross and an outline of its origins drawing on the work of scholars like Petrie. Moran's approach was factual, distant and restrained. In the handbook it was left to Roderic Quinn's brother, journalist and politician Patrick Edward Quinn to help the Cardinal's native born Catholic flock to feel some connection between their sunlit

---

29   The Monasterboice Cross in Sydney, One of the World's Wonders, *Catholic Press* 8 September 1904.

Australian urban lives and this silent replica from the Christian life of a misty, distant island lived out a thousand years back in time. Quinn described the bright colours of the many exotic stalls of the fair selling their wares but of how 'over it all, dark and rude and strange, towered the Cross of Monasterboice':

> Somehow this magnificent symbol of Christianity, made so long since, so far away, brings home to us the antiquity and permanence of the Catholic faith. Standing here in this modern hall it is instinct with the message of faith. Long ago in Irish vale, or on Irish hillside, beneath such crosses they gathered at even-glow to hear the words of some travelling bishop read from a book of gold ornate with the patient beautiful work of prayerful hands, they gathered … the ancestors who have passed into the night of oblivion, the simple Irish Catholics of one thousand years ago.[30]

And much more in the same vein.

In 2010 the National Museum of Ireland put on a temporary exhibition of their replica high crosses, an exhibition which went with great acclaim to Japan. A museum press release wrote of how the Irish of the turn of the twentieth century, when these replicas were made, through such objects could see into a past beyond the Anglo-Norman invasion, to 'a cultural heritage other than one linked to the British Empire'.[31] For Moran this was surely the message of the Monasterboice cross at the centre of his great 1904 St Mary's Fair. Here was the Irish spiritual empire on display more powerful, in the Cardinal's mind surely, in its ancient religious and ethnic connections than the sight of a British battleship in Sydney Harbour or narratives of Good Queen Bess and the Armada in the state public schools.

Much of the physical evidence of Moran's efforts in this area of highly charged public spectacle has vanished. While the National Museum in Dublin still has all their high cross replicas, the one made for the 1904 Fair in Sydney has disappeared. In 1919 it stood against a

---

30   *St Mary's Jubilee Fair, 1904,* 23–4.
31   Irish High Crosses 2010, segment in Notes to the Editor, National Museum of Ireland media release, online at https://bit.ly/3kofhYV.

wall inside St Mary's Cathedral itself and it was still there in 1925, but there is no mention of it after that in Sydney's Catholic newspapers.[32] The objects Moran had on display for the Fair cannot be produced by the Sydney Archdiocesan Archives and must, sadly, also be accounted as missing.[33] When Moran brought the four coffins of the remains of the early English and Irish Catholic prelates to St Mary's in 1901 he had them placed in the Chapel of the Irish Saints not far from the high altar, a clear symbolic positioning of these men as the founders of the church in Australia. They have subsequently been moved away to the crypt where Moran himself lies buried.[34] But the opening of St Patrick's Cathedral in 1897, the reburial of the founding Catholic prelates of Sydney in St Mary's on St Patrick's Day 1901 and the exhibition at the Fair of 1904 with the Monasterboice high cross at its centre can all be remembered as public spectacles when the Irish ecclesiastical empire, or if one prefers the Hiberno-Roman ecclesiastical empire, was both interpreted, and on two occasions given dramatic visual form, by its top Australian showman, Patrick Francis Moran.

---

32 *Freeman's Journal* 31 July 1919; *Freeman's Journal* 19 March 1925.
33 Jo Robertson, Catholic Diocese of Sydney Archives, *pers. comm.*
34 This removal is described in Cologan, Joseph and Marley, Monsignor V. 1971 Description and Guide, *St Mary's Cathedral Sydney 1821–1971*, edited by Patrick O'Farrell, Sydney: Devonshire Press 204–5. It is not clear from the text if the original burials in the chapel were at the time (1901), meant to be permanent.

12
Remembering Easter 1916: Australian Links to the Irish Rebellion

Anne-Maree Whitaker

On 26 April 1916, a year and a day after the Gallipoli landing, the London *Times* reported:

> At noon on Monday serious disturbances broke out in Dublin. A large body of armed men occupied Stephen's Green, took possession of the post office, and held houses in the neighbourhood and on the quays.[1]

The report was copied by the press in Australia the next day, and Irish Home Rule supporters in Sydney and Melbourne were quick to condemn the Rising as 'sectional pro-German rioting'.[2] In the end it proved to be considerably more than that.

The 1916 Easter Rising was the most significant revolt against British rule in Ireland since the United Irishmen Rebellion of 1798. The Irish Volunteers, along with their women's auxiliary Cumann na mBan and youth organisation Na Fianna Éireann, joined with the trade-union-based Irish Citizen Army to take over large parts of Dublin

---

1 *The Times* 26 April 1916.
2 *The Age* (Melbourne) 28 April 1916.

for almost a week. Over 500 people were killed and 2600 injured, and 200 buildings were destroyed by British bombardment.[3]

The Rising might have been deemed a failure but for the British reaction. Between 3 and 12 May, fifteen of its leaders were executed and the tide of public opinion turned. 'The prisoners include many intellectuals of the Irish literary movement', the *Sydney Morning Herald* noted.[4] Archbishop James Duhig of Brisbane declared: 'Irish Queenslanders, who have loyally and generously supported the cause of Empire and its Allies, are grievously disappointed and saddened by hasty executions.'[5] The British reaction snatched defeat from the jaws of victory. As Yeats wrote in his Poem 'Easter 1916': 'MacDonagh and MacBride/And Connolly and Pearse/Now and in time to be,/Wherever green is worn,/Are changed, changed utterly:/A terrible beauty is born.' Several Australian newspapers approvingly quoted the *Manchester Guardian*'s comments:

> The death sentences ought now to cease. Enough has been done for an example and a warning, and there is no need for another 'bloody assize.' Mr. Redmond and Sir Edward Carson have pleaded for clemency for the rank and file, but where is the line to be drawn? It is monstrous that a military tribunal sitting in secret should be allowed to determine a great and critical matter in hot blood.[6]

The Easter Rising not only shook the British Empire's foundations and enthused independence movements elsewhere, it was also a pivotal event in the movement towards Irish Independence. As such its remembrance and commemoration over the period of a century reflect the evolving relationship between the Irish past and present. Mark McCarthy's study *Ireland's 1916 Rising: Explorations of History-Making, Commemoration and Heritage in Modern Times* discusses how the event

---

3   Ferriter, Diarmaid 2015 Why the Rising Matters, *Irish Times* 23 September 2015. Collins, Lorcan 2016, *1916: The Rising Handbook*, Dublin: O'Brien Press 112.
4   *Sydney Morning Herald* 4 May 1916.
5   The Plea for Clemency, *The Age* 11 May 1916.
6   For example, *Tribune* (Melbourne) 11 May 1916; *Examiner* (Launceston) 8 May 1916.

has remained a perpetual influence in the making of modern Ireland. He finds that in many ways, Easter Week was never allowed to become history or stand still, as it continued to resonate in current affairs. McCarthy's analysis explores 1916 as a perpetually shifting site of memory due to the changing politics of commemoration and the constant pressure of current political needs and realities.[7]

The centenary of the Easter Rising in Dublin was commemorated by Irish government and community events throughout 2016, principally focused on Easter Week and on the actual anniversary dates.[8] Official activities included the presentation of copies of the Proclamation of the Republic to all schools for formal reading, wreath-laying in the Kilmainham Gaol Yard where the executions took place, and a military parade watched by a crowd estimated at 250,000 people. The national broadcaster RTÉ organised a day of music, re-enactments and talks in Dublin on Easter Monday, and other activities were held around the country.[9] A citizens' group, Reclaim 1916, organised a poetry competition and held a pageant outside the GPO in central Dublin on Sunday 24 April (the actual centenary date of the Rising) which attracted 40,000 people.[10]

As might be expected, the centenary of the Easter Rising sparked a rash of publications. The National Library of Ireland's catalogue lists 2749 books, of which over 200 have appeared in the five years before the centenary. Among these was a series of biographies, '16 Lives', studying the sixteen men executed in the aftermath of the 1916 Rising.[11] While the American connections of Tom Clarke and others have long been known, it is from these new studies that the first inklings of Australian connections of Rising leaders Commandant Ned Daly, Major John MacBride and others emerged.[12]

---

7   McCarthy, Mark 2016 *Ireland's 1916 Rising: Explorations of History-Making, Commemoration and Heritage in Modern Times*, London and New York: Routledge.

8   Easter Sunday fell on 23 April in 1916, but on 27 March in 2016.

9   Irish Government 1916 2016 http://www.ireland.ie/programme.

10 Reclaim 1916 http://www.reclaim1916.ie/.

11 The 16th was Roger Casement who was hanged in London on 3 August 1916.

12 Litton, Helen 2013 *Edward Daly*, Dublin: O'Brien Press 21–8; Fallon, Donal 2015 *John MacBride*, Dublin: O'Brien Press 20.

Other works focused on the cultural milieu from which the Rising emerged. Eminent Irish historian Roy Foster's *Vivid Faces: the Revolutionary Generation in Ireland, 1890–1923* follows on from Robert Wohl's landmark study *The Generation of 1914*, which concentrated on the generational consciousness of young men from across Europe whose lives were interrupted, if not obliterated, by World War I. Foster considers that the participants in the 1916 Rising were inspired by trends such as cultural revival, militarism and radicalism which were common to many parts of Europe, America and the British Empire.[13]

An important advance in historical resources on the Easter Rising and subsequent War of Independence and Civil War was the release of the Irish Bureau of Military History paper records in 2003.[14] This is a collection of 1773 witness statements (totalling 36,000 pages), 334 sets of contemporary documents, forty-two sets of photographs and other primary source material that was collected between 1947 and 1957, relating to the period 1913 to 1921. The collection was digitised in 2011 and is now available on the internet.[15] Another significant collection held by the Irish Military Archives is the Military Service Pensions Collection, comprising applications for service pensions for the Revolutionary period with comments by referees and other information. This material is also available online.[16]

The Easter Rising's Australian ramifications have, perhaps surprisingly, received little attention from scholars. Patrick O'Farrell's pioneering survey, *The Irish in Australia*, did not even list the event in its index.[17] More recently Jeff Kildea has examined the involvement of Australian soldiers in the events of the Rising in Dublin, while Rory Sweetman has looked at the reaction of the Australasian Catholic

---

13   Foster, R. F. 2014 *Vivid Faces: the Revolutionary Generation in Ireland, 1890–1923*, London: Penguin.
14   Ferriter, Diarmaid 2003 'In such deadly earnest': the Bureau of Military History, *Dublin Review* 12, 36–64.
15   Bureau of Military History, Irish Military Archives http://www.bureauofmilitaryhistory.ie/index.html
16   Military Service pension collection, Irish Military Archives https://bit.ly/3mxNXcW.
17   O'Farrell, Patrick 1986 *The Irish in Australia*, Sydney: University of NSW Press 328, 333.

hierarchy to the event.[18] As Glenn Calderwood has explained, the Rising's impact in Australia was largely overshadowed by the World War I conscription referenda and the activities of Melbourne's Archbishop Daniel Mannix.[19] But there is more to tell about Australia's links to the Easter rising than the Australian reaction. Several of the Rising's leading figures had family ties to Australia stretching back to the 1850s, while after the Rising rank-and-file participants emigrated to Australia and contributed to public life in their new homeland over many decades.

First to the Australian background of the Easter Rising leaders. It is certainly a curiosity, but nothing more, that Roger Casement's grandfather drowned in the Melbourne Corporation Baths and his uncle was held up by Ned Kelly.[20] The death of Major MacBride's brother Francis in the Liverpool Asylum in south-west Sydney in 1932 was simply the end of an uneventful career as a stockman in outback New South Wales over the preceding four decades.[21] On the other hand the intervention of the Australian branch of the Daly family undoubtedly changed the destinies of their Irish relatives, including two of the men executed after the Easter Rising. They were Commandant Ned Daly, who commanded the Four Courts Garrison, and his brother-in-law Tom Clarke, the first signatory of the Proclamation of the Irish Republic. This document became the ideological cornerstone of the independence movement and later of the Irish State.

---

18   Kildea, Jeff 2003 'Called to Arms: Australian Soldiers in the Easter Rising 1916', *Journal of the Australian War Memorial* 39; Sweetman, Rory 2008, 'Who Fears to Speak to Easter Week? Antipodean Irish Catholic Responses to the 1916 Rising', *The Impact of the 1916 Rising: Among the Nations*, edited by Ruan O'Donnell (Dublin: Irish Academic Press), 71–90.

19   Calderwood, Glenn 2006 A Question of Loyalty: Archbishop Daniel Mannix, the Australian Government and the Papacy, 1914–18, *Footprints* 2, 12–48.

20   Inquests, *The Age*, 31 January 1863, 5; The Kelly Outrages, *The Age* 12 December 1878, 3.

21   Whitaker, Anne-Maree 2018 Major MacBride's Australian relatives, *Cathair na Mart* [Westport Historical Society journal] 35, 56–9.

The Daly Family

Ned Daly's uncle James exemplifies the successful migrant returning to his native land to contribute to the well-being of the family members he left behind. Sponsored by an uncle, he arrived in Sydney from Limerick in 1855, aged twenty-three. He spent five years in New South Wales, where he married Honora MacMahon in 1857 and started a family. When the gold rush began at Lambing Flat in 1860 Daly travelled to the district. However, in 1862 he and his family moved to the French colony of New Caledonia where he took up cattle farming, was also an employee of the Société le Nickel company and later a director of the Barrau trading company.[22]

Also, in 1862 James's eighteen-year-old brother Michael followed him to Sydney, and then joined him in New Caledonia in 1865. Meanwhile their brothers John and Edward, who remained in Limerick, joined the Fenians, a clandestine organisation which advocated the use of physical force to end British rule in Ireland. They were arrested in late 1866 but John was released in time to participate in the ill-fated Fenian Rising the following year. John escaped to America where he became active in Clan na Gael, the American Fenian organisation.[23]

By the 1880s Edward and John were working in Sussex, and in 1884 John was arrested again and sentenced to life imprisonment for treason. Edward died of a heart condition in 1890, leaving his pregnant wife with eight daughters under the age of fourteen. When their ninth child was born it was a son, who was named John Edward after his uncle and father but usually known as Ned. Although local supporters set up a fund to assist the family they were soon in financial difficulties, until the timely return of Uncle James from Australia in 1894.[24]

James Daly's return to Ireland followed that of his brother-in law Patrick MacMahon in 1888. MacMahon travelled with his wife from Sydney to Italy, France, England, Scotland and Ireland. While in Paris

---

22 Mr James Daly, of New Caledonia, *Freeman's Journal* (Sydney) 23 September 1899, 26; Aldrich, Robert 1990 *The French Presence in the South Pacific 1842–1940*, London: Macmillan Press 154.
23 Litton, *Edward Daly* 17–8, 24.
24 Litton, *Edward Daly* 18–22.

he called in to Hennessy's to order 100 cases of brandy, and his return trip to Sydney was made via the United States. MacMahon's return migration was both business and personal, the voyage of an emigrant who had succeeded in his new country and could afford to indulge in an expensive journey.[25] James Daly's return on the other hand was motivated by duty rather than indulgence. Following the death of his wife in early 1893 he returned to Ireland on what he later described as a 'special mission' to secure his brother John's release from gaol.[26]

On James Daly's arrival in London in early 1893 he met with leading figures of the Irish Parliamentary Party at the House of Commons including Tim Healy, T. D. Sullivan, Justin McCarthy and John Dillon. The first outcome of these meetings was the overturning of a ban on visitors to his brother John in Portland Prison in Dorset, when James was given special permission by British Home Secretary Herbert Asquith. He was accompanied to Portland by another Irish MP, William Abraham, the newly elected member for North-East Cork. In fact, this was merely the first move in a campaign by James to secure John's release.[27]

While MacMahon kept a diary of his trip, the account of James Daly's return migration six years later is more indirect. Apart from newspaper reports, which are numerous, the most informative account is found in the autobiography of his then fifteen-year-old niece Kathleen. Naturally the young girl locates James in the domestic setting rather than describing his political activism. Kathleen records that James assisted his brother Edward's widow and children, moving them into a large two-storey house with extensive grounds and obtaining jobs and apprenticeships for the older girls. Kathleen expressed an interest in musical training, but Uncle James opined that it was a waste

---

25   McInerney, Bill 1984 A Sixmilebridge Emigrant, *Dúchas na Sionna* [Shannon Heritage Group] 8, 7–12.

26   Mr James Daly, of New Caledonia, *Freeman's Journal* (Sydney) 23 September 1899.

27   Mr James Daly, of New Caledonia, *Freeman's Journal* (Sydney) 23 September 1899; More Visitors to John Daly, *Manchester Courier*, 9 September 1893, 3; Return of John Daly's brother from Australia, *Kerry Sentinel*, 13 September 1893.

of money. Instead she was apprenticed to a dressmaker and soon established her own business.[28]

James Daly spoke at several major meetings in support of an amnesty for the Fenian prisoners, including one at Bodyke in County Clare in December 1894, and another at Mallow, County Cork in May 1896. He proved to be a formidable orator, excoriating the Redmond brothers, leaders of the Irish Parliamentary Party, and accusing them of having 'foully sold' his brother. At the Cork rally he quoted William Redmond's letter to the Sydney *Daily Telegraph* from which Redmond now seemed to be retreating. 'He [Daly] was afraid that the cause of amnesty was dead (no, no), and that Mr Redmond had killed it (groans)', the press reported.[29] The staunch Fenianism of the Limerick Dalys was not shared by James, who supported the Irish Parliamentary Party and used his connections with them in the campaign for John's release. On one occasion Tim Healy MP arrived at the Daly home looking for James, and Edward's widow confronted him: 'Are you that awful man that uses such bad language?' Healy politely replied 'Yes ma'am, I am that awful man.'[30]

As well as maintaining relations with the Irish politicians, James Daly also cultivated the press. He gave exclusive interviews to the Limerick-based correspondent for the Dublin newspaper *Freeman's Journal*, and in March 1896 passed on for publication a letter from John.[31] The letter was immediately published, and was then copied by other newspapers in Ireland, Britain and Australia.[32] The letter referred to James as Jim and Jimmy, and also mentioned their sister 'Lollie' (Laura). John reported his affection for substitute pets such as a spider, but then affirmed that his photo of James helped him 'in a great way to destroy that awful feeling of all-aloneness that kills a man slowly but

28   Litton, Helen editor 1991 *Revolutionary Woman: Kathleen Clarke, 1878–1972: An Autobiography*, Dublin: O'Brien Press 20.
29   The Great Meeting at Bodyke' *Dublin Freeman's Journal* (Dublin), 5 December 1894; The National Cause in Cork, *Freeman's Journal* (Dublin) 25 May 1896.
30   Litton, *Revolutionary Woman* 19–20.
31   *Freeman's Journal* (Dublin) 30 March 1896.
32   For example: A Convict's Christmas, *North-Eastern Daily Gazette* (Middlesbrough, England), 10 April 1896; Letter from John Daly, *Catholic Press* (Sydney) 16 May 1896.

surely'. At Christmas he had toasted James's photo with an empty pint tin. He also expressed concern that he may not be released in time to see his frail elderly mother, who 'would rather have seen her two sons lying dead at her feet than that their names should be connected with anything unworthy of their country'.

Another huge public meeting was held in London in June 1896, attended by numerous MPs and clergymen. James was scheduled to speak but had to withdraw due to the ill-health of his 88-year-old mother.[33] Eventually in August 1896 James travelled to Portland to meet John at the prison gate and take him to James's daughter's home in Paris to recuperate from the hunger strike which helped John win his release. On his return to Ireland the following month, John was welcomed with a huge torchlight procession through the streets of Dublin followed by another in his native Limerick. James had announced his intention of returning to Australia in a press interview, but added, that 'everything would depend upon the time of his brother's release from Portland'. By early 1898, with John fully recovered and undertaking a speaking tour in the United States, James decided to head home.[34]

After the release of John Daly and others in 1896, there were only two remaining Fenian prisoners in England, Henry Burton and Thomas Clarke. Campaigning for their release continued and in September 1898 John Daly travelled to London to meet Clarke at the gates of Pentonville Prison in London. In Daly's new role as Lord Mayor of Limerick he persuaded the council to confer the freedom of the city on Clarke, who came to accept the honour in early 1899 and stayed in the Daly home for several weeks. In this time, he formed an attachment to John's niece Kathleen, and after an extended courtship they were married in New York in 1901, with Major MacBride as the best man.[35]

On a visit to Sydney in September 1899, James Daly called in to the office of the *Freeman's Journal* newspaper where he gave an expansive

---

33 Great Amnesty Demonstration in London, *Freeman's Journal* (Dublin) 25 June 1896.
34 Litton, *Edward Daly* 27–8; Interview with Mr James Daly, *Freeman's Journal* (Dublin) 13 August 189; Mr James Daly leaves for Australia, *Irish Examiner* 5 May 1898.
35 Litton, Helen 2014 *Thomas Clarke*, Dublin: O'Brien Press 60–1, 64–70, 79–80.

interview about his life and the current prospects of New Caledonia. He returned to Nouméa and died there on 19 October 1900 at the age of sixty-eight, although the family in Ireland misremembered the place name as 'New Mayo, Australia'. His young nephew Ned, the future Commandant, was still only nine years old. James's death was covered in the Irish newspapers, with one report noting that he 'was held in high esteem by a wide circle of friends'.[36]

Meanwhile Michael Daly remained in New Caledonia and seems never to have returned to Ireland. Family legend states that he made and lost three fortunes. Michael sent a telegram of congratulations to John on his release from gaol addressed simply 'John Daly, Limerick', which was duly delivered.[37] Michael died in Newtown, Sydney, in early August 1921 and is buried in Rookwood Cemetery in an unmarked grave. His wife Louise and daughter Eileen are buried nearby.[38] John Daly survived his nephew Ned Daly and niece's husband Tom Clarke by less than two months, dying in Limerick on 30 June 1916.[39]

May Gahan (later O'Carroll)

The second aspect of Australian links to the Easter Rising is the emigration of rank-and-file participants to Australia. Recent studies estimate that over ten per cent of the rebel forces in the Easter Rising were female. Their involvement attracted newspaper reports such as 'Women fighting for the Rebels' in the *Aberdeen Daily Journal*, which commented: 'They were wearing the dark green uniform similar to that of the male insurgents and slouch hats. They consist largely of young women, but there are a number of older ones among them.'[40] While women served equally with the men in the Irish Citizen Army, the Irish

---

36   Litton, *Edward Daly* 28; Mr James Daly, of New Caledonia, *Freeman's Journal* (Sydney) 23 September 1899, 26; Death of Mr James Daly, *Freeman's Journal* (Dublin) 6 December 1900.
37   The Release of Mr John Daly, *Irish Examiner* 25 August 1896.
38   Litton, *Edward Daly* 21–2, 28; Funeral notice, *Sydney Morning Herald* 10 August 1921.
39   Death of Mr John Daly, *Freeman's Journal* (Dublin) 1 July 1916.
40   *Aberdeen Daily Journal* 1 May 1916.

Volunteers had a parallel women's organisation, Cumann na mBan, with female leadership. Thanks to the Irish Military Archives pension records it is now possible to trace the emigration and changes of name of many female participants in the Easter Rising.[41]

One of these women was Mary Gahan, usually known as May, who was born in Dublin on 22 February 1899, the daughter of Robert Gahan and his wife Mary (née Murray). She and her older brothers Mattie and Joe became involved in Irish republican organisations from an early age, with May joining Cumann na mBan in 1913 at its foundation. During Easter Week seventeen-year-old May served at Stephen's Green under Lieutenant Constance Markievicz and Commandant Michael Mallin, and on carrying a despatch to the GPO was sent by Commandant-General James Connolly with another message to the Imperial Hotel nearby. After the Rising she was arrested and imprisoned for several weeks in Kilmainham Gaol before being released.[42] May married John O'Carroll from Tipperary on 6 May 1917 at St Agatha's, Dublin, and they opened a restaurant called the Republican Bar, which 'was a rendezvous for Republicans, not to mention gun smugglers.'[43] May continued her work for the IRA through the War of Independence, with her premises subject to constant raids by the British authorities. She fought on the Republican side in the Civil War, and was arrested in May 1923 and imprisoned in Kilmainham Gaol and the North Dublin Union, during which she staged two hunger strikes. Captain Frank Thornton later said: '[She] was a most active member of Cumann na mBan, and rendered very good service throughout the whole period of the War to the Truce', adding 'she was a very fine character'.[44]

---

41 Collins *The Rising Handbook* 82, 128. Another example is Whitaker, Anne-Maree 2016 Margaret Fleming: Irish Rebel to Sydney Schoolteacher, *Descent* 46 (4), 182–5.

42 Mary O'Carroll, Military Service Pension Application, 34E8257, Irish Military Archives.

43 *Sydney Morning Herald*, 6 May 1947; John Kenny, Witness statement 1693, Bureau of Military History, Irish Military Archives 17–8.

44 Mary O'Carroll, Military Service Pension Application, W1RB1494, Irish Military Archives.

May and John left for Liverpool, England after her release in November 1923. They went on to New Zealand before moving to Sydney in around 1929. John opened a barber's shop in Darling Street, Balmain, and became active in Irish community affairs. At a rally in the Sydney Domain in 1932 he gave a fiery speech which was extensively quoted in the *Sydney Morning Herald*, which sarcastically described it as 'a speech in which England was all bad and Ireland was all chastity'.[45]

In 1938 John ran as an independent for the NSW Parliament in the Balmain electorate, gaining 18.9 per cent to the ALP candidate's 72.1 per cent.[46] When the victor, John Quirk, died in December the same year his widow Mary was endorsed by Lang Labor, with John O'Carroll nominating again as independent Labor. At this second attempt he gained 19.7 per cent, and thanks to him and another independent candidate the Labor vote slumped by 4000 or 35 per cent.[47] Although John O'Carroll and the other independent alleged irregularities on polling day, Mary Quirk became the second woman elected to state parliament and went on to represent the seat for eleven years.[48]

Meanwhile May O'Carroll was a foundation member of the Hands Off Ireland Organisation formed in 1932, holding the position of Organiser.[49] The group conducted annual Easter commemorations at the 1798 Memorial at Waverley Cemetery in Sydney's Eastern suburbs, and held social functions at the Manchester Unity Hall at Gladstone Park, a stone's throw from the O'Carroll home. Letters and telegrams about various campaigns were also sent to Australian and Irish politicians, many of them signed with the Irish form of May's name, Maire Ó Cearbhaill.[50] The Hands Off Ireland Organisation (HOIO)

---

45 Irish Rally in the Domain, *Sydney Morning Herald*, 18 April 1932.
46 Atlas of NSW http://atlas.nsw.gov.au/public/nsw/home/map/elections.html .
47 The Balmain By-Election Result, *Australian Worker* (Sydney) 18 January 1939; Balmain By-Election, *Singleton Argus* 16 January 1939.
48 Conduct of Election, *Sydney Morning Herald* 17 January 1939; NSW Parliament https://bit.ly/3hFavo8.
49 Mary O'Carroll, Military Service Pension Application, 34E8257, Irish Military Archives.
50 Hands Off Ireland Organisation, Commonwealth Investigation Branch, series B741, item V/26197, National Archives of Australia.

discontinued its Waverley commemorations in 1947, but continued functioning until 1951.[51]

The first evidence of the Sydney Irish community commemorating the Easter Rising came in April 1929 when an apparently short-lived group called the ex-IRA Social Club held an Easter Commemoration at the 1798 Memorial at Waverley Cemetery. The O'Carrolls were not named as participants.[52] Later that year Irish community attention again focused on Waverley Cemetery with the unveiling of a memorial to Edmund McSweeny, an Irish National Association (INA) stalwart and one of the Irish Republican Brotherhood leaders interned in Sydney during World War I.[53]

Even though the 1798 Memorial was to an earlier Irish rebellion, its size and ornate decoration made it a fitting site for Irish political commemorations. In 1927 a fence and gates decorated with martial symbols such as spears, axes and a shield were installed at the Memorial.[54] The first reported INA Easter Rising commemoration at the 1798 Memorial in Waverley Cemetery was held in 1930.[55] The INA commemoration was normally held on Easter Sunday at 3 pm, and has continued in various forms to the present.

The rival HOIO annual event was held each Easter Sunday at 11 am and took the form of a wreath-laying, last post and reveille, and

51   Irish rallies commemorate Easter heroes, *Catholic Weekly* (Sydney), 1 May 1947; Column 8, *Sydney Morning Herald* 25 June 1951.

52   Easter Week Meeting at Waverley Memorial, *Freeman's Journal* (Sydney) 28 March 1929; '98 Patriots Honoured: ceremony at Waverley, *Catholic Press* 11 April 1929.

53   Edmund McSweeny Memorial Unveiling Ceremony at Waverley, *Catholic Press* 31 October 1929; Edmund M'Sweeney Memorial Unveiling Ceremony at Waverley, *Freeman's Journal* (Sydney) 31 October 1929; O'Keeffe, Garrath 1997 Australia's Irish Republican Brotherhood, *Journal of the Royal Australian Historical Society* 83(2) 136–152.

54   Wooding, Jonathan M. 2007 'It was in Human Nature to Love One's Native Land and Make Sacrifices for it': Monumental Commemorations and Corporeal Relics in 1920s Irish-Australia, *History Australia*, 4 (2), 39.8–39.14.

55   Easter Week Commemoration at Waverley Cemetery, *Workers' Weekly* 2 May 1930. The organisation is not named, but its President was 'P. McMahon' whose link with the INA is confirmed in A Wet St Patrick's Day: How Sydney Celebrated It, *Freeman's Journal* (Sydney) 20 March 1930.

one or more speeches. The O'Carrolls were featured in a number of reports. In 1936 May was the wreath-layer: 'Mrs O'Cearbhaill carried on her arm an old tattered uniform of dark green, as worn by the Cumann-na-m-Ban (League of Women) during the Easter-week rebellion.'[56] In 1938 one of the speakers was ' Shaun O'Carroll' and two years later as 'Sean O'Cearbhaill' he laid the wreath.[57] May was the speaker in 1939 and 1941.[58] The last report of an HOIO commemoration was in 1946 when the wreath was laid by Sean Heuston O'Cearbhaill, John and May's eleven-year-old son.[59]

May and John O'Carroll had fourteen children, of whom ten lived to adulthood: Robert Emmet (1919), Eileen Markievicz (1920), Cathleen Clare (1930), Patricia Josephine (1931), Maureen Cyril (1933), Seamus Connolly (1934), Sean Heuston (1935), Liam Mellows (1936), Eamon de Valera (1937) and Peadar Clancy (1942). Robert was named after the United Irish rebel leader of 1803, while Seamus and Sean were named after two of the leaders executed in 1916. Liam and Eamon were named after prominent Republican leaders in the Civil War. Peadar was named after one of May's commanding officers who was summarily executed by the British on Bloody Sunday in 1920.

The children all displayed musical talent, and many followed careers in music. Robert, Cathleen and Eamon were violinists; Eileen, Patricia and Peadar specialised in the harp; Maureen was a cellist; Sean played the trombone; and Seamus and Liam the trumpet.[60] Cathleen won a scholarship and travelled to London in 1951 with Joan Sutherland where she enjoyed great success. At the age of twenty-three

56 Irish Memorial: The Rising In 1916, *Sydney Morning Herald* 13 April 1936, 2. As identical text appeared in a number of publications it is assumed the reports relied on press releases issued by HOIO.
57 Annual Ceremony at '98' Memorial, Waverley, *Freeman's Journal* (Sydney) 21 April 1938; Irish Commemoration. The Easter Rising, *Catholic Press* 28 March 1940.
58 Irish Remember the Dead. Easter Week Demonstration, *Freeman's Journal* (Sydney) 20 April 1939; Easter Week Recalled at Waverley, *Freeman's Journal* (Sydney) 17 April 1941.
59 Easter Tribute at Irish Hero's Tomb, *Catholic Weekly* 2 May 1946.
60 Patrick, S. Where fiddle, harp, trombone, trumpet and Irish laughter mingle, *Australian Women's Weekly* 20 January 1954.

Cathleen was appointed leader of the Royal Academy of Music orchestra, receiving a glowing tribute from NSW Premier Joe Cahill.[61] May had applied for an Irish Government military-service pension as soon as they were introduced in 1934, and by the time her claim was allowed the lump sum enabled her to purchase a house at 75 Laycock Street, Bexley, soon after World War II. After serving in the Australian Army during the war, John O'Carroll died in 1956 and was buried in an Australian war grave in Woronora Cemetery in southern Sydney.[62] May returned to Ireland in 1966 for the fiftieth anniversary of the Easter Rising, joining 600 other veterans to review a military parade which drew 200,000 people into the centre of Dublin.[63] She lived for another twenty-two years, attending the annual Easter commemoration at Waverley proudly wearing her medals. May died on 30 April 1988, the seventy-second anniversary of the end of the Easter Rising. Her daughter Patricia played the harp at her funeral, and the Irish flag and her medals were on the coffin.[64]

Sydney's centennial commemoration of the Easter Rising in 2016 was organised by the INA and held at the 1798 Memorial at Waverley Cemetery. The event included a formal procession from the cemetery gates, a Mass concelebrated by Bishops David Cremin and Terry Brady, and speakers including Irish Consul General Jane Connolly and Sinn Féin MP for West Belfast Paul Maskey. The main oration was given by former NSW Public Service Association office-bearer and *Gaeilgeoir* Muiris Ó Súilleabháin. The Proclamation of the Irish Republic, first read by Patrick Pearse outside the GPO at the start of the Rising, was read out on this occasion by Sean O'Connor who also read it sixty years earlier at the 1956 Waverley commemoration. The INA wreath was

---

61   Young Woman Chosen to Lead Orchestra, *Sydney Morning Herald* 9 February 1954.
62   WWII service number NX174612; NSW death certificate, 22531/1956.
63   Higgins, Roisin, Holohan, Carole and O'Donnell, Catherine 2006, 1966 and All That: The 50th Anniversary Commemorations, *History Ireland* 14(2), 31–6.
64   An earlier paper discussing May O'Carroll was Whitaker, Anne-Maree 1996 Veterans of the Irish War of Independence in Australia, *Irish-Australian Studies: Proceedings of the Eighth Irish-Australian Conference*, edited by Richard Davis et al. Sydney: Crossing Press 413–20.

laid by Sean Heuston O'Carroll, seventy years after he had previously performed this task, and on this occasion, he was joined by Cormac Smyth, whose grandfather Paddy Mahon was a sniper on the roof of the GPO during the Rising.[65]

Conclusion

The Australian connections to the Easter Rising resonate through a century of Irish-Australian history. From the chain migrations of the 1850s through to the eve of the Rising, Irish emigrants to the Australasian colonies found opportunities for successful careers which would have eluded them in their native land. The urge to return was able to be satisfied for those such as James Daly, who embarked on a political career in his sixties which helped to free his activist brother from gaol. James also intervened to provide a stable home environment for his fatherless nephew, Ned, and his eight sisters.

Following the Irish Civil War many of those on the losing Republican side resorted to emigration. Few made it as far as Australia, which was often the destination chosen because it was as far away as could be envisaged from Europe. The woman veteran considered in this article, May O'Carroll, not only continued her political work but even gave her sons defiantly Irish names after prominent Irish Republican figures.

Re-examination of the Easter Rising for its centenary opened up a wide range of research possibilities, facilitated by newspaper digitisation and the availability of digitised records on the internet which can be utilised by researchers in any part of the world. No longer are topics or research questions defined by the traditional historical narrative. In the case of Australian links to the Easter Rising the new sources reveal that there is far more to recount than the activities of Archbishop Mannix.

---

65   O'Flynn, Denis P. 2016 *INA President's Report 2015–2016*, Sydney: Irish National Association 1.

13
Dancing Bodies, Living Memories: Irish Immigrants in Sydney

Jeanette Mollenhauer

In dance and song we gift and mourn our children
They carry us over the ocean in dance and song.[1]

These words appear in the souvenir program of the Irish-dancing stage show Riverdance: the children of whom these words speak are the emigrants who have left Ireland to forge new lives in other parts of the world.[2] The couplet concerns the Irish diaspora, estimated by the former President of Ireland Mary Robinson, in 1990, to number 70 million people.[3] The words describe the emigrants as having taken dance and song with them as a means of remembering Ireland and the people still living there. It is said that 'the elicitation and presentation of embodied cultural memories fleshes out the story of

---

1   *Riverdance*, Concert Program, 2003.
2   I have previously described Irish migration to Australia and Irish dancing in Australia in Mollenhauer Jeanette 2015 Competitive Irish Dance: Culture and Community. *Australasian Journal of Irish Studies* 15, 35–54; Mollenhauer, Jeanette 2017 Irish Dancing in Sydney: Global Patterns, Local Practices, *Journal of Intercultural Studies* 38(2), 213–27.
3   President of Ireland, 2016. *Address by the President, Mary Robinson, on the Occasion of her Inauguration as President of Ireland, 3rd December 1990.* https://bit.ly/2FF5QWi

a people':[4] this chapter is concerned with the chronicle of the people who have left Ireland to settle in Sydney, Australia, and the ways in which Irish dancing has provided them with modes of mnemonic connection to Ireland. Dancing has always been intimately woven into the narratives of Irish settlers in Australia: it is a social adhesive, reminding immigrants that there are others who share both ancestry and affection for Ireland, and collectively turning hearts and minds towards the former homeland. The multiple layers of meaning embedded within the dancing need to be teased out so as to thicken the immigrants' stories and present a more polished account of the people of Ireland who left their birthplace, whether forcibly or by choice, to begin new lives in Sydney.

Migration stories are both nuanced and multi-faceted, so to interpret the meanings contained within them, several theoretical paradigms will be appropriated. The dancing practices themselves will be explored using theories of embodiment and emplacement. Immigration is an experience of the body, and so is dance; the bodies of immigrants who dance are rich in information concerning the experiences of leaving one's home, making another home in a distant location and maintaining emotional links with the former homeland by joining a traditional dance group in Sydney. Nostalgia theory is used to explain the purpose of reminiscence, even when immigrants have contently settled into new surroundings. The memories of migrants have journeyed across time and space, and often it is the roots of those memories which is privileged. Yet, complementary facets are revealed when memory is also 'studied through the reconstruction of its routes', especially when those memories are closely linked with processes of migration.[5] Both roots and routes are considered important in the narratives of Irish immigrants and their dance practices in Sydney: bodies have moved in migration and are still moving in dance, while memories have their roots in Ireland but have developed, and been

---

4   Stoller, Paul 2009 *The Power of the Between: An Anthropological Odyssey*, University of Chicago Press 47.
5   Erll, Astrid 2011 Travelling Memory, *Parallax* 17(4), 4–18: 11.

shaped by, the routes taken by those same bodies as they have migrated then settled in Australia.

The story of Irish immigrants in Sydney will unfold throughout this work. First, it is necessary to explain the origin and nature of the various forms of dancing which may be classified as 'Irish'. To begin the historical narrative, archival materials are sourced to demonstrate some of the history of dancing amongst the Irish community in Sydney. The subsequent section presents a choreological analysis of the role of the dancing body in eliciting memories of Ireland through the movements, steps and motifs of Irish dancing. Finally, data collected from first, and second-generation Irish immigrants, who currently live and dance in Sydney, is presented, so grounding the story in the current era. Through each section of the narrative, affective connections with Ireland, as elicited through Irish dancing, are privileged.

The Different Genres of 'Irish Dancing'

Several forms of Irish dancing were brought from Ireland to Australia, and a pause is needed to outline the various genres included in 'Irish dancing' before continuing with the narrative.[6] Step dancing is the form of dance which is most publicly recognised (as a result of the various stage shows). It is a solo genre, which in its current mode of practice consists of: first, dances which are performed in soft leather shoes which make little sound when in contact with the floor, such as in the initial dance performed by Jean Butler in Riverdance; and second, those which are danced in shoes with fibreglass tips, making percussive sounds when the floor is struck, as in the dancing performed by Michael Flatley. Towards the end of the nineteenth century, when the Gaelic League sought means through which to foster feelings of nationalism amongst the population of Ireland, they chose step dancing as one of the Irish cultural activities to be promoted among the population.[7] Since 1929,

---

6   Mollenhauer, Irish Dancing in Sydney 216.
7   Foley, Catherine 2001 Perceptions of Irish Step Dance: National, Global, and Local, *Dance Research Journal* 33(1), 34–45: 35; Foley, Catherine 2013 *Step Dancing in Ireland: Culture and History*, Farnham: Ashgate 134.

An Coimisiún le Rinci Gaelacha or the Irish Dancing Commission (IDC) has governed all aspects of this genre on a global scale.[8] Currently, there are IDC rules governing all aspects of the dancing around the world: teacher registration, examinations, competitions, metronome speeds, costumes and make-up.

An older form of step dancing is called *sean nós* dancing and was taught by itinerant dance masters, who developed their own unique styles.[9] It is a percussive dance form, but the dancing feet are kept close to the floor, in contrast to the elevation from the floor which is required in modern step dancing. Set dancing has been practised for about 500 years, and was developed from the French cotillions and quadrilles, which were taken about by the itinerant dance masters and had localised forms and idiosyncrasies applied to them.[10] A predetermined number of figures form one dance, which is executed by four couples facing each other, thus dancing in a square set. Céilí dancing was the social dancing prescribed by the Gaelic League, who collected dances which they deemed suitable for public consumption: the dances they chose stood for the supposed purity of Irish culture, as opposed to the set dances which had been developed from foreign influences and were, therefore, not subject to Gaelic League approval.[11] Set and *céilí* dancing are informally connected on a global scale in that there is an archive of written notation, meaning that the dances are taught in a consistent manner around the world.

Dancing and Irish Immigrants

Having described the various genres of dancing which are classified as 'Irish', this section draws on various archival resources to present the historical part of the overall narrative and it begins with the earliest days

---

8   Foley, Perceptions, 36.
9   Brennan, H. 1999 *The Story of Irish Dance*, Lanham MD: Roberts Rinehart 59
10 Brennan 23.
11 Foley, Catherine 2000 The Irish Ceili: Appropriation, Community and Identity. Paper presented at the 21st Symposium of the ICTM Study Group on Ethnochoreology, Korcula, Croatia (no pagination).

of non-Indigenous settlement in Sydney.[12] Irish prisoners were amongst the first European settlers in Australia, with the first flotilla of boats arriving in January 1788.[13] Each ship had a doctor on board, who was required to keep a log of the health and activities of the prisoners in his care. Multiple records demonstrate that dancing was one activity which was undertaken by the prisoners when they were taken up to the deck for their brief period of fresh air each day.[14] While the records do not specify that it was Irish dancing, it is known that many prisoners were from Ireland and, therefore, it is reasonable to assume that they were performing a dance from Ireland. It is not hard to imagine that one prisoner might start to dance, choosing his or her favourite, and that once the unique rhythm sounded out on the deck, even if generated with bare feet, the familiarity of the sounds would have encouraged others to join in. In addition to the physical benefits of increased circulation and respiration rate, encouraging the inhalation of fresh sea air, the dancing added an important layer of emotional unity to the group and would, perhaps, have reminded them of the homes in which they learned those dances and the loved ones who still occupied those homes.

Later, when free settlers began to emigrate from Ireland to Australia, they too turned to dancing as a form of entertainment throughout the long voyage.[15] On the night before an emigrant ship departed from Ireland, a form of wake would be held, and one of the main activities was dancing.[16] The process of parting was seen to be similar to the process of death for, in those times, emigration meant never seeing loved ones again.[17] So, dancing was one of the

---

12 Mollenhauer, Competitive Irish Dance, 38–9; Mollenhauer, Irish Dancing in Sydney 215
13 O'Farrell, Patrick 1986 *The Irish in Australia*, Kensington: University of NSW Press 22.
14 McMahon, Ann 2011 *Convicts at Sea*, Hobart: Artemis 69–70.
15 McConville, Chris 1987 *Croppies, Celts & Catholics: The Irish in Australia*, Melbourne: Edward Arnold 39.
16 Morrison, J'aime 2001 Dancing between Decks: Choreographies of Transmission during Irish Migrations to America, *Eire-Ireland: A Journal of Irish Studies, Spring-Summer 2001*, 83–97: 87.
17 Miller, Kerby 1985 *Emigrants and Exiles: Ireland and the Irish Exodus to North America*, Oxford University Press 558.

final activities in which prospective emigrants engaged prior to leaving Ireland; hence, to dance during the journey, and after re-settlement, provided a sense of continuity for them. The dancing and music set the Irish travellers apart from the others. On a ship bound for the United States, one Welsh man remarked that 'indulgence, frivolity and instability are the special characteristics of the Irish … During the whole journey when the sea was quiet there was nothing to be heard except their singing, dancing, shouting and noise'.[18] In the midst of the arduous sea journey, dancing was a means through which Irish emigrants connected with each other, reviving their spirits and raising enthusiasm for the times which lay ahead.

In the early days of the settlement which eventually became known as Sydney, there were various accounts of Irish dancing taking place. Social dance evenings quickly became common activities for the upper echelons of the community, and dances of Irish origin such as *The Waves of Tory* and *The Walls of Limerick* were regular inclusions on the event programs.[19] An early mention of a step dance teacher is made in August 1829, when it was noted that there was 'an Irish dance master carrying on his profession in Kent-street (sic)'.[20] Throughout the remainder of the nineteenth century, detailed reports of Irish dancing are somewhat sporadic, but there is ample evidence of the continued practice of dancing being central to Irish community activities. Meetings of the Irish National Association and Catholic Church gatherings often included performances of Irish dancing.[21] The sights and sounds of the costumes, steps, motifs and music served to personify Ireland for the gathered crowd, reminding them of their shared origins and communal memories.

Sydney newspapers in the early twentieth century were brimming with references to competitive Irish step dancing. At this point in time, news of the activities of the Gaelic League and its agenda of nationalism would have reached Australia. For almost the first thirty years of that

---

18 Morrison 94.
19 Cullinane, John 2006 *Aspects of 170 Years of Irish Dancing in Australia*, Cork: John P. Cullinane 15–6.
20 *Sydney Gazette and New South Wales Advertiser* 8 August 1829.
21 O'Farrell, *The Irish in Australia* 124, 258.

century, debate concerning the nature and quality of solo dancing, as conducted in Australia, was evident in various Sydney newspapers. The discourse began in the *Freeman's Journal* on 7 July 1900 when a Mr Purtill, prior to his retirement from competitive dancing, issued a challenge to 'any man' in Australia to dance against him in the performance of seven dances: *Jig, Reel, Slip Jig, St Patrick's Day, The Blackbird, Job of Journeywork* and *Brien the Brave*.[22] Two weeks later, someone wrote to challenge Mr Purtill's authority and experience, stating that he (the writer) had been involved with step-dancing in Ireland and had seen many champions perform.[23] He doubted that Mr Purtill could dance as well as those champions, although he himself did not take up Mr Purtill's challenge to participate in a dance competition.[24]

A particularly emotive exchange commenced in 1926; in a letter to the *Freeman's Journal* on 18 November that year, it was said that 'Irish dancing as it is generally done in Australia is the most corrupted phase of Irish art, and all lovers of the beautiful should be grateful to the Gaelic League for trying to raise it to its proper standard'.[25] The same newspaper, on 13 January 1927, contains a counter-argument: 'I consider the dancers who did the "athletic exercises" as stated by the critic, are the true performers of the traditional Irish style as was taught in Ireland 50 years ago'.[26] The month of February 1927 contains several more letters on the subject, the last being published in the *Freeman's Journal* on 24 February 1927, in which the writer poses a question: 'What the public wants to know is, what style of Irish dancing is in accordance with the traditional canons of the art and the spirit and character of the Irish times of which the various step and figure dances are the physical expression and why?' In the final letter of this series in March 1927, the opponent suggests that the writer of February's

22 A dance called *Brien the Brave* is not known in Ireland (Catherine Foley, Irish World Academy of Music and Dance, University of Limerick, personal correspondence, September 2016). The other dances are still performed in competitions, although currently the slip jig is danced only by females.
23 Apart from Purtill, the other writers used pseudonyms so their gender is unknown. I use the pronoun 'he' for convenience.
24 *Catholic Press* 21 July 1900.
25 *Freeman's Journal* 18 November 1926.
26 *Freeman's Journal* 13 January 1927.

letter should publish an article on 'the origin, history, development and traditional characteristics of Irish figure and step dancing'.[27] A note from the obviously frustrated newspaper's editor, placed under this letter, states that 'this correspondence is now closed'.[28]

There are several observations which can be made from this somewhat heated altercation. The first is that it is remarkable that Irish dancing was the subject of discussion in a newspaper, although the *Freeman's Journal* was at one time called *The Catholic Weekly* or *The Catholic Freeman's Journal,* so there would have been a high percentage of its readership during that era who could claim Irish heritage. The second is the depth of passion which is evident in the writings; whichever view is held, it is clear that all of these authors were devotees of Irish dancing, although it is not always clear whether they were dancers, musicians, parents or seasoned amateur assessors of dance performances. The third, and most pertinent here, is the manner in which the writers privilege their notions of the traditional origins of the dancing whenever they refer to the Gaelic League, the pedagogical practices employed in Ireland or the history and expansion of Irish dancing. This is the case whether the writer was taking a conservative or a progressive view of the dancing; both sides claim affinity with dancing as they remember it being practised in Ireland.

With notable clarity, the writer of the letter on 24 February 1927 remarked concerning 'the spirit and character of the Irish times of which the various step and figure dances are the physical expression'.[29] This comment is amazingly congruent with much current scholarship concerning Irish dancing. The writer was, in effect, describing Irish dancing as an embodiment of Ireland and Irishness. In the following section, I outline some of the modern theories concerning the Irish-dancing body and the ways in which it serves as a locus for the propagation and perpetuation of memories of Ireland.

---

27 This is the first mention of figure (*céilí*) dancing in the exchange. Perhaps it was included as a test of the other person's knowledge of multiple genres of Irish dancing.
28 *Freeman's Journal* 3 March 1927.
29 *Freeman's Journal* 24 February 1927.

Bodies, Senses and Places

This section is concerned with the body, and the way the body moves when performing Irish dancing. A theoretical discussion of embodied and sensory practices in Irish dancing serves to bridge the gap between past and present.[30] Bodies danced on the convict ships, as described already in this paper, and are still dancing today, as will be covered in the final section. To be a human being is to have a body, and our bodies are trained in a variety of tasks during our lives: to write our names, ride a bicycle, wash the dishes. Embodiment is a universal human experience: it is both 'a purposive, active, learned and reflexive way of being in the world' and 'a way to actively bring the world into focus'.[31] Bodies also move, and dance, of course, is a collection of movements, whether those movements are pre-determined or spontaneous. So, by analysing dance, we are able to comprehend some of the ways in which people are positioned within, and relate to, the world around them.[32]

The interpretation of bodily movements may be mediated through an existing reservoir of knowledge which is dependent on one's cultural heritage background.[33] The idiosyncrasies of the relevant cultural tradition are ingrained in the stylised motions of each genre, hence a dance form which is unique to a given cultural group represents part of the 'ephemeral *repertoire* of embodied practice/knowledge' of that group.[34] Dancers performing traditional dances are embodying culturally specific memories through which the knowledge which belongs to that culture may be transmitted.

We perceive and react to our environment through the body's senses, so a study of embodiment should include the role of sensory input, not only from the five commonly acknowledged senses of sight,

---

30 Mollenhauer, Jeanette, 2017 Embodied Emplace Embraced: Performing the Chain Sword Dance of Blato (Croatia) in Sydney, Australia, *Journal of Emerging Dance Scholarship*, 5, 1–28:5.
31 Conger, A. 2015 Bodies of Knowledge: Cultures of Embodied Knowing among American Dance Majors (Unpublished doctoral thesis) Indiana University, Bloomington IA 13; 35.
32 Conger 243.
33 Connerton, Paul 1989 *How Societies Remember*, Cambridge University Press 74
34 Taylor 19 (italics in original)

hearing, touch, taste and smell, but also kinaesthesia, the sense through which a body knows where its individual parts are located, and where the body as a whole is located in relation to other bodies and objects in our surroundings. These senses are put to use by both dancers and audience members; even while sitting and watching a dance performance, people can experience empathic sensations and imagine themselves performing the dance.[35] As already stated, embodied practices such as dance are culturally mediated, so it follows that the network of sensory stimuli which are present in a performance is also determined by cultural background. Therefore, members of that cultural group are able to discern specific meanings in the sensory stimuli presented in a performance.[36] Sensory encounters are thus able to 'serve as mnemonic devices of selfhood and belonging to the larger community'.[37]

The complementary notion of emplacement considers the ways in which bodies populate affect and transform spaces:[38] physical places may 'become written on the body [and] become part of us, quite literally'.[39] The nature and meaning of an empty space is, most often, completely different to the same space when it is full of bodies, whether those bodies belong to the dancers or the audience members who have come to observe the dance. As noted elsewhere, 'the complex interactions between bodies and senses' serve to configure memories of place and space:[40] as the dancers and audience members draw on their habituated senses, their bodies are connected to deeply felt passions,

35   Reason, Matthew & Reynolds, Dee 2010 Kinaesthesia, Empathy and Related Pleasures: An Inquiry into Audience Experiences of Watching Dance, *Dance Research Journal* 42(2), 49–75: 50.
36   Howes, David 2003 *Sensual Relations: Engaging the Senses in Culture and Social Theory*, Ann Arbor MI: University of Michigan Press 53–4.
37   Low, Kelvin & Kalekin-Fishman, Devorah 2012 Afterword: Towards Transnational Sensescapes, *Everyday Life in Asia: Social Perspectives on the Senses*, edited by K. Low & D. Kalekin-Fishman, Farnham: Ashgate 195–203: 199.
38   McCormack, David 2008 Geographies for Moving Bodies, *Geography Compass* 2(6), 1822–36: 1823.
39   Farrar, Margaret E. 2011 Amnesia, Nostalgia and the Politics of Place Memory, *Political Research Quarterly* 64(4), 723–35: 725.
40   Mollenhauer, Embodied Emplace Embraced 14.

perceptions and familiarities.[41] The senses act 'as referential markers which connect the home of the past with home in the present';[42] put simply, they help us to remember.

A dance performance (whether private or public) may be analysed by asking 'what is seen, heard, felt (both touch and kinaesthesia), smelled and tasted?' Admittedly, the senses of smell and taste may not be directly awakened through the dancing itself, but, for example, may be stimulated through specific foods which are habitually served on a particular occasion when dancing takes place. So, in Irish dancing, it is that which the bodies (of both dancers and audience members) see, hear, touch and feel which reminds them of past experiences. Consequently, when a performance of dancing is mounted, there is a system of sensory mnemonics which turns the collective consciousness of Irish immigrants towards Ireland.

The most prominent visual cue is costuming. Competitive solo dancers have always dressed in costumes which, in some way, link them to Ireland. It may be the colours, the adornment of a Tara brooch, or the embroidered knotwork which was inspired by the artistry of *The Book of Kells*. Step-dancing costumes may currently appear to be more theatrical than traditionally inspired, yet the vestiges of Ireland are still to be found in the embroidered designs.[43] Social (set and céilí) dancers do not wear costumes except for public performances; the current costumes of the *Sydney Irish Céilí Dancers* feature bright green shirts and blouses, a colour which immediately identifies them as Irish in the minds of audience members.

The physical formations of the social dances provide visual stimulation of notions of home and close community contact. Before the dance begins, the dancers may often be standing in a square set, where every dancer is facing in towards the others, or in a longways set where a row of women face a row of men.[44] Such formations are intimate and

---

41   Main, Kelly and Sandoval, Gerardo 2015 Placemaking in a Translocal Receiving Community: The Relevance of Place to Identity and Agency, *Urban Studies* 52(1), 71–86:83.
42   Mollenhauer, Embodied Emplace Embraced 14.
43   Cullinane, *Aspects* 85; Mollenhauer, Competitive Irish Dance 42.
44   Gender numbers may be unequal in a group and it is usually the case that there is an excess of women, so some women may then need to dance in men's positions.

inclusive; they foster a communal spirit. Once the dance begins, motifs with names such as 'dance at home' and 'house around' act as reminders of past times and serve to embed Ireland into the dancing.[45]

The sight of individual dancing bodies also stirs the memory. The presence of an upright torso and head, with the arms locked into position by the side, is an immediate visual link to 'Irish dancing' and indeed, these postural features have formed the basis for multiple caricatures in popular media.[46] However, the parodies are constructed from a basis in truth: for someone with Irish heritage, the sight (and feeling) of that particular posture, where the focus of movement is located in the feet while the rest of the body is still, can elicit thoughts of the former days in Ireland. Such musings may even extend as far back as those times when Irish people were subject to British rule and sought avenues, such as dance, through which to demonstrate resistance and independence.[47] Or, for recent immigrants, it may simply remind the viewer of their own dance lessons as a child in Ireland. In a modern context, the vibrant athleticism of the Riverdance performers 'conjures up the image of Irish bodies on the move, conquering the world'.[48] Irish-dancing bodies, with the postures, movements and the formations which coalesce into the choreographies, form a powerful visual aide-memoire: Ireland is there, in plain sight.

Another trait which is associated with step dancing is its percussiveness. What Michael Flatley achieved in Riverdance was a focus on the multiple ways in which the feet can be used in sonic production of the rhythms of Ireland. The older form of séan nós dancing was also based on a dancer's prowess in producing a rhythm and blending that rhythm with the musical accompaniment. In rural

---

45   Foley, Catherine 2011 The Irish Ceili: A Site for Constructing, Experiencing and Negotiating a Sense of Community and Identity, Dance Research 29 (1), 43–60: 56; Mollenhauer, Irish Dancing in Sydney 220–1.

46   Popular television shows which have caricatured Irish step dancing include Kath & Kim (Australia), Father Ted (UK) and Third Rock from the Sun (USA). A simple web search leads to many sites with cartoons, for example https://bit.ly/3mnsins

47   Wulff, Helena 2005 Memories in Motion: The Irish Dancing Body, Body & Society 11, 45–62: 58.

48   Wulff 59.

homes, a door would be taken down and placed on the floor so that the wood could enhance the sonic qualities of the moving feet.[49] In both *séan nós* and step dancing, the pounding rhythms of feet moving in either jig or hornpipe time is suggestive of only one place: Ireland. Additionally, Irish dancing of all genres is most often accompanied by music, whether live or recorded, and the unmistakeable sounds of the tin whistle or uilleann pipes speak of their origins in Ireland.

The sonic scenery created by musicians and dancers may transform the arena, in which the dancing is taking place, into an Irish space. Sounds have the means of employing 'our affective, emotional and intuitive selves',[50] thus engaging both minds and spirits. The ability of human bodies, to 'sense rhythms and anticipate certain communicative patterns operates in ways that help sense a collective identity',[51] serves to unify participants at a dance event in their collective reminiscences,[52] which have been stimulated through hearing the sounds of Ireland in the dance and its musical accompaniment.

Finally, the feeling of the dancing bodies further develops remembrances of Ireland. The formations described earlier, such as the square set, often come together into a circle of dancers, all of whom hold the hands of the people either side of them, or they may come into a tighter circle with arms clasped behind neighbours' backs so that maximum spinning speed is more easily attained. The touch of the other dancers suggests connection, unity and community; it provides a concrete connection to others who share similar memories of places, people and events in Ireland. Bodies moving together, especially in synchronised rhythms, exert strong influence on the affective state of dancers and audience alike. As dancers seek unity in both rhythm and gradation of their movements, the sense of communion is heightened

---

49   Breathnach, Breandán 1996 *Folk Music and Dances of Ireland: A Comprehensive Study Examining the Basic Elements of Irish Folk Music and Dance Traditions*, Cork: Ossian 49; Brennan 77.

50   Boyd, Candice & Duffy, Michelle 2011 Sonic Geographies of Shifting Bodies, *Interference: A Journal of Audio Culture*, www.interferencejournal.com/.

51   Duffy, Michelle, Waitt, Gordon, Gorman-Murray, Andrew & Gibson, Chris 2011 Bodily rhythms: Corporeal capacities to engage with festival spaces. *Emotion, Space and Society* 4, 17–24: 19.

52   Mollenhauer, Embodied Emplace Embraced 17.

and the overall mood is raised.[53] In plain terms, dancing together with others becomes more enjoyable when movements are synchronised. Again, audience members are not left out; they may share the enjoyment as their bodies experience 'kinaesthetic empathy' whilst watching the dancing.[54]

A dance event, then, contains many markers of the particular cultural group to which the dance genre belongs; it reflects the historical, political and social discourses of that group.[55] Attention to the ways in which bodies move can help us to understand much about the members of that group, the situations in which they find themselves, and their attitudes to those situations. Irish immigrants dance to reconstruct Ireland and renegotiate their hybrid identities which are a blend of the Ireland of their memory and the Australia of their present cognition.

Memory Evocation and Recent Immigrants

Here in the final part of this chapter the focus is on the current cohort of Irish-dance practitioners in Sydney, and the role that dance plays, amongst Irish immigrants, in the provision of personal connections with their ancestral homeland, Ireland. To understand this role, the voices of first and second immigrants need to tell their own stories, in their own words. Dancers, musicians, teachers and parents from three Irish dance groups in Sydney were interviewed, using a semi-structured technique, in 2014 and 2015 about their dancing and what it means to them.[56]

The primary theme which emerged from the narratives of Irish immigrants in Sydney was that they have chosen to dance so as to maintain a personal affective link with Ireland through perpetuation

---

53 McNeil, William H. 1995 *Keeping Together in Time: Dance and Drill in Human History*, Cambridge MA: Harvard University Press 155–6; Collins, Randall 2004 *Interaction Ritual Chains*, Princeton University Press 76.
54 Reason & Reynolds 50.
55 Kaeppler, Adrienne 2010 The Beholder's Share: Viewing Music and Dance in a Globalized World. *Ethnomusicology* 54 (2), 185–201: 192.
56 As part of a broader ethnography for doctoral research at The University of Sydney.

of an Irish cultural practice in Sydney.[57] When asked 'What does your participation in Irish [step/set/ céilí] dancing mean to you?' some of the replies were: '[Dancing] was a huge part of the culture in my childhood and in my adolescence [in Ireland]'(Theo,[58] dancer). 'There's definitely, for me, a connection to my Irish heritage' (Andrea, dancer). 'For me it's is a lovely connection [with Ireland]' (Deirdre, parent). '... because of my family being from an Irish background and I was keen to keep that culture in the family' (Jessica, parent). 'It would mean a lot to them [grandparents in Ireland] because they've done it [danced] all their lives' (Maeve, dancer).

These comments cover family heritage, culture and traditions, physical locations and socialisation, all with the thread of Ireland and Irishness running through them. Dancing allows these immigrants a small means of ensuring that their past selves are not overwhelmed by the present realities of life in Australia. It provides a focus for their memories of earlier parts of their lives, and a place within which to commune with other Irish immigrants who share similar reminiscences.

Nostalgia refers to the human tendency to position oneself in relation to home, which is perceived as the locus of significance, attachment and ideals.[59] It may operate at two levels: individuals bring their unique perspectives, remembering what was significant to their lives; and societies remember, collectively, their history.[60] Shared memories are forged through communal recollection of a past which was inhabited by many individuals, and are then appropriated to configure a shared self-understanding.[61] The longing may not be for a mere geographical location; it may also be for the loss of social ties along with the accompanying security of the values and beliefs bound up in that community.[62]

---

57 Mollenhauer, Irish Dancing in Sydney 222.

58 Pseudonyms have been assigned to all participants.

59 Wu, Jing 2006 Nostalgia as Content Creativity: Cultural industries and Popular Sentiment, *International Journal of Cultural Studies* 9, 359–68: 360

60 Shelemay, Kay 2006 Music, Memory and History, *Ethnomusicology Forum* 15(1), 17–37: 18.

61 Brockmeier, Jens 2002 Remembering and Forgetting: Narrative as Cultural Memory, *Culture and Psychology* 8(1), 15–43: 18.

62 Boym, Svetlana 2001 *The Future of Nostalgia*. New York, NY: Basic Books 53.

Perpetuation of traditional artistic practices such as dance serves to forge links with the former homeland. Dancers may be reminded of specific sensory experiences of that place as they dance.[63] They may experience deep longing for the homeland;[64] audience members' connections with the past being may be reinforced through witnessing a performance of dance,[65] and dance and music may possess the ability to evince memories of past times with loved ones and in communities.[66] When a group collectively recalls the past, as in the case of a diasporic dance group performing a traditional choreography, the dancing contributes to the enhancement of intra-community solidity.[67] Memories serve to bind people together.

Nostalgia also has a role in connecting the past and the present; it acts as both an agent of spatial embedding in the present, and a facilitator of place-making for the future. It recalls past events and interprets those events through the prism of contemporary understandings,[68] so functioning as a tool which may give agency in the processes of self-understanding. Nostalgia represents a 'desire of being there *here*'.[69] Members of the Filipino community in the United States have stated that 'our movements and choreographies continue to be some of the most precious resources for rewriting the past, *as if it*

63 Bottomley, Gillian 2002 Polyphony, Polythetic Practice and Intercultural Communication in Greek-Australian Creative Work, *Journal of Intercultural Studies,* 23 (1), 47–57: 53.

64 Duarte, Fernanda 2005 Living in 'the Betweens': Diaspora Consciousness Formation and Identity among Brazilians in Australia, *Journal of Intercultural Studies* 26 (4), 315–35: 321.

65 Ram, Kalpana 2000 Dancing the Past into Life: The *Rasa, Nrtta* and *Raga* of Immigrant Existence, *The Australian Journal of Anthropology* 11 (3), 261–73: 267.

66 Wrazen, Louise 2005 Diasporic Experiences: Mediating Time, Memory and Identity in Gorale Performance, *Canadian Journal for Traditional Music* 32, 43–53: 47.

67 Tabar, Paul 2005 The Cultural and Affective Logic of the Dabki: A Study of a Lebanese Folkloric Dance in Australia, *Journal of Intercultural Studies* 26 (1–2), 139–57: 143.

68 Stock, Femke 2010 Home and Memory, *Diasporas: Concepts, Intersections, Identities*, edited by K. Knott and S. McLoughlin, London, UK: Zed Books 24–8: 24.

69 Hage, Ghassan 1997 At home in the Entrails of the West: Multiculturalism, 'Ethnic Food' and Migrant Home-Building, *Home/World: Space, Community*

were still a part of us, still connected'.[70] In the same way, the memory of connections with Ireland is embedded in the dance practices of Irish immigrants in Australia.

Maintaining links with a former homeland was, for some time, assumed to prohibit the development of affiliations to the society in which a person is currently living; it was thought that transnational links were incompatible with acculturation to new geographical and social surroundings. However, it is now understood that these two aspects of immigrants' lives may not only exist concurrently, but may be mutually advantageous.[71] The research respondents' participation in Irish dancing does not mean that they do not appreciate their lives in Australia, nor does it mean that they feel no loyalty to the Australian nation. It simply allows them a point of contact with the past; a way in which they can, through the bodily movements and sensations generated by dancing, acknowledge that their Irish heritage still has salience in their current lives. They want to move forward, but they also want to remember.

Conclusion

The story of Irish dancing in Sydney is a story which has been, and still is, propelled by memories. From the first prisoner ships, carrying frightened convicts, to modern citizens of the twenty-first century, memories of Ireland are central to, and evoked by, the various forms of Irish dancing which are practised in Sydney. The cultural representations embedded in Irish dancing have served to encourage

---

and Marginality in Sydney's West, edited by H. Grace, G. Hage, L. Johnson, J. Langsworth, & M. Symonds, Sydney: Pluto Press 99–153: 108 (italics in original)

70 Gonzalves, Theodore 2010 *The Day the Dancers Stayed: Performing in the Filipino/American Diaspora*, Philadelphia PA: Temple University Press 146–7 (italics in original).

71 Tsuda, Takeda 2012 Whatever Happened to Simultaneity? Transnational Migration Theory and Dual Engagement in Sending and Receiving Countries, *Journal of Ethnic and Migration Studies* 38 (4), 631–49: 640.

individuals and bind communities together through collective reminiscences about Ireland as their former homeland.

This chapter has not covered every facet of immigrants' memories: it has not dealt with those who may long for an idealised past which has gone and can never be replaced,[72] and it has only focused on what is remembered, rather than those matters which have been forgotten or overlooked.[73] Furthermore, Irish-dance genres are now practised by many who do not have Irish heritage, and the form of emulative nostalgia which has been observed amongst these dancers has been described elsewhere.[74] The focus of this work has been on Irish immigrants and the positivity of thought and affect which is generated through the perpetuation of Irish dancing in Australia. The immigrants who dance in Sydney are '*carriers* of memory'; they are 'the individuals who share in collective images and narratives of the past, who practice mnemonic rituals, display an inherited habitus and can draw on repertoires of explicit and implicit knowledge'.[75] They represent Ireland to themselves and to each other.

Migrants' memories are important to them; the comments of those who were interviewed attest to this: Irish immigrants in Sydney have been able to weave nostalgia into their experiences of resettlement, which in turn has led to 'the building of symbolic capital ... continuity and coherence' in the lives of individuals and communities.[76] Nostalgia can also be 'valued as potentially democratic, opening up new spaces for the articulation of the past and acting as a mode of assimilating this to the rapidly changing modern environment'.[77] The process of migration, whether by convict ship or aeroplane, is a rupture of the

72   Krupinski, Jerzy 1984 Changing Patterns of Migration to Australia and their Influence on the Health of Migrants. *Social Science Medicine* 18 (11), 927–37: 933
73   Erll 14.
74   Mollenhauer, Competitive Irish Dance 43–4; Mollenhauer, Irish Dancing in Sydney, 222–3.
75   Erll 12 (italics in original).
76   Holyfield, Lori, Cobb, Maggie, Murray, Kimberley, & McKinzie, Ashleigh 2013 Musical Ties That Bind: Nostalgia, Affect, and Heritage in Festival Narratives. *Symbolic Interaction* 36(4), 457–77: 469.
77   Pickering, Michael & Keightley, Emily 2006 The Modalities of Nostalgia. *Current Sociology* 54, 919–41: 923.

continuity of life: the psyche searches for the familiar and the beloved, and finds comfort in the shared memories of home, which are brought to life, or embodied, when people dance. The dancing is a nexus of past and present, memory and currency; it is a way of retaining links with the former life while simultaneously working out a new identity in the current circumstances of life.[78]

Irish migrants have, for centuries, spread across the world, and Irish dancing has accompanied those migrants wherever they have travelled, including Sydney. Memory, too, has become globalised, and 'today, memory and the global have to be studied together, as it has become impossible to understand the trajectories of memory outside a global frame of reference'.[79] The geographical distance between Australia and Ireland remains unchanged since the first flotilla of ships arrived in 1788, but the practicalities of modern travel and communication have permanently altered the migration experience. While the modern immigrant in Sydney may use email or Skype to instantly communicate with relatives or friends in Ireland, their affective connections with Ireland are not dissimilar to those of the early settlers. Bodies continue to dance, and the dancing still embodies Ireland and Irishness: through dancing, memories of Ireland are nourished *and* give nourishment in return.[80]

---

78   Fortier, Anne-Marie 2000 *Migrant Belongings: Memory Space Identity.* Oxford: Berg 157.

79   Assman, Aleida & Conrad, Sebastian 2010 *Memory in a Global Age: Discourse, Practices and Trajectories,* Basingstoke: Palgrave Macmillan 2.

80   Parts of this work have been submitted in fulfilment of the requirements for the degree of Doctor of Philosophy at The University of Sydney.

About the Authors

Lorna G. Barrow (Fsascot) completed her PhD at the University of Sydney in 2008. She currently works as a casual academic at Macquarie University in Sydney in the Modern History Department. She is, broadly speaking, a keen observer of Scottish History in general; however, her main research interests lie in the history related to the royal women of fifteenth- and sixteenth-century Scotland; she has published widely in this area. Lorna is a joint editor of the *Journal of the Sydney Society for Scottish History*, and an active committee member of the Celtic Studies Foundation at Sydney University.

Elizabeth Bonner (the late) was a historian specialising in the Early Modern History of Scotland and France. A graduate (BA, PhD) of the University of Sydney, she was the recipient of the Chevalier de l'Ordre des Palmes Académiques, and a Fellow of the Society of Antiquaries of Scotland. She passed away on 31 May 2020 in Sydney, Australia.

William Christie is Professor and Head of the Humanities Research Centre at the Australian National University, Director of the Australasian Consortium of Humanities Research Centres, and a Fellow of the Australian Academy of the Humanities. He was founding President of the Romantic Studies Association of Australasia (2010–2015) and his work in Romantic studies has been widely published. His *Samuel Taylor Coleridge: A Literary Life* (2006) was awarded the NSW Premier's Biennial Prize for Literary Scholarship in 2008 and subsequent publications include *The Letters of Francis Jeffrey to Thomas and Jane Welsh Carlyle* (2008), *The Edinburgh Review in the Literary Culture of Romantic Britain* (2009), *Dylan Thomas: A Literary Life* (2014), and *The Two Romanticisms and Other Essays* (2016).

Cairns Craig is Glucksman Professor of Irish and Scottish Studies at the University of Aberdeen, and has been Director of the Research Institute of Irish and Scottish Studies at Aberdeen since 2005. Before that he was Professor of Modern and Scottish Literature at the University of Edinburgh. He is the author of *Muriel Spark, Existentialism and the Art of Death* (2019), *The Wealth of the Nation: Scotland, Culture and Independence* (2018), *Intending Scotland: Explorations in Scottish Culture since the Enlightenment* (2009), *Associationism and the Literary Imagination* (2007) and *The Modern Scottish Novel* (1999). He was General Editor of the four-volume *History of Scottish Literature* (1987) and is currently an editor of the *Journal of Irish and Scottish Studies* and the *Journal of Scottish Thought*.

James Donaldson was born in Edinburgh, Scotland, and attended the Royal High School of Edinburgh. Following his migration to Australia in 1951, he worked on pastoral properties in the Riverina of New South Wales. He attended the University of Sydney, graduating in Arts in 1965 and in Divinity, with First Class Honours and the University Medal in 1969. He completed a Master's Degree in Theology; and later a Doctorate in San Francisco in 1976. He was Visiting Scholar at Princeton Theological Seminary in 1993. He is a former President of the Probus Club of Melbourne; a member of Metropolitan Golf Club and plays lawn bowls with the Melbourne Cricket Club and Old Scotch Collegians. He is the Honorary Secretary for Australian Affairs for the Society of Antiquaries of Scotland.

Sybil Jack was born and educated in the UK, taking degrees at Oxford before moving to Australia in 1961. She became first senior tutor in Economic History in the economics faculty at Sydney University, then lecturer, and eventually associate professor, in History, as well as for a time Dean of the Faculty of Arts. Since retirement she has continued to work and publish in her primary research area of sixteenth-century British history and in Australian history, especially the history of science and technology and the history of forests and gardens. Sybil also assists in the work of the Australian and New Zealand Society for Medieval and Renaissance Studies (which she helped to found), the Sydney Medieval and Renaissance Group, the Foundation for Celtic Studies, the Sydney Society for Scottish History, and the Scottish Australian Heritage Council.

John Kennedy studied Early English Literature and Language at the University of Sydney in the 1960s, and was awarded a PhD by that University in 1986 for a thesis on an Old Norse/Icelandic topic. Brepols published his book on translating the Icelandic sagas in 2007. Much of his academic career before retirement in 2007 was spent teaching and researching in the field of Information Studies at Charles Sturt University, where he continues to have adjunct lecturer status. In retirement his research interests include the medieval Norse interactions with the predominantly Celtic lands, and modern national responses to Norse and Celtic heritages as reflected in coin issues.

Dymphna Lonergan is a research fellow in Humanities at Flinders University and an editor of the online magazine *Tinteán*. She was born and raised in Ireland, calling both Ireland and Australia 'home'. Her primary research interest is the Irish language in an English setting. Her book *Sounds Irish: The Irish Language in Australia* is available from Lythrum Press, Adelaide. In 2019, she contributed two chapters and co-edited the Wakefield Press publication, *Irish South Australia: new histories and insights*.

Jeanette Mollenhauer is an independent scholar who completed the first doctoral project about Irish dance in Australia in 2017. Her work has been published in several high-profile journals including the *Journal of Intercultural Studies* and the *Dance Research Journal*. A first monograph, *Dancing at the Southern Crossroads: An Early History of Irish Step Dance in Australia,* will be published in 2020. Jeanette is a member of numerous academic organisations, including the Irish

Studies Association of Australia and New Zealand and the International Council for Traditional Music (ICTM), and serves on the ICTM's Archives Committee. She is also a community dance teacher and current Vice President of Folk Dance Australia.

Tessa Morrison was formerly Senior Lecturer at the School of Architecture and Built Environment at the University of Newcastle. She has written extensively on Isaac Newton and architecture, and on utopian cities. Her books include *Isaac Newton's Temple of Solomon and his Reconstruction of Sacred Architecture* (2011) and *Unbuilt Utopian Cities 1460 to 1900: Reconstructing Their Architecture and Political Philosophy* (2015).

Val Noone is a Fellow of the School of Historical and Philosophical Studies at the University of Melbourne and is the author of the first full-length study of Gaelic culture in southeast Australia entitled *Hidden Ireland in Victoria*. Recently he edited an annotated version of *Nicholas O'Donnell's Autobiography* (2017), in which O'Donnell goes beyond personal autobiography to clan biography, providing a rare detailed account of a chain migration, in this case, of some one hundred people from O'Donnell and Barry clans of Limerick to Australia.

Richard Reid is a retired high school teacher, museum educator, museum curator and public historian. In 2011, with three assistant curators, he put together the National Museum of Australia's exhibition, 'Not Just Ned—a True History of the Irish in Australia', the first such comprehensive exhibition of its kind in one of the major destinations of the nineteenth- and twentieth-century Irish diaspora.

Katherine Spadaro was born on the Isle of Lewis in Scotland, which gave her early exposure to Scottish Gaelic, although most of her life has been spent in Australia. She has a PhD in Applied Linguistics (Second Language Acquisition) and has been involved in adult language education in many different roles, both in Australia and overseas.

Anne-Maree Whitaker is an independent historian based in Sydney, Australia, with a PhD in Australian history from Macquarie University, examining United Irishmen transported to New South Wales in the period 1800–1810. Anne-Maree has written ten books and numerous journal articles, with a particular interest in Irish-Australian and Australian-Catholic topics. Her chapter in this volume is one of several studies which have arisen from an investigation of links between Ireland and Australia associated with the 1916 Easter Rising. She is a Fellow of the Royal Australian Historical Society and the Royal Historical Society (UK), and a life member of the Irish National Association of Australasia.

Jonathan M. Wooding is the Sir Warwick Fairfax Professor of Celtic Studies at the University of Sydney. His research interests centre on pilgrimage, travel, monastic settlement and the cult of saints in the early Celtic world. His publications include: *Communication and Commerce Along the Western Sealanes* (1996) and (with A. Grimley), *Living the Hours: Monastic Spirituality in Everyday Life* (2010).

Index

Index

Index

Sinclair, Catherine 179
Sinclair, John
  Old and New Statistical Accounts of
    Scotland 8
Skene, William Forbes 20–21
Smith, Reverend Edward 186
Smollett, Tobias 72
South Africa 197
Spencer, Herbert 64
Spender, Stephen 86, 95
St Killen's church 21
St Mary's Cathedral 223–225, 229–231,
  236
St Patrick's Day 11, 223–225, 228–229
Stafford, Fiona 72
Stewart, Balfour 78–80
Stewart, Rev Colin 172–173, 184–185
Stewart, Sir John 150–151, 154–155,
  160
Stuart, Bérault 152–154, 159–160
Stuart, Robert 160
Stuarts of Aubigny 146, 159
superstitions 3, 18, 29–30
Sweetman, Rory 240

Tait, Peter Guthrie 77–80
tapestries 146–147, 161
taste 60, 64–68, 71, 262–263
Teraphim 29
Theodore Jacobsen's Foundling
  Hospital 46
Thermodynamics 80
Therry, John Joseph 230
Thomas, D. J. (father) 92
Thomas, Dylan 5, 85
  18 Poems 86, 90
  A Portrait of the Artist as a Young Dog
    94
  Deaths and Entrances 95
  Under Milk Wood 88, 97–99

Thomson, Deas 184
Thomson, Derick 197
Thomson, William see Kelvin, Lord
  translation 197, 209, 216
Tudor, Henry 157–157, 166
Tudors 148, 160, 164
Tyndall, John 76–79

Unionists see Ireland: Unionists of
Unitarianism 92
United Irish League 10, 207
United States of America
  New Harmony 50–51
urbanism 33–34, 55–57
Urbánek, Zdeněk 100

Vikings 128, 143–144
Villages of Unity and Cooperation 43,
  50–51

Wales 5–6, 40, 85, 91–101, 136
  Swansea 5, 85, 94
Watkins, Vernon 101
Watson, George 60
Waverley Cemetery 228, 248–251
Webster, Bruce 21
Wells, H. G. 79
Whitbread, Samuel 47
Whitwell, Thomas Stedman 48–51
Williams, Raymond 99
Wilson, David 82
Withers, Charles W. J. 178
Wohl, Robert 240
Wood the Younger, John 38
World War I 208, 240–241, 249
World War II 164, 251
Woulfe, Patrick 213
Wu, Jing 1, 13

Yeats, W. B. 5, 60, 74–82, 128, 210, 238

285